PUBLICATIONS
OF THE
ARMY RECORDS SOCIETY
VOL. 5

THE MILITARY CORRESPONDENCE OF FIELD-MARSHAL SIR WILLIAM ROBERTSON,

CHIEF OF THE IMPERIAL GENERAL STAFF, DECEMBER 1915–FEBRUARY 1918

The Army Records Society was founded in 1984 in order to publish original records describing the development, organisation, administration and activities of the British Army from early times.

Any person wishing to become a Member of the Society is requested to apply to the Hon. Secretary, c/o The National Army Museum, Royal Hospital Road, London, SW3 4HT. The annual subscription entitles the Member to receive a copy of each volume issued by the Society in that year, and to purchase back volumes at reduced prices. Current subscription details, whether for individuals living within the British Isles, for individuals living overseas, or for institutions, will be furnished on request.

The Council of the Army Records Society wish it to be clearly understood that they are not answerable for opinions or observations that may appear in the Society's publications. For these the responsibility rests entirely with the Editors of the several works.

Sir William Robertson by Francis Dodd, 1918.
By permission of the Trustees of the Imperial War Museum

THE MILITARY CORRESPONDENCE OF FIELD-MARSHAL SIR WILLIAM ROBERTSON, CHIEF OF THE IMPERIAL GENERAL STAFF, DECEMBER 1915–FEBRUARY 1918

EDITED BY

DAVID R. WOODWARD

PUBLISHED BY

THE BODLEY HEAD

FOR THE

ARMY RECORDS SOCIETY

1989

A C.I.P. catalogue record for this book
is available from the British Library

ISBN 0–370–31415 8

Printed in Great Britain for
The Bodley Head Ltd
20 Vauxhall Bridge Road, London SW1V 2SA
by Mackays of Chatham PLC
Set in Linotron Ehrhardt
by J&L Composition Ltd
Filey, North Yorkshire

First published 1989

CONTENTS

ACKNOWLEDGMENTS

Editing this volume was a most rewarding and pleasurable endeavour. More than once, however, the editor was reminded of a remark once made by A. J. P. Taylor: 'Writing history is like W.C. Fields juggling. It looks easy until you try to do it'. This statement rings no less true for editing a volume of historical documents.

I owe a great debt of gratitude to the many people and institutions who helped me complete this project. I am especially grateful to Lord Robertson of Oakridge who granted me full access to his grandfather's papers and assisted me in many ways. Field-Marshal Robertson's only surviving child, Lady Vincent, graciously provided me with an intimate glimpse of her father's personality. Patricia J. Methven and her excellent staff at the Liddell Hart Centre for Military Archives, King's College London, could not have been more understanding and cooperative. The same can be said of the staffs of other repositories too numerous to mention. The Marshall University history department secretary, Beverly Bunch, instructed me in the use of a word processor and assisted me in other valuable ways. Two history graduate students, Carl Wolfe and Philip Paine, spent many hours checking my typescript against the original documents. Roderick Suddaby, who has befriended so many researchers in the Department of Documents at the Imperial War Museum, provided some invaluable leads. Professor Stuart Kaufman of the University of Maryland, editor of the Samuel Gompers Papers, shared his vast editorial experience with me. My colleague at Marshall University, Professor William Palmer, read the manuscript, offered suggestions, and provided me with a sympathetic ear. My wife, Martha Cobb Woodward, proofread the manuscript, helped decipher Field-Marshal Robertson's handwriting, and provided warm encouragement. Marshall University granted me a sabbatical during the first half of 1987 to conduct my research in Great Britain.

Reproduction of documents in the Royal Archives appears by gracious permission of Her Majesty the Queen. Crown copyright material in the Public Record Office is reproduced by permission of the Controller of Her Majesty's Stationery Office. The other following individuals or institutions have generously allowed the editor to reproduce documents in their possession and/or copyright: Lord Robertson of Oakridge; Mrs. Belinda Bell; Lord Hankey; Mr. Andrew Rawlinson; the Earl of Derby; the Warden and Scholars of New College, Oxford; the Master, Fellows and Scholars of Churchill College in the University of Cambridge; the Trustees of the Liddell Hart Centre for Military Archives, King's College, London; the Clerk of the Records and the House of Lords Record Office; the Trustees of the National Library of Scotland; the Bodleian Library; the British Library; the Trustees of the Beaverbrook Foundation; the Trustees of the Imperial War Museum; and the India Office Library and Records, British Library.

I have made every effort to avoid infringing upon the copyright of any individual or institution and regret any possible oversight in this regard.

To all who helped with this volume, my sincere thanks.

David R. Woodward
Marshall University
January 1989

ABBREVIATIONS USED FOR DEPOSITORY CITATIONS

H. of Lords RO: House of Lords Record Office
IWM: Imperial War Museum
LHCMA: Liddell Hart Centre for Military Archives
NLS: National Library of Scotland
PRO: Public Record Office
RA: Royal Archives

INTRODUCTION

From Private to Chief of the Imperial General Staff 1877–1915

William Robert Robertson was born on 29 January 1860 at Welbourn, Lincolnshire.[1] He was the eldest son of Thomas Charles Robertson, the village tailor and postmaster, and Ann Rosamund Johnson. Educated in the village Anglican school, he entered domestic service at age thirteen, for a time serving as a footman in the service of the Cardigan family at Deene Park, Northamptonshire. Little is known of his employment as a servant from 1873/77, and he makes no mention of it in his autobiography. A few months shy of eighteen, the minimum age for enlistment, he took the Queen's Shilling on 13 November 1877 from a rules-bending recruiting sergeant in Worcestershire, where he had been employed by the Vernon family at Hanbury Hall, near Droitwich. His age was ascribed as eighteen years and two months.

News that Will had sought his fortune with the 16th (Queen's) Lancers was not warmly received in Welbourn. His mother, a formidable and deeply religious person, made clear her unhappiness. The army was 'a refuge for all Idle people', she wrote. 'I would rather Bury you than see you in a red coat'.[2] His mother's reaction was quite understandable. With no advantage of wealth, class or social connections, Robertson's choice of an army career seemed a particularly bad one. The Victorian army was essentially a dynastic rather than a national institution, virtually belonging to senior army officers, the aristocracy and the royal family. Officers came from the middle and especially the upper class and were products of public schools. A gentleman and an officer were synonymous. As late as 1913, only two per cent of regular officers commissioned that year had advanced through the ranks. Even fewer rankers, an average of from four to five a year, were promoted from the ranks in the 1870s and 1880s.[3]

Robertson's first eleven years in the ranks were filled with personal successes but were not without blemish. Every offence in the army was then considered a 'crime' and the offender was imprisoned. Robertson was 'crimed' three times, but still gained promotion to troop sergeant-major in 1885. He excelled in troop competitions in skill-at-arms, winning all the first prizes in sword, lance and shooting in 1886. No ranker perhaps worked any harder improving his knowledge of soldiering. He read all of the limited materials available to him on tactics, strategy and past wars. He knew the drill books from A to Z. To make every moment count, he paid a comrade a few pence to read to him while he cleaned his kit. His dedication and raw ability impressed his superiors, and he was encouraged to seek a commission. Having passed the required written and oral examinations, Robertson was gazetted in 1888 second lieutenant and posted to the 3rd Dragoon Guards.

Robertson never doubted that he had the ability, but he was all too aware that he did not really have the financial means to afford a cavalry officer's lifestyle. He survived on the margin because his new regiment was serving in India where pay was higher and expenses for officers less than at home. Robertson was still forced to cut his expenses to the bone, drinking water instead of alcohol and abstaining from smoking after meals because a pipe, for which he could afford tobacco, was not allowed at mess. His penury helped him discover that he was gifted in languages. Cash awards were given by the Indian government to those who passed examinations in native languages. While his fellow officers slept during the oppressive heat of the day, Robertson worked with native tutors to master Urdu, Hindi, Persian, Pushtu, Punjabi, and Gurkhali. His language prowess, which was almost unheard of for a cavalry subaltern, gained him a posting with the intelligence department of Simla, which collected information on the North-West frontier.

His knowledge of Chitral, a mountainous state bordering India, led to his appointment in 1895 to the intelligence staff of the Chitral Expedition to rescue a British garrison being besieged in that state. This campaign almost cost him his life. On a reconnaissance mission, he was attacked by a native guide. At a range of some ten yards, he was fired upon from the rear by both barrels of a 12-bore breechloader. Miraculously unscathed, Robertson fell when he dismounted on the narrow mountainous path. From a half-sitting position, he had to ward off an attack from his own sword, which Robertson, suffering from dysentery, had given to the guide to carry. 'As there was neither time nor opportunity to draw my revolver while this vigorous sword practice was taking place', Robertson later wrote, 'I could only scramble to my feet and floor the fellow with my fist'.[4] While recovering from his severe wounds in the hospital, he was promoted to captain. He also received the Distinguished Service Order and a mention in despatches for his service in this campaign.

Robertson's career advancement, impressive as it had thus far been, would probably have been limited in the future if not for two events. First, in 1894, he married Mildred Adelaide, the second daughter of Lieutenant-General Charles Thomas Palin of the Indian Army. His marriage to Mildred, which bridged a major social divide, helped smooth some of his rough edges and made easier socialising with his 'social superiors'. Second, the British army at the turn of the century was about to become a modern, larger-scale, technically-orientated fighting force in which professionalism was increasingly required and expected from its officer corps. For the first two decades of Robertson's service, despite the Cardwell Reforms, the British army was traditional in the worst sense. It was an amalgam of imperial forces without an expeditionary force or a general staff. Polo commanded more attention from the typical cavalry officer than the serious study of warfare or competency in staff work. The army's Commander-in-Chief, 1856–1895, the Duke of Cambridge, Queen Victoria's cousin, seemed determined to train officers to fight in the wars of the eighteenth and early nineteenth centuries, once telling officers during a lecture at Aldershot, or so it has been alleged: 'Why should we want to know anything about foreign cavalry? We have better cavalry of our own. I fear, gentlemen, that the army is in danger of becoming a mere debating society'.[5] Robertson, the quintessential professional, could not have been a junior, energetic and ambitious officer at a more opportune time.

The end of the conservative, largely retrograde, thirty-nine year tenure of the Duke of Cambridge as Commander-in-Chief in 1895 coincided with a momentous step in Robertson's career. In 1896 Robertson was nominated by the commander-in-chief in India to attend the Staff College at Camberley, about a mile from the Royal Military College. Robertson had to surmount two considerable obstacles to gain entrance to the institution which was responsible for instructing many of Britain's World War I generals. No ranker had attended Staff College since its inception in 1858. And the entrance examination, which included mathematics and required Robertson to know either German or French, was certain to be difficult for someone who was largely self-taught and could not afford to take leave from his duties in the intelligence branch. 'By rising regularly every morning between four and five o'clock, in winter as in summer, I was able to get through a large amount of spade work, crude and ill-directed though it might be, before going to office for the day', he later wrote.[6] Tutors and his educated wife also helped him.

The Staff College Robertson attended, 1897/98, with sixty-three other officers, was undergoing progressive changes and had exceptional leadership from two officers, Henry J. T. Hildyard, the Commandant, and George F. R. Henderson, a brilliant professor of strategy and tactics, whom Robertson worshipped. Robertson and his fellow students represented the elite of the army's junior officer corps. From 1895/98, Brian Bond has written, 'a galaxy of future stars passed through'.[7] A. J. Murray studied with Robertson in the Junior Division in 1897 while the Senior Division included Allenby, Haking, Edmonds, Haig, Macdonogh, Dyer, Capper and Forestier-Walker.

Robertson was assigned to the intelligence branch of the War Office when he left the Staff College. With the outbreak of the South African War, he was posted to Lord Roberts's headquarters to work under Henderson in intelligence. The role of intelligence, however, was little understood by his superiors; after experiencing nine months of frustration in South Africa, he was ordered back to the War Office. Robertson no doubt regretted that circumstances dictated that he spend most of the South African War in London. His experiences in wartime London, especially his interaction with the civil authorities, however, surely served him well as CIGS in Britain's next war. Not that he enjoyed the home front, which he described as 'the depressing and uncongenial atmosphere common to official life in London in time of war'.[8] When the intelligence branch of the War Office was enlarged, Robertson was chosen head of the foreign section. In 1903 he was promoted to full colonel. In 1905 his appointment as head of the foreign section was extended until the end of January 1907. Robertson's responsibilities included extensive travel and he visited lands such as France, Belgium and the Balkans where British soldiers would fight during the Great War. He also made a serious study of Britain's world strategic position, especially Germany's growing threat to British interests. Robertson's expanded role was a reflection of the quickening pace of the modernisation of the army, which included the creation of a proper general staff, of which the intelligence branch was a part, in 1904.

In May 1907 Robertson became Assistant Quartermaster-General of the Aldershot Command. A few months later he was promoted to Brigadier General, General Staff, of the same command under General Sir Horace Smith-Dorrien. It was at Aldershot that Robertson came to know George V, who attended troop manoeuvres there several times as Prince of Wales before succeeding to the throne.

In 1910 Robertson achieved another first in the army. Although some, including Sir Henry Wilson, had expressed concern about Robertson's lack of 'breeding', he became the first ranker to be chosen Commandant of the Staff College. His selection for such an important post was a strong statement about the growing professionalism of the army. At the Staff College, Robertson continued the same method of instruction that he had used at Aldershot. He sought to make the training of officers less theoretical and more practical. Since his mission was to train officers 'not only for staff work but also for the duties of command', he tried without success to change the name of the Staff College to 'War School'. His predecessor at Camberley, the easy-going, even flippant, Wilson, had delivered provocative and imaginative lectures on broad questions of strategy and politics. This was definitely not Robertson's style. 'It was the difference between the agile greyhound and the tenacious bull-dog—Wilson, expansive, giving himself out to those above him; Robertson, repressive, drawing others in towards himself; Wilson's eyes searching the horizon, Robertson's closely scanning the objects at hand',[9] one of their contemporaries has written. Robertson was concerned with acquainting officers with battlefield conditions, how theories of war were actually applied to defeat an enemy. 'Details, so-called, were thought to be petty and beneath the notice of the big-minded man', he later wrote, 'and yet they are the very things which nine hundred and ninety times out of a thousand make just the difference in war between success and failure'. On one subject, Robertson and Wilson could not have been in more agreement—the probability of war with Germany. Students at the Staff College toured continental battlefields, and training exercises simulated a German drive through Belgium. Perhaps the best example of Robertson's common sense approach to warfare was that officers were trained to conduct a withdrawal as well as an offensive.[10]

During his last year at Camberley, Robertson received recognition which greatly moved him. Accompanying George V on army manoeuvres, he was informed that the King wanted to make him a Knight Commander of the Victorian Order. Not knowing exactly what was expected of him, Robertson was understandably ill-at-ease. 'I was more than surprised, somewhat nervous, and quite ignorant as to what I was expected to do, but Wigram came to the rescue, drew the sword he was wearing, handed it to the King, and told me to kneel down. Having duly knighted me the King put out his hand, and not knowing what else to do I shook it, rising to my feet at the same time. I ought to have kissed it, of course, as a sign of homage, but the King was probably quite as pleased to see me shake it'.[11]

In October 1913 Robertson, now a major-general, left the Staff College to become Director of Military Training at the War Office. While at the War Office, Robertson played a role in the Curragh Incident during which elements within the army became politically involved to a degree not seen since Cromwell. The mutual distrust and suspicion between civil and military authorities provoked by this incident clearly contributed to the often antagonistic relationship between 'frocks', especially Liberal 'frocks', and 'brass-hats' during the Great War. Robertson's account of this divisive event suggests that he was largely above the fray and was convinced that the army would never be employed in Ulster. Yet Robertson was prepared to resign, placed obstacles to moving troops in his capacity as Director of Military Training, and unquestionably supported the Gough brothers, who were leading opponents of military coercion to impose Home Rule on Ulster.[12]

World War I quickly pushed the Irish Home Rule question into the background. Field-Marshal Lord Kitchener was appointed Secretary of State and took charge of the War Office. Sir John French, Britain's best cavalry commander during the South African War, a man of true grit, was appointed Commander-in-Chief of the British Expeditionary Force. Robertson, who was expected in wartime to become the chief staff officer of the home defence force because of his position as DMT, was able to join the BEF when there was a reshuffling of army positions. Archibald Murray, originally designated as Quartermaster-General of the BEF, became French's Chief of Staff. Robertson, selected to take Murray's place as QMG, was thus given an unexpected opportunity to demonstrate his considerable military qualities during the stress of battle.

'Wully' Robertson was fifty-five years old when he crossed the Channel on 14 August. Stocky and powerfully built, he was in excellent physical condition. Flat-footed, his step was heavy and deliberate. He has been described as an 'ambulating refrigerator'.[13] He had a thick moustache and a prominent jaw and chin. Beneath his bushy eyebrows, his eyes were dark and penetrating. He spoke in a deep, gruff voice. No less imposing than his physical presence was his forceful personality. Robertson's common sense approach, ability to see the essentials of a question, and his organisational ability were legendary within the army. These qualities, along with his moral courage, work ethic, judgment of men, common touch, and professionalism, made him one of the most respected senior officers in the army. But he could be a difficult man. Lacking in subtlety, he did not attempt to conceal his emotions. When angry it was said that his countenance took on the appearance of an approaching storm. 'I frequently trembled lest the food were not of the proper English kind, the carriage not properly warmed, or the bottle of whisky not forthcoming on the special French train I had often in later days to order for him,' one of his subordinates has written.

> When a misfortune of this sort occurred his chin would go into his collar, a second chin would appear under it, his eyes would go dark, his whole face assume a quite terrifying wooden aspect, while the hand tucked into the Sam Browne belt flapped gently like a fin. And then out came the grunt, like a cork out of a bottle, releasing the flow of words, the 'telling off' which he generally shot at you without turning his head as he strode by. No, he was not always easy to deal with. His manners were not good either. He had a way of slamming the door in your face while you were still speaking that endangered your nose and was disconcerting in the extreme.[14]

Robertson feared no man; and he could be as abrupt, even rude, with his superiors as he was with his inferiors. He did not mask his contempt for ideas on military questions, especially those emanating from amateurs, that differed from his own. It is often suggested that Robertson would have had much improved relations with the civil authorities had he been articulate. This view bears revision. With friends, Robertson was a good and at times amusing conversationalist. Furthermore, Robertson's correspondence, much of which was dictated, his cogent lectures at Camberley, and the minutes of committees at which he spoke, do not demonstrate any lack of fluency. Quite the contrary. The truth is that Robertson refused to be drawn into debate with politicians on military questions.[15] They wanted to talk in general, and to him, high-sounding and unrealistic terms; he in strategic principles and specific questions of application. Hence he chose his subjects carefully, and was slow and deliberate in his discussions with politicians. It was, thus, not any inability to express himself clearly that hampered his relations with political leaders such as Lloyd George, but his refusal to indulge the politicians in their dialectical reasoning and their use of compelling metaphors. 'It would have been as easy to make one of Henry VIII's yeomen armed with a quarterstaff understand the meaning of tact', Spears has written, 'as to make him realise that a little mansuetude and affability would have helped him mightily in his difficult and most responsible task'.[16] Nonetheless, Robertson was a dominant figure for most of the war. In M.P.A. Hankey's words, 'He knew what he wanted, and he nearly always got his way'.[17]

Robertson was put to a severe test during the long, and at times, panicky retreat of the BEF from Mons. His foresight in making plans to transfer British bases from the Channel to the Atlantic coast and his flexibility in finding ways to supply troops in headlong retreat enhanced his reputation.

When Archibald Murray was sent home, Robertson was chosen as his successor at general headquarters, but not before some behind-the-scenes manoeuvering had taken place. Sir John French had wanted Wilson to replace Murray, whose health had failed. Prime Minister Asquith, who had not forgiven Wilson for his intrigue with Unionist leaders against his government during the Curragh incident, and Kitchener, however, strongly vetoed this suggestion. Sir Douglas Haig, then Commander of the First Army, who was considered for the post, demurred and made very clear his preference for Robertson over Wilson. Haig's support of Robertson at this juncture of the war was to be the beginning of perhaps the most powerful and influential partnership in British military history. It is a relationship that should be explained. Robertson and Haig were never close friends. Strikingly different backgrounds and personalities along with Haig's aloofness precluded that. 'The Iron Ration', as opposed to 'Wully', was

Haig's private nickname for Robertson.[18] A common view on how the war should be conducted and their professionalism created the bond that held the two men together. They vigorously opposed the deployment of British military resources away from France and Belgium, believing that the war could only be won or lost on the western front. 'Here we can beat the German,' Robertson wrote to the King's equerry, Clive Wigram. 'No more d__d silly eccentric Dardanelles fiascos, pretty well doomed to failure & in no circumstances likely to help in decisive result. Fancy our fighting on a front from Calais to Constantinople'.[19] No two senior officers in the army had been more single-minded in their studious and serious approach to the profession of soldiering. A widespread view in 1914/15, perhaps shared by them, was that they were the two best professional soldiers produced by the prewar army.

Robertson had been reluctant to become French's Chief of Staff because he knew that he was not the first choice of the Commander-in-Chief. He also, like Haig, did not have a high regard for French's generalship. French's lack of Staff College training and his consequent ignorance of the crucial role of staff work in modern war, along with his mercurial personality and high-strung temperament, made him a poor choice to direct the large-scale operations being conducted by the BEF.[20] Robertson did not keep his unfavourable opinions of French to himself. As early as June 1915, he was telling Hankey of the 'reckless and impossible things' Sir John was contemplating.[21]

Robertson was equally concerned and vocal about the conduct of the war in London in 1915. Kitchener's new armies were being readied, but there was uncertainty that they would be sufficiently committed to the western front. Increasingly, civilians were influencing grand strategy with their amateur opinions which usually emphasised the political over the military aspects of military operations, with the Dardanelles and Gallipoli campaigns being the most notable examples. The Imperial General Staff, whose proper role was to provide an overall strategic plan, was practically moribund. Without competent and decisive leadership, misunderstood and ignored by Kitchener, the Imperial

General Staff was having no impact on the conduct of the war.[22] Bluntly stating his case, Robertson informed the King through his secretary and adviser Lord Stamfordham:

> The Govt. must receive the best military advice at home (Hankey & Callwell are I suppose the chief advisers. Ridiculous!) The S. of S. for War has not the time to study matters & formulate advice, in addition to his other work. The General Staff, with a trusted & competent head, should be allowed to function & do the work for which it was designed, & which it alone can do. It has been obliterated. Having the views of the different C's in C., & the advice of the General Staff at home, the Govt. will be in a position to see where they are & what they can best do. The present method of the higher conduct of the war can only lead to disaster.[23]

Archibald Murray's appointment as Chief of the Imperial General Staff in late September did not mollify Robertson. Murray prepared strategic appreciations for the government in favour of concentrating on the western front, but Robertson thought him 'wobbly'[24] and constitutionally unable to stand up to Kitchener in the realm of grand strategy.

Haig and Robertson were in agreement about the necessary changes in the British high command. Haig should replace Sir John and Robertson should return to the War Office as Chief of the Imperial General Staff. Haig's support, along with wire pulling from Buckingham Palace, was no doubt important in Robertson's selection as Chief of the Imperial General Staff in December 1915. Probably more important, however, was the belief on the part of Asquith and other ministers that Robertson was the best soldier available to offer the government sober, unequivocable and informed strategic appreciations. As early as June 1915, he had begun to provide London with his views on grand strategy and its formulation. He had written:

> A sound military policy cannot be properly formulated unless the General Staff at the War Office is placed in a position which ensures due consideration being given to its views. If no

> trained minds are brought to bear on the many questions that arise, the Cabinet will inevitably be influenced by those members who are the most persistent in pushing forward their views. These members may be the least qualified to express an opinion.[25]

His most important paper, which perhaps more than anything else made him CIGS, was a tightly-argued memorandum 'on the Conduct of the War' which he sent to Asquith on 6 November. Robertson expounded in this paper the strategic position from which he would never deviate in his advice to the government. Germany, he argued, could best be defeated where her main army could be found, France and Flanders. There were no short cuts to victory in any subsidiary theatres. As for the necessary machinery to win the war, he came right to the point:

> We are now conducting four distinct campaigns, and we hold in England large disposable reserves. It is essential in these circumstances that there should be one military authority responsible for advising His Majesty's Government regarding military policy in all theatres. The officer selected for this all-important part must be trusted by the Government to carry out his duties without interference, and if he cannot be so trusted he should be replaced. Experience has shown that in a war of the magnitude of the present one it is undesirable to combine in one person the functions of supreme military adviser and of War Minister.[26]

This last sentence was a direct hit at Kitchener, whose unsteady, often contradictory, military advice had destroyed his reputation with the civilians.

In early December, Asquith decided to appoint Robertson CIGS, but left the precise details of his relationship with Kitchener to be negotiated between the two men. Robertson was apprehensive for he barely knew the Secretary of State for War. As he expressed it years later, 'I was not particularly a Kitchener man, never having served with him anywhere except on Lord Roberts' staff in South Africa'.[27] If anything, Robertson believed that he needed Kitchener more than Kitchener needed him. 'I am an unknown man in the country', he wrote Wigram. 'K. with me would be a great help. Without him I would be nobody in the eyes of the public'.[28] Robertson's desire that Kitchener stay on in his post did not prevent him from insisting that the Secretary of State for War's authority be restricted, for all practical purposes, to the feeding and clothing of the army. Robertson demanded that the CIGS become the responsible military adviser to the government, issue all orders to commanders-in-chief in the various theatres on their behalf, and be in direct touch with these commanders with no interference from the Army Council. No CIGS, before or since, had demanded or received such autonomy within the War Office. Yet Robertson got what he wanted. His position as the supreme military adviser to the government was given the full force of law by an order in council issued by the King in January 1916. The only concession to Kitchener was that Robertson's orders to the commanders would be issued under the authority of the Secretary of State for War.

Robertson's triumph meant that the Imperial General Staff could now provide professional strategic and technical assessment of proposed military operations. Certainly, Robertson's, that is to say, the Imperial General Staff's ascendancy meant a substantial improvement in the often haphazard way in which military ventures had been embarked upon in the past. On the other hand, Robertson's dominance meant that British strategy for the next two years would have little or no flexibility. Granted, coalition warfare, the German advantage of interior lines, and the emerging shipping crisis already severely limited Britain's freedom of action. Britain's commitment to France on the continent could not have been altered without disastrous military and political consequences; the railways that linked Germany to her allies virtually neutralised British seapower; and unrestricted U-boat warfare made it difficult to feed the nation, let alone ship and supply troops in outlying theatres. On the other hand, Robertson, more often than not, refused to give an unbiased appreciation of military operations. His bluntly expressed criticisms of proposed or expanded military operations in Palestine, the Balkans, Italy and elsewhere were often clear-headed and proven correct by events. At times, however, as reflected in this volume of his military correspondence, he 'cooked' the advice he gave, refused to employ his considerable abilities to show how subsidiary military operations with which he disagreed might be made more realistic, and through personal and private letters sought to prevent military assessments from his commanders-in-chief opposed to his own views from reaching the civilian war leaders.

Robertson Correspondence And Editorial Method

The bulk of Field-Marshal Sir William Robertson's military correspondence can be found in the Robertson Papers which are deposited at the Liddell Hart Centre for Military Archives, King's College London. The major part of these papers was given to the Centre in February 1965 by Robertson's son, General Lord Robertson. These papers constituted the primary source for Victor Bonham-Carter's biography, *Soldier True*. A second deposit of Robertson papers, apparently not seen by Bonham-Carter, was made to the Centre in July 1969 by Marshal of the Royal Air Force Sir John Slessor. These personal and semi-official files had formerly been in the possession of Sir William Robertson's private secretary, C. C. Lucas. Letters from other repositories, including the Royal Archives and National Library of Scotland (Haig Papers), have also been included in this volume with the intention of providing as balanced and as comprehensive a picture as possible of Robertson's tenure as Chief of the Imperial General Staff, December 1915 to February 1918. Since it is assumed that this volume will be read, documents have also been chosen which help to convey a sense of the unfolding of events and policies. Particular attention is given to themes that have previously interested students of the higher conduct of the war, such as civil-military relations, manpower questions, conflict over higher strategy, the role of the national press, and the Robertson-Haig relationship.

Emphasis has been given to Robertson's private communications, including his 'R' or secret and personal telegrams. With very few exceptions, documents that are readily available and printed in full have been excluded. Although Robertson's numerous and important general staff appreciations have been omitted, the nature and location of such memoranda when mentioned in his correspondence have been (when possible) given in the chapter notes at the end. With few exceptions these memoranda are available at the Public Record Office at Kew. Given the scale and importance of the British military effort in France and Flanders and the special relationship between the two men, it is not surprising that Robertson's correspondence with Sir Douglas Haig constitutes the most substantial and revealing part of the Robertson Papers. This is reflected in the editor's selection of documents. It must also be noted that copies of Robertson-to-Haig letters in the Liddell Hart Centre for Military Archives often do not include alterations that appear in letters received by Haig and that are in the Haig Papers deposited in the National Library of Scotland. When there are differences, other than minor changes of punctuation, the editor has used the letter in the Haig Papers.

Documents are arranged chronologically. Each correspondent's rank or title is that borne at the time the document was written. All correspondents are identified in the Biographical Notes. Source references are placed at the end of each document. In the interest of readability or the conservation of space, documents have been silently standardised. The salutation and complimentary closing of letters have been left out. The place of origin and date are placed at the top right. Whether holograph or typescript and other distinctive aspects of the document are indicated on the top left. Other silent adjustments are the omission of material marked out by the author and the spelling out of abbreviations (Adjutant-General for A.G., for example) except in the case of easily recognisable individuals who were often called 'L G' instead of Lloyd George and 'K' instead of

Kitchener. With these above exceptions, the text of holograph letters, or correspondence in the author's hand, has been left as is, including inconsistent capitalisation, misspellings, stray dashes, and other errant characteristics. This preserves the individual relationship between the authors and their written words.

Substantial omissions are indicated by a row of asterisks, minor omissions by an elipsis.

Robertson's illegible handwriting can usually—but not always—be deciphered by the practiced and determined reader. The historian, not to mention those with whom he frequently corresponded, is exceedingly fortunate that Robertson dictated many of his letters. Ellipses within brackets [. . .] indicate an indecipherable word; a question mark preceding a word in brackets signifies uncertainty or speculation on the editor's part.

CHAPTER I

Chief of the Imperial General Staff: 'Three-hundred Yards of the Seat of Political Government'

Robertson entered the War Office as CIGS on 23 December 1915, in his own words, 'with a profound sense of anxiety'.[1] The responsibilities he assumed were without precedent in British military annals. As he later wrote Lord Northcliffe: 'I have to deal with five commanders-in-chief abroad, one at home, and about a dozen Allies, and to conduct my business with my Head Quarters within three-hundred yards of the seat of political government. It is a task which no man in the world, to my knowledge, has ever attempted before, and I hope that no other man will ever have to attempt it'.[2]

The Allied generals at the Inter-Allied Military Conference at Chantilly on December 6–8 1915 had unanimously decided upon a policy of co-ordinated offensives in 1916 in their principal theatres: Russian front, Italian front, and Franco-British front. Robertson's first priority was to gain his government's approval of a major British effort on the western front. He was equally determined to force upon the civilians a more realistic manpower policy. British losses were certain to be high in the coming battles and Robertson believed that Haig, who had replaced French as Commander-in-Chief of the BEF as part of the shakeup of the British high command that had brought Robertson to Whitehall, must be given the men he required through the adoption of compulsory service.

Given the growing strain on British shipping, war materials and men, Robertson was especially concerned about the 'side shows', or military ventures away from the western front that were supported by some civilians because they believed in indirect warfare or because of political considerations, or both.[3] As Haig advanced his preparations to attack on the Somme during the first half of 1916, Robertson kept a wary eye on these so-called 'easterners'. Efforts to expand the war against Turkey in Mesopotamia, Palestine and Arabia were either thwarted altogether or limited. The Balkans proved to be another matter—largely because of coalition politics that were not a factor in the British military effort against Turkey. The War Committee, the Cabinet's subcommittee which directed war policy, accepted Robertson's advice to abandon completely the Gallipoli campaign. But some of the British troops being evacuated from Gallipoli were sent to Salonika to rescue Serbia—and there they stayed as part of an international army despite Robertson's vigorous protests. By mid-1916, there were five British divisions in the Allied army at Salonika. Robertson had the support of most British ministers, Lloyd George being a notable exception, for reducing or even withdrawing the British forces from the Balkans after Serbia's collapse. But the French government strongly resisted, making what developed into a campaign against Bulgaria in Macedonia a litmus test of Anglo-French solidarity. The result was an often acrimonious tug-of-war between London and Paris. 'Of all the problems which brought soldiers and statesmen into conference during the years 1915–1917 the Salonika Expedition was at once the most persistent, exasperating, and unfruitful',[4] Robertson later wrote.

Lloyd George, who joined Arthur Balfour in initially opposing a major British offensive on the western front in 1916, posed the greatest threat to Robertson's control of British grand strategy. An ardent 'easterner', Lloyd George became the head of the War Office following Lord Kitchener's death. Although Lloyd George resisted becoming the Secretary of State for War 'under the humiliating conditions to which poor Kitchener had been reduced',[5] and scored many debating points in an exchange of letters in late June with the CIGS over the Kitchener-Robertson compact,[6] Robertson emerged with his powers intact.

Robertson's frequently harsh characterisation of Lloyd George and other political leaders found in his correspondence is not surprising. His views were typical of the attitude of the senior British officer corps towards the 'frocks', whose political compromises, intrigues, posturing, apparent indecisiveness, and use of the press were anathema to Robertson, Haig and other senior officers. To them crooked dealing and politicians were one and the same. Yet Robertson often found himself playing politics, cultivating the press and working behind the scenes with the King and politicians who were sympathetic to his views, in order to keep the government behind his and Haig's 'western' strategy and to influence the national debate on manpower. In the midst of a grave political crisis over compulsory service,[7] Robertson lunched with Geoffrey Robinson, the editor of *The Times*, in Smith Square on 14 April. Robinson's notes of their discussion reveal that Robertson was as contemptuous of Unionists as he was of Liberals:

> Great pressure had evidently been brought to bear upon him to agree to a compromise. He told me that he had seen half a dozen Ministers that morning and was worn out with their talk. Of Bonar Law he spoke with great contempt, saying that he was in a state of pitiable funk. Austen Chamberlain he thought useless, Selborne very disappointing, Lansdowne a good man grown old and weak. Of the Unionist Ministers the only man of whom he spoke with any approval was Curzon, whom he thought a big man with broad views; but he said that even Curzon did not seem able to 'get a move on'. His opinion of Asquith was very much the same as all of us hold—very clever, very skilful at holding his Cabinet together, possessed of a remarkable power of throwing off anxiety, but a pure politician without drive or initiative. He thought Lloyd George perfectly sound on this recruiting question ... All through our talk Robertson kept returning to the difficulty of 'getting a move on'. He was much impressed by the difficulty of the soldiers in the dealings with the politicians, saw that the soldiers could not safely assert themselves too much for fear of losing popular sympathy, while the politicians could nearly always outwit them in argument. He seemed inclined to welcome pressure to have the Army Council's general views on the subject made public. 'Certain detailed figures might have to be suppressed, but there need be no concealment about the broad question'.
>
> I told him that, so long as he and his colleagues at the War Office stuck to their guns, there need be no real difficulty about 'getting a move on' outside.[8]

Despite—or perhaps because of—his direct and crusty ways, Robertson enjoyed considerable success in achieving his objectives in London's very political environment. His efforts to modify aspects of Haig's plans with which he disagreed, however, proved to be a more delicate and in the end much less successful venture. The difference between his limited as opposed to Haig's grandiose conception of what the BEF could achieve in the stalemated siege warfare on the western front was so great that Robertson was driven to deviate from his strongly-held principle that the CIGS, far removed from the smoke of battle, should not interfere with a commander-in-chief's direction of a campaign. Unlike Haig, who hoped to achieve a breakthrough and aimed at distant objectives in 1916, Robertson believed that the BEF should conduct what have been called 'bite and hold' operations against the Germans. To limit British casualties and inflict maximum loss on the enemy, Robertson favoured limited infantry objectives, emphasis on the artillery, and the methodical defence of captured trenches to inflict heavy losses on the counter-attacking enemy.[9]

Robertson's uncharacteristically tactful and circumspect approach to his differences with Haig as revealed in his correspondence is easily understood. Robertson believed that he must avoid at all costs a division within the British high command. Any breach between himself and Haig, he believed, would be quickly exploited by Lloyd George and other 'amateur strategists' to the detriment of the army and sound military policy.

1

General Sir William Robertson to General Sir Douglas Haig

[Typescript with additions in other hand] War Office
26 December 1915

I found things here even in a greater state of muddle and chaos than I had feared, and it will take me some time to get them right. But I think I am making some progress, and will get properly going in the course of a week or so.

***

I also hope in the course of a day or two to inform you as to when you may expect new divisions from here. Quite roughly, and without committing myself in any way, as far as I can gather it would seem that I may be able to send you the remaining 4 new divisions at the rate of about one a month, commencing in January. This is exclusive of the one already under orders, regarding which a telegram was sent to you yesterday. I am turning my attention now to completion of the formation of the 13 Territorial Force Divisions still in this country. They are very much below strength, and require several things to fit them for the field. Our chief difficulty is, of course, as regards men; and this the Cabinet will decide or at any rate will consider tomorrow. I am putting before them the General Staff's view of the requirements to carry on the war as you suggested that I should, and they will not get these requirements so far as I can ascertain at present except by introducing compulsory measures.

The question of the evacuation at Helles[10] has been favourably received by the War Committee, but as originally the Gallipoli evacuation was referred to the Cabinet, and the Cabinet declined to agree to the evacuation of Helles the present question of evacuation has, of course, to be referred back to the Cabinet. They will consider it on Tuesday. All soldiers are for the evacuation but the sailors are not. It is rather monstrous to think that we should have to keep 50,000 men at Helles merely for the sake of looking after hostile submarines; which is what it amounts

to. The First Sea Lord[11] even went so far as to say that if we came away from Helles, the Germans might put a big gun there and bombard the Naval establishments at Imbros, 15 miles away. I reminded him of the futility of the German long guns with respect to Dunkirk, and he had no more to say. Generally speaking the Navy seems to be adopting a very helpless attitude.
P.S. *Don't* tell the French the 14th Division is *not* to leave you. In certain circumstances it *might*, and in any case I want to use the threat of moving it (as I many times have) as a lever for clearing out of Salonica.

LHCMA, Robertson Mss, I/22/3

2

General Sir William Robertson to General Sir Douglas Haig

[Holograph] War Office
Private 31 December 1915

I have greatly neglected you but I have been very busy. I have spent nearly two hours daily discussing with K the Command in Egypt. Result today is that he has gone to the Prime Minister proposing *2* Commanders & taken my written protest. What will be the outcome I do not know. K says he will resign if his proposal is not adopted. And the whole trouble is caused by the fact that he does not wish to put anyone over Maxwell.[12] Never mind.

I am just sending a War Office letter telling you what big guns you may expect to get in the next 3 months. L George has also promised to tell me our prospects as regards ammunition. You should economise 6″ Howitzer ammunition and you ought to send home at once any of these howitzers requiring repair. He tells me he can repair them in 2 months.

I hope to tell you soon what you may expect in the way of New Divisions & 2nd line Territorial Force Divisions. It is a difficult problem to solve. One division wants men; another rifles; another breeches etc. Therefore it is not easy to say which will be ready first or when. I am kept hard at it by many matters which ought to have been settled months ago. There is dreadful need of superior control of the war & our money though plentiful has its limits. There has been no coordination of the different departments. K has been working up to 70 Divisions. L George has ordered material for 100 Divisions. The Chancellor of the Exchequer[13] did not till yesterday know either of these things! Now he says the money will not run to it & I do not think it will. Clearly he cannot do impossibilities and the Government must decide what force they will maintain. There is great waste going on. The want of a military plan has lead to very great expenditure in sea-transport for instance. No less than 17 fat mounted Brigades have for long been allotted to Home Defence. Altogether more than 100,000 are on the Home Defence order of battle. Of course they are not nearly all efficient but they count as men. In many ways we are using our resources in the worst possible way. We have heaps of men as it is, but there is no intelligent plan for using them. What I am now aiming at is to find what number of men we can raise & *pay for*; then what we need for Home Defence; then the remainder will be for you I hope. I wish we could get away from Salonika but so far the French hold us there. Rub this in every time you see Joffre.

I am doing all right on the War Committee but it is difficult to keep ones temper. At the last meeting Balfour weighed in with a proposal that as the Western Front was so strong we should transfer all possible troops to cooperate with Russia on the Eastern front! Words failed me & I lost my temper.[14]

LHCMA, Robertson Mss, I/22/4

3
General Sir William Robertson to General Sir Douglas Haig

[Typescript with additions in other hand]

War Office
4 January 1916

I have been more busy than ever the last few days. Not being able to go back on the Prime Minister's pledge to bring out single men before married, certain politicians seem to be aiming at rendering compulsion useless by making out that although we may have power to take the men we cannot pay for them and they cannot be spared from their trades sufficiently to keep up the necessary exports and so provide the money we need with which to subsidise our allies. I was on a Committee nearly the whole of yesterday, and Cabinet Councils meet nearly every day and all day. The arguments I advanced were that we need every man we can get, that it is for the Government to say how many they can pay and how many they can find. The idea of some politicians was to abolish some, if not all, of the 2nd Line Territoral Force divisions now at home, 13 in number which we are preparing to send out later. But I do not think this will be done. I have shown many directions in which economy can be effected, and how there would be very little saving if any divisions were abolished, to say nothing of the money which has been already expended upon them. In the course of a few days I hope to be able to tell you what the result of it all is.

In the meantime I am still trying to re-organise the Army in Egypt. It is a terrible job.

***

May I ask you *not* to discuss with Lord K, when he comes, matters which can best be dealt with by me. It may add to my difficulties. I hope to come and see you week after next. Good luck.

LHCMA, Robertson Mss, I/22/7

4

General Sir William Robertson to Lieutenant-Colonel Clive C. Wigram

[In other hand] War Office
<u>Private</u> 12 January 1916

I have been attending a Cabinet Committee meeting for the last week, with not quite satisfactory results. The attitude of some ministers is rather to find out what is the smallest amount of money and smallest number of men with which we may hope, someday, to win the war, or rather not to lose it, whereas the proper attitude is to see what is the greatest number of men we can put into the field in the shortest possible period of time, after thoroughly organising Labour, eliminating all occupations not essential to the vigorous prosecution of the war, and making full and appropriate use of every man and woman in the country. There is a desire to cut down some of our existing Divisions—67 plus the 3 in India. No one can say what men we shall need except that we may need every one. If we do not exert our maximum effort this year with the object of gaining decisive victory & so dictate our own terms of peace, we shall probably have to conclude later an unsatisfactory peace, making our subsequent existence intolerable and have to maintain a large and ruinous army in readiness for the next struggle. I have tried to make all this clear to the committee, but am doubtful what the Cabinet will do. If any of the existing Divisions are cut down, the result may well be fatal.

RA, Geo. V, Q. 838/ 71

5

General Sir William Robertson to General Sir Douglas Haig

War Office

[Typescript] 14 January 1916

***

I hope my letter of yesterday has not misled you in regard to what Lloyd George is after with respect to the amount of ammunition required.[15] I am far from wishing you to say anything that might afterwards be construed into asking for too small an amount. Of course you must have ample, but I do not think that very much is to be learned from the French requirements as their methods and guns are totally different from ours. We all know that they blaze away far more than we do and if anything with less result. I am inclined to suspect that Lloyd George is preparing for future trouble in that he is beginning to see that he will not turn out in the time the enormous amount about which he has talked so much. I shall send you an official letter tomorrow showing his forecast for the next few months.

There is a good deal of talk on the War Committee and elsewhere about your having more Cavalry than you need. This is because of the various investigations now proceeding as to the directions in which economy can be effected. I have represented that the proportion of Cavalry you have to other arms is very much below the normal proportion though of course the conditions are not at present normal. I have always added that they may become normal some day. I shall be glad to have your views on this matter. I did not think you would care to decrease the amount of Cavalry you have, but on the other hand you may be of a different opinion and think that you can dispense with some or the whole of the Indian Cavalry Corps.

LHCMA, Robertson Mss, I/22/15

6

General Sir William Robertson to General Sir Douglas Haig

War Office

[Typescript] 16 January 1916

I shall try to get over during this week to see Joffre, and shall call and see you first. I hope that you will be able to go with me to see him. I cannot say yet on what day I shall come but I hope probably between Wednesday and Friday. If those dates would be inconvenient to you I shall be glad if you would send a wire. I will let you know definitely as soon as I can when I propose to go. As you will have gathered from my recent letters to you the opinions of the powers that be here vary a good deal as to what our policy should be, notwithstanding the so-called conclusions that they have come to.[16] But in addition to this I find that Joffre is very much in the hands of his politicians, and I hear that he is thinking that Russia will not be ready before July and therefore that the French will not go off before then, while in the meantime the British should prosecute a wearing down system on a rather extensive scale. Incidentally he seems to leave entirely out of the question what the enemy may do, and I am inclined to think that the enemy will go for Russia early in May and try to finish with her next summer, in which case we should have to go off before July. In general things seem to becoming rather mixed, and also seem to necessitate our taking hold of them. For these reasons it appears that the sooner I see Joffre and talk things over with him the better. At the Chantilly Conference he was all for going off in March. It would not be right nor so useful for me to see him without your being present. You and I could put our heads together over-night and then tackle him next day.

LHCMA, Robertson Mss, I/22/16

7

General Sir William Robertson to General Sir Douglas Haig

[Typescript with
additions in other hand]
War Office
Private
24 January 1916

***

I had a very pleasant visit and also a very instructive one. I must come over as frequently as I can, and I hope that some of your people will also come to see mine here whenever they can. We must rigorously avoid forming into two separate parties. Each must know all about the other's difficulties. I found while with you that even in the short time that has lapsed I have got out of touch to some extent.

It was very kind of you asking my boy[17] to join your Staff. I spoke to him yesterday and although he very much desires to push along in his own line he feels the opportunity you offer is much too good to be refused, and he therefore would be very glad to come if you still wish to have him. He is at present not in a specific appointment and therefore is free practically any day you may wish to have him. It would be convenient if he were allowed to come to England for two or three days before taking up his work so that he may get certain articles of kit that he should have with you. I am very grateful to you for thinking of the boy.

The Munitions Meeting with the French is I think to take place at Paris on Thursday or Saturday next. I will tell you definitely later. You must not forget that what Lloyd George is out for is to prove that we at any rate will not have sufficient ammunition to enable us to get going properly until well on into the summer. Your General Staff representatives should be alive to this aspect of the matter. Lord K is particularly keen that I should attend in order to see that Lloyd George does not in any way queer our pitch. I suggest that either Kiggell or Butler should be there if you can spare one of them. It is rather your pigeon than mine and I did not wish to go at all but Lord K was suspicious of what Lloyd

George may attempt to do. It would be a very good thing if Joffre had a representative there and perhaps you can arrange this. I am saying nothing to Joffre or Clive on the matter because it would be better that you should make the arrangement if it can be made. Whether it can be made or not depends upon the rather intricate relations existing as between Gallieni and his lot and Joffre and his people.

LCHMA, Robertson Mss, I/22/18

8

General Sir William Robertson to General Sir Douglas Haig

War Office

[In other hand] 27 January 1916

***

I have just seen Chalmers of the Treasury. He is a good fellow, and fully with us. He lost his two sons at Ypres last year. I have known him for some time. He discussed the financial situation, which he says is really very serious. What we need, he says, in order to preserve our credit is a victory, and we must avoid doing anything which may have the appearance of failure as this would act greatly against our credit. Of course I said nothing as to our plans. But it is well you should know the great importance all our proceedings have on the financial side as well as others. I make out we can go on as now, more or less for most[18] of this year but certainly not beyond it. It is in the meantime, very necessary to make every economy possible. To omit to do this will be tantamount to committing suicide. We cannot continue on the same lavish scale as heretofore. You will receive some letters in a few days on economy, and I know you will do all you can to ensure it.

LHCMA, Robertson Mss, I/22/19

9

General Sir William Robertson to General Sir Douglas Haig

[Typescript with holograph additions]
Secret

War Office
Whitehall, S.W.
28 January 1916

Many thanks for your letter of the 26th, I shall be very glad to stay with you on Sunday night on my way back from Paris, as I am anxious to have another talk with you. I have been thinking much over our last conversation.

As I have told you, the War Committee is not altogether whole hearted on the question of an offensive on the Western front and it is quite definitely opposed to an attack on our part which is independent of a general Allied offensive.

On the other hand, Joffre wishes you to begin a wearing-down attack in April, though the date of the general offensive is quite unsettled. It seems to me that there are seeds of friction in this state of affairs. The French very naturally consider that they have hitherto borne the brunt of the fighting, and, as we know, they are getting short of men. They, therefore, want you to bear the brunt of the preparation for an offensive on the West and have some reason on their side. If we cry off the preliminary wearing-down attacks the French will probably consider that we are not playing the game and are trying to avoid the losses involved. On the other hand, if Joffre trys to force on our War Committee his proposals for a preliminary offensive by us it may very well lead to trouble with our Government.

What is wanted is, in my opinion, a general coordinated scheme of operations for the Allies (see P.S.) and the best machinery for getting this seems to be the re-assembly of the Chantilly Conference of the Commanders-in-Chief, or their representatives.

I suggest the following outline for the Allied scheme:

(i) All the Allies should be ready as early as possible in the Spring, so that a German offensive can be dealt with if necessary;

(ii) The date of the Allied offensive, provided the enemy does not interfere, as it is very probable he will, should depend mainly upon when Russia is ready;

(iii) As the French and we can almost certainly be ready before the Russians the offensive on the Western front should precede that on the Eastern front by some three or four weeks, i.e., the time it takes Germany to transfer a considerable body of troops from one front to the other;

(iv) The wearing-down attacks, which we are, I think, all agreed are advisable, should precede the main offensive on the Western front, but should be so timed as to lead up to and culminate in the main offensive, and these wearing-down attacks on the Western front might be undertaken mainly by us.

We could then hope to have some fresh divisions, either from home or the Mediterranean, ready for our part in the main offensive.

I suggest that some general scheme of this kind should be prepared and agreed upon as soon as possible, whether it can be carried out or not must depend upon the situation at the time and chiefly upon the enemy's action. I think it is particularly important that the French should be brought to see that wearing-down attacks are of no value unless they are intended to prepare for and directly lead up to the main attack, and our War Committee should understand that a combined scheme of offence does not necessarily mean that all the Allied attacks must be simultaneous in point of time.

I send this on ahead so that you can think it over before I come. I am, of course, particularly anxious not to appear to be upsetting any of your arrangements with Joffre, but on the other hand we [?cannot] risk friction in the future.

P.S. The agreed Allied plan made before at Chantilly was that all should go off together as far as possible, and all try to be ready by March. Now Joffre seems to be departing from it, by wanting us to go in alone at very considerable strength in April. I will discuss with you the best way of putting Joffre right.

NLS, Acc 3155, no. 104, Haig Mss

10

General Sir William Robertson to General Sir Douglas Haig

[Typescript with additions in other hand]

War Office
1 February 1916

I have again had a long talk with Lord K regarding drafts. There is a good deal of ignorance in this office as to what is the true state of the case. There are many ramifications and the matter is not an easy one to understand. Lord K is going to see me and the Adjutant-General[19] together tomorrow to see if something can be done, at any rate as regards the Territorial divisions. But it will not be possible to bring these battalions up to 1,000 strong all at once. As I have said before the men are simply not in existence, *trained* men. No doubt there is a considerable number of men in 2nd Line and 3rd Line Territorial units, but there are exceedingly few of them trained. To take the few trained men away would mean practically scrapping these divisions altogether for a long period, and as you yourself told me before I left France we must aim at putting a large number of divisions into the field and of course we must get them into the field this summer. We have to consider which is the quickest way to get them into the field, and certainly to take *all* trained men away from these divisions would mean that the latter would not be able to go into the field much before the end of the year. The lack of rifles is one of the main reasons for not turning out more *trained* men. We cannot get the rifles. I hope all will be well in due time.

The difficulty is increased by the fact that Territorials cannot be transferred from one formation to another except they volunteer, while as regards regulars they also cannot be placed, it is said, in practice, in *any* unit. If this is so it is equally true to say that in practice it is impossible to keep all units up to strength, because if certain units can receive only a certain kind of man and that certain kind of man is not forthcoming it is quite clear that that unit may often be below strength. Legally, men of the regulars can be placed anywhere and it is for consideration whether more cannot be done in this way in France than is being done. It is the only alternative to weak battalions in some cases, that is unless we can count on practically an unlimited number of men and that we cannot do. I hope some good will come of Lord K's talk to the Adjutant General. Personally I am of opinion that the matter of personnel is second in importance to no other question at the present time and that to get the best value there is only one solution—that one you and I are agreed about and perhaps it may materialise shortly. I am doing what I can in the matter.

In the meantime, however, I would like to say a word as to the disposal of the personnel now in France. Although several of your battalions are under strength, several of your brigades are over strength because you have more than four battalions in them. I am now considering what is the best thing to do with these surplus battalions. What will be done with them I cannot yet say but what we shall not be able to do will be to maintain more than four battalions in a brigade at war strength.

I notice in your Strength Return that a large number of men are shown in Column B, varying between 9 and over 200. These great numbers away from battalions probably give rise to many of the reports as to the weak state of the battalions. I cannot imagine what the numbers include in some cases, because they vary so. There would seem to be need of investigation.

I notice too that the 'Drafts at Base' include men in entrenching battalions, but here again we cannot keep entrenching battalions going as well as authorised units.

The Prime Minister tells me that you have been asking for more labour battalions. I fear there is no chance of your receiving any until all ordinary battalions have been made up to war strength. We cannot take more than a given number of men away from industries and you agree that the first thing to do is to bring up fighting battalions to their war strength.

In general I may say that we have now reached the stage at which we have to proceed very carefully as regards personnel. Hitherto whenever units have been asked for they have been supplied as soon as they could be got together. In future I fear it will be necessary to do with fewer additions other than ordinary formations. As I daresay you know the Germans recently have been sending some of their labour battalions into the ranks, and at present we are certainly not in a position to raise many additional ones if any.

The Quartermaster General[20] has recently been taking up the question as to the reduction of men on the Line of Communication. I have thought for months past that considerable reductions could be made there and I hope you will do all in your power to effect reductions. No doubt everything is done very well in the Administrative Services, but the time has come to consider whether we should not try to do better in the fighting line at the expense of doing less well in rear. The whole question is one of men, the number of which is limited. I do not expect any reply to this. I will continue all I can to get you drafts. I can do no more.

LHCMA, Robertson Mss, I/22/20

11

General Sir William Robertson to General Sir Douglas Haig

[Typescript with holograph additions] War Office, 17 February 1916

I am sorry I kept you waiting so long on Sunday morning but Joffre sprung rather a bomb upon me. He told me that his Government had been considering the question of sending another 100,000 men to Salonika, which with the 200,000 now there plus 100,000 Serbians would make up a force of 400,000 for the purpose of making a demonstration northwards in order to keep the Bulgars, Germans etc. away from attacking Rumania. He is really rather tiresome in this matter because he knows that the operations would be foolish and useless yet apparently will not so tell his Government openly. Apparently it is the politicians who are at the bottom of the trouble. They seem to think that if anything goes wrong with Rumania the French Ministry will be turned out, that is all they care about. He told his people that he could not find any troops from France but that we might be able to find them from ours in Egypt. I was very straight with him and told him that I should oppose this to the utmost of my power, and I am working hard at this end to make our people take a firm stand if and when this French proposal comes forward, as I understood from Joffre it is likely to do. The fact is that we are not taking nearly sufficient lead in the conduct of the war, considering the great amount we are contributing towards it. I enclose a paper[21] on this subject which may interest you. We discuss it next week. I believe the Foreign Office think that I have been trespassing on their preserves, but that I do not mind. We must take charge of the thing in politics in the same way as we are gradually beginning to do in military affairs. I think you managed Joffre excellently. They always ask for far more than they expect to get, and you gave practically nothing. They really are rather difficult people to deal with.

***

NLS, Acc 3155, no. 104, Haig Mss

12

General Sir William Robertson to Lord Curzon

War Office

[Holograph] 2 March 1916

I am sure General Haig would not mind my allowing you to see the enclosed. I fear we have people in London, in high places, who need encouragement to take a less gloomy view of matters. After all we can but do our best, and although foolish optimism is dangerous, pessimism—even if justified—is unpardonable in leaders, civil as well as military. A pessimistic commander in the field is *never* tolerated. I am thinking of our Foreign Office and to some extent of the Admiralty, and often wish they would not so frequently paint for themselves—often quite without grounds—haunting pictures of what may happen to us. This great war will be won by fortitude and stout-hearts—if we have not them in high places we shall lose, or at any rate deserve to lose.

I am just off to see Joffre.

P.S. You will understand the enclosure is for your information alone. Also this letter.

India Office and Records, Mss Eur F 112/117, Curzon Mss

13

General Sir William Robertson to Lieutenant-General Sir B. T. Mahon

Dictated [typescript with holograph additions]

War Office
6 March 1916

***

I have just got your telegram saying that Sarrail has been ordered to undertake offensive operations and I have sent you a reply. Until you hear from me you can take it that I am not out for any offensive operations in the Balkans. Such operations would be unsound from every point of view, and the day they are sanctioned I shall leave the War Office. I know the Balkans pretty well, I also know the Germans, and I know where a decision will be got, and that certainly will not be in the Balkans. I do not intend to have anything to do with British soldiers being engaged in killing Bulgars and getting killed themselves in return.

P.S. Always let me know if I can help you. Sarrail is a wrong'un I should say. Too much of the politician about him.

LHCMA, Robertson Mss, I/35/74

14

General Sir William Robertson to General Sir A. J. Murray

War Office

Dictated [typescript] 6 March 1916

I have no news of importance to send you this time. I saw Joffre last week and he still declines to consider a withdrawal from Salonika. The reason is that he is so much in the hands of the politicians. If we withdrew from Salonika the futility of having sent the troops there would be apparent to the French public and the French Government would get into trouble. The whole thing is a French political rant. I think the only way of getting some troops from Salonika will be to decline to send any more from Egypt, and this I shall probably do after you have sent three or four divisions away. I must have a little reserve in Egypt to meet eventualities in India or elsewhere in the East, and although I am prepared to run any amount of risk I do not intend to run it so long as we and the French each have five divisions sitting in Salonika doing nothing. The French are even more tiresome than before.

I may say that the Verdun business has been magnified unduly by the French. They were caught napping as usual and with few or no trenches, they lost their heads and began to chatter and in general behaved as the French always do. No doubt the Germans tried to see what they could do, but they ought not to have been able to do anything like what they did had the French taken reasonable precautions. I should imagine that the German losses are no greater than the French and their's are all to the bad.

***

LHCMA, Robertson Mss, I/32/9

15

General Sir William Robertson to General Sir Douglas Haig

Dictated [typescript with holograph additions]

War Office
6 March 1916

I had the usual kind of talk with Joffre. Apparently he has no idea of ever taking the offensive if he can get other people to take it for him. So far as I can make out he has no longer any confidence in himself. I am going to tell the Prime Minister all that I learnt and the class of work done by the French round Verdun.

***

After my visit last week to French General Headquarters I am more convinced than ever it is we who will have to finish this war, and therefore in every way we possibly can we must take the lead or at any rate refuse to be led against our own judgment. I am preaching this here every day to all the powers that be. I hope I am getting a little more manliness and courage into some of those in higher places.

***

P.S. I have not much use for Castelnau.

NLS, Acc 3155, no. 105, Haig Mss

16

General Sir William Robertson to General Sir A. J. Murray

[In other hand]

War Office
8 March 1916

I was at a war committee meeting this morning, and have come away very depressed because of the lamentable display of inability to govern on the part of the Ministers. There was a very unseemly wrangle between Fisher (who had been brought in for the morning), and the Lords of the Admiralty, & Whitehall is full of Sandwich men calling for Fisher. The whole disgraceful proceeding is got up by Fisher and Winston,[22] apparently. No doubt the Admiralty require shaking up, but not in this manner. Winston has just applied to be relieved of his command because his Parliamentary duties call for him here! Asquith is seeing him. The second topic was paucity of shipping, lazy and striking workmen, fear of restricting imports, declining store of food supplies. We have *ample* resources of *all* kinds if only Government would but govern and make the resources available. The conscription bill is proving a farce.

Macready & I are attending to it, & will shortly go to the Government about it if matters do not improve.

Fortunately purely military matters are not now interfered with, but I am very anxious as to everything else, & it is that which counts for much in this war of Exhaustion.

I am writing this with the object of saying that practically anything may happen to our boasted British Constitution before this war ends, and that the great asset is the army—whose value will be fixed largely by the extent to which we at the top stick together & stand firm.[23]

British Library, Add 52461, Murray-Robertson Mss

17

General Sir William Robertson to General Sir A. J. Murray

Dictated [typescript with holograph additions]

War Office

Private

15 March 1916

I attended the Conference at Chantilly on Sunday last but nothing much happened worth repeating to you. A month ago

Joffre was urging me to send six divisions from Egypt to Salonika with a view to taking the offensive in the Balkans, aided by 100,000 Serbians when they were ready. Of course I would do nothing of the kind and I never shall. I am determined on that. Verdun however has brought him to his senses and he now asks me to send no more troops to Salonika but to send all the divisions from Egypt to France, six of them to get there by 15th April. I have no intention of doing this either and I told him so. I told him quite plainly that although I shall be prepared to take risks I am not going to take any in the East so long as we have 200,000 men at Salonika doing nothing. I have told him that I would send five from Egypt and no more, for an indefinite period of time. So when we get the five from Egypt we are going to review the Salonika matter again. I am trying to put pressure on him to bring away troops from Salonika by refusing to bring more out of Egypt. My influence over him is governed by the strength of my reserve, and once I hand it over to him I shall be helpless. I have no intention of doing so. Until Kut[24] and the Eastern situation have become clearer five divisions from Egypt is my limit. I know I can trust you however to get all the divisions ready so that they may be sent whenever they are required. I feel strongly that Egypt must be regarded as my general reserve, and of course the troops there *must be ready for action*. So I hope you will push along getting the divisions ready as quickly as possible so that they may be sent wherever they are needed. It seems to me that there is a very large mass of troops of different sorts in Egypt and now that you have got supreme command you will I hope unravel the muddle, let me know definitely what you want and for what purpose, and then I shall know what I have got as a general reserve. Kindly let me have your views on the whole question, officially, as soon as you can. We want *men* badly. Can't get the recruits we need. Men, men.

***

The Turk is having a good deal of hustle at the present time and would like to throw up the whole business I believe, but of course Constantinople is the obstacle. But for that I believe he would throw in his hand at once.

Very much depends upon what happens at Kut. It is a poor

show there and very little courage and determination are being displayed. I still hope for the best and am applying all the ginger I can.

Briefly my policy is to get as many troops away from Salonika as possible and as soon as I can. Refuse to take offensive action in the Balkans unless the situation changes very much. To keep Egypt reasonably secure. To keep a reserve in Egypt for India as long as it seems likely to be required. To get everybody else to France.

P.S. This being a private letter *don't* refer to it if and when you write officially on the points I have mentioned.

British Library, Add 52461, Murray-Robertson Mss

18

General Sir William Robertson to David Lloyd George

Dictated — War Office
[typescript] — 16 March 1916

Lord Kitchener has informed me that the question of giving Rumania some machine-guns was discussed by the Cabinet this morning and that you were asked to obtain my opinion on the subject before acting. I can only say that I not only object but feel it my duty to protest against any guns being given to Rumania until we and our Allies are properly equipped with them. We are in great need of these guns for Home Defence. We need more in France and other theatres. India needs these guns; and so do our Allies. Fifty guns may not seem to be a large number, but they would be most welcome to Lord French and also to India.

LHCMA, Robertson Mss, I/33/5

19

General Sir William Robertson to General Sir Douglas Haig

Dictated [typescript with holograph additions]

War Office
22 March 1916

I enclose copies of two papers[25] which explain themselves, for your personal information. I do not know what luck I shall have in regard to either of them, but I am endeavouring to keep on a straight and simple road, and shall not abate one jot of my purpose to get you men. I daresay this question of men may break up the Government before we have finished, and perhaps that is not to be altogether regretted. At any rate we must have the men. There is great agitation in London these last few days in regard to men. Since we have had Macready here he has been able to get to work and get us some definite figures and we all know now where we are. The present Military Service Act[26] is a farce and a failure. It was a regular political dodge, and of course political dodges will not stand the stress of war with Germany. We want men.

I go to Paris on Sunday to attend this Conference, not that I wish to go except for the reason of keeping my eyes and ears open. I do not propose to say a word unless I am compelled. When there I am hoping to make some progress as regards Salonika but very much doubt it. You see we are tied up with the French Government and have not a free hand to bring our troops away. If we had I would bring some of them away at once.

LHCMA, Robertson Mss, I/22/31

20

General Sir William Robertson to General Sir A. J. Murray

Dictated
[typescript]

War Office
5 April 1916

***

We are having troublesome times here in regard to personnel and I am giving the Government no peace. When we shall get your Territorial Force divisions up to strength I do not know. However, you are safe enough for some months yet I think. Kut is the place that troubles me most because if Kut goes well all will be well in the East. If it does not there is no telling what might happen.

At the Paris conference last week I had a heated discussion with Joffre in front of Asquith and Briand in regard to Salonika, but again I failed to bring the divisions away. Apparently there is a great deal of Finance as well as Politics mixed up in this French enterprise, and the French have no idea at all of coming away if they can help it. A week or two before Verdun Joffre asked me to send six more divisions to Salonika, but he soon altered his tune when the German got going, and now he is for sending no more British troops to Salonika. That is as far as we have got. I feel that this fellow Sarrail will get us into a mess there before he has done, and I hope that Mahon will be careful and not lose any more British lives than possible in foolhardy enterprises.

I am delighted to see how you keep packing people home. We have plenty of work for them to do—bar the generals and of them we have got more than enough. It means that they are not only idle but mischievous as you can understand.

LHCMA, Robertson Mss, I/32/19

21

General Sir William Robertson to General Sir Douglas Haig

War Office

[Holograph] 26 April 1916

***

I have had a busy time lately, but have managed to win, I think. On May 27th we get compulsion I think—*if* the Government stick to their word—for they will not get 50,000 unattested unmarried men (out of an estimated 200,000 *available*) by May 27 & 15,000 a week—or nearly 70,000 a month—afterwards. They decided not to table the bill *now*, but rather to break up the Government, which meant at any rate a winter before a bill could be produced, & perhaps not then be passed. Under the arrangement made they say they will stand united for the bill on May 27th if the numbers are not forthcoming—as they will not.

With regard to your operations. The French people are *most* trying. Clive has wired to say he comes on Friday & will ask what guns & ammunition will be available on May 15. June 1. June 15. For Joffre's [?information]. I have told him to apply to you. You know all I know, and more. Besides I do not mean to come in between you & Joffre. It is best to leave him entirely to you. As far as I can make out the French are making practically no preparation for business on your right. But *I know you will keep your eye on them and not embark alone on a foolish enterprise.*[27] It is disheartening they do not act more sensibly and sincerely with you. What good do they expect to get from trying to inveigle you into an abortive offensive? It is a great comfort to me to have you on the spot.[28]

Kut is all up. A more mismanaged expedition never was—except Gallipoli.[29]

Hope you are keeping fit. We have had much excitement in Ireland[30] and in *London*, because it was feared some Germans would land in Ireland![31] I reminded them that 2½ million Germans were in France & yet the French were not so excited! They are just cowards. They really are. They regard me as an optimistic ass when not as a stupid soldier. They think—& nearly say—that all soldiers are stupid. They are much annoyed with *all* soldiers, because we have now got them into a corner, & finally have the upper hand.

NLS, Acc 3155, no. 105, Haig Mss

22

General Sir William Robertson to David Lloyd George

War Office

[Holograph] 2 May 1916

The bill[32] introduced today should more than compensate you for the rubbishy Press attacks of the last week or two. The great thing is to get the bill, and for it the Empire's thanks are due to you alone.

H. of Lords RO, Lloyd George Mss, D/18/8/12

23

General Sir William Robertson to Lieutenant-General G. F. Milne

R [telegram]

SECRET War Office

Personal and Secret 8 May 1916

Joffre is proposing combined offensive from Salonika and to this we and our Government have always been opposed. I have told Joffre I must have your views before we can definitely agree and that Sarrail must disclose and discuss his plans with you. He has told Sarrail to do this. Of course we must co-operate with our

Allies to the full extent possible but this would not justify our undertaking futile and costly operations. It is not a platitude but vital necessity to employ fullest energy on main front and it is not justifiable to throw good money after bad by assuming offensive merely for sake of doing something. I wish you comprehensively and seriously to consider Balkan situation and possible developments of offensive having special regard to men and munitions, communications, transport, mountain artillery, and much additional shipping which we might find impossible to provide.

I prefer you should not open the question but wait for Sarrail to speak to you and in meantime send me such views as you can. Should the proposed operations be eventually adopted we shall insist upon your relations with Sarrail being similar to those obtaining between French and British in France and you in no sense being under Sarrail's orders. Plans should therefore admit of British troops being kept together and having their own mission. There are many factors of which I am ignorant but on general grounds and subject to your views I am unable to think otherwise than that extensive offensive operations would be very difficult and be unlikely to succeed and probably prove a costly failure. Above is not for communication to Sarrail but for your guidance and personal information.

LHCMA, Robertson Mss, I/14/16

24

General Sir William Robertson to General Sir A. J. Murray

Dictated — War Office
[typescript] — 18 May 1916

... I think we shall keep Davies[33] at home, and as regards Mahon I can only confess that he ought not to have been sent to you. But it was the only way in which I could get him replaced at

Salonika. We are having a deal of trouble with the French again in regard to this place and they are urging us to commence offensive operations. Mahon is not at all up to Sarrail and in any case he is not the kind of man we want there. Sarrail is trying to get us committed to an offensive by indirect means and I want them to be scotched.

***

I had a big fight about the Conscription Bill, but the Army Council backed me up to a man and we proved too much for the Cabinet. It was a great victory, and although the Bill is hedged about with all kinds of exemptions etc. I think we shall now manage to get the men we want. I am paying constant attention to your drafts and hope that we shall soon bring your divisions up to strength. I think we shall. There has been a great improvement here since Macready came, but as you know trained drafts cannot be produced in a day. What with training, the want of rifles etc. etc. it takes many months to put the men into the field. However, things in general are improving and I hope and believe that in another two months time the whole show will be going much better.

***

LHCMA, Robertson Mss, I/32/28

25

General Sir William Robertson to General Sir Douglas Haig

Dictated [typescript] War Office
Secret 18 May 1916

If we can arrange sea transport I hope it may be possible to commence moving the 4th and 5th Australian divisions from Egypt during the first week of June.

I think I have already told you that I have received a letter from Joffre advocating offensive operations in the Balkans. I have been waiting to ascertain more particulars in regard to the operations, and was about to answer Joffre when the French Government weighed in with a request of the same nature to our Government, and suggesting that two divisions from Egypt destined for the Western front should be sent to Salonika to reinforce the troops there previous to the offensive being undertaken. Joffre has said nothing regarding the latter. It is very difficult to deal with people like the French. Tomorrow I hope to send, for your personal information, a copy of the reply which has been sent to the French Government. I expect there will be rather serious trouble about this matter, and I shall be glad if you would give me the benefit of your observations as soon as you receive the reply I am sending to you. I feel that we really must stick to our ground on this occasion, but it is such a serious matter that I would like to know what you think. If we embark on a Balkan campaign the result may be very serious indeed in regard to the war as a whole. Joffre told Maurice the other day that before Verdun he had hoped to put 40 divisions into his offensive, whereas now he looks forward to putting only 25 in, and he added that if fighting continued at Verdun he might in the course of two or three months be able to put no divisions in at all. I do not know how this tallys with your conversations with him.

LHCMA, Robertson Mss, I/22/36

26

General Sir William Robertson to Major C. C. Lucas

1765 Mayfair
4, South Street
Park Lane

[Holograph] [Undated[34]]

I am *most* anxious the King shall *not* move in the matter for the present, or he will give me away & do himself no good. There is lots of time. There is really no reason to tell *him*, & I'd rather he were not told, as it will only worry him, & perhaps for nothing. The story is long & rather complicated & therefore I send you to tell *Wigram*. We can keep him afterwards informed of events. Perhaps it may all bust up. The War Committee conclusions *may* give the King a handle, & if so he can use it if he likes. On the other hand they may *not*. I don't know what will appear. Perhaps very little as the thing is so sub-rosa. Any how His Majesty should not move till he hears of it from some other source than me, unless I tell Wigram the coast is clear. On the whole I think Wigram had best await the War Committee conclusions before saying anything to His Majesty, & when he gets them *if they say nothing*, he had better still wait till he gets the word go from me. It is no use worrying the King without reason, & I hope there may be none.

RA, Geo. V, Q. 1200/13

27

General Sir William Robertson to Lieutenand-Colonel Sir M. P. A. Hankey

Dictated [typescript with additions in other hand]

War Office
25 May 1916

I am concerned regarding the supply of information to the War Committee.[35] The question was raised a short time ago, and it was more or less decided that I should regularly make verbal statements, perhaps a little more fuller than in the past. I am most anxious to give the War Committee all the information they ought to have. I can honestly say that I have no secrets in regard to them. But what I wish to suggest is that it would be useful to the Committee and probably conducive to the despatch of subsequent business if it were an accepted rule that at each Meeting I would begin with a short statement of all information that I think would be useful to the Committee. The Committee could then ask for anything more they wished to have, and I should always of course be glad to tell them anything I can. Under present arrangements sometimes I make a statement and sometimes I do not. If the statement were made regularly at each Meeting the Committee would be kept regularly and fully informed. For yesterday's Meeting, for example, I spent a considerable amount of time previously preparing some notes and maps that I proposed to give to the Committee, but the War Committee Meeting proper did not open before 12.30., and then went on to Lord Robert Cecil's question which continued to about ¼ past 1. Other business had then to be transacted, and generally the time was no longer appropriate for making my statement. I wish you would think this over and if you consider necessary speak to the Prime Minister. I really believe it would help the Committee very much if the rule I have suggested were usually adopted, and I myself would like it because I would then feel more satisfied than I now do that I am keeping the Committee fully informed of all I think they ought to know. Perhaps the Navy should also give an account of their stewardship. If more time were devoted to matters above indicated and in making the Committee more au courant with the real Naval, Military Situation, and less time devoted to matters which could equally well be settled, largely, beforehand by the Departments mainly concerned, I believe great good would accrue.

LHCMA, Robertson Mss, I/33/21

28

General Sir William Robertson to General Sir Douglas Haig

War Office
[Holograph] 28 May 1916

***

The more I think of the future the more I feel we need to be, relatively, much stronger than at present in artillery. The French, too, give me the impression that they do not see the end of the war before next year and intend to go easy this year. Therefore I do not, at my end, propose to cause the Government to think of a great offensive promising far reaching effect, but to show them the necessity of our cutting in soon so as to assist & encourage our allies, and to well strafe the German. This, I understand you to agree, is the correct point of view to take. I think it is.

In a few weeks *we must consider the reduction in the number of Cavalry divisions.*[36] I can, at a pinch, always find you some cavalry from England, who meanwhile are useful there.

NLS, Acc 3155, no. 106, Haig Mss

29

General Sir Douglas Haig to General Sir William Robertson

General Headquarters
British Army in
[Holograph] the Field
Secret 29 May 1916

. . . As regards what you say regarding the future, the objectives at which I am aiming are:

1. Train Divisions

Build up reserves of ammunition & military resources of all kinds.

Wear out the enemy by raids & every means.

2. Be ready to support the French by a resolute attack when required by the military situation, and at the same time prepare to exploit to the utmost any success gained—

3. But, while attacking keep in view the necessity for putting troops in favourable positions for a campaign in the spring of 1917 so as to make sure of success next year—

(I mean don't forget the difficulties of the Ypres salient; nor go down into the mud beyond the Pozières ridge, unless we have the force to take up to a line on the heights beyond the valley at le Sars)—

As to reducing cavalry, I have already given orders to consider how we can reduce the cost of their keep in the coming winter—If we can't effect economy then some must go, but I have an inward feeling that events will make us regret a reduction in mounted troops. It seems to me that troops & matériel are so imbedded in the ground in trench warfare, that a general retreat will be most difficult. We ought therefore to be prepared to exploit a success on the lines of 1806—[37]

I hope you got back all safe & sound & were none the worse for your trip.

NLS, Acc 3155, no. 106, Haig Mss

30

General Sir William Robertson to General Sir Douglas Haig

[In other hand]

War Office
2 June 1916

Again today it has been brought to my notice in a forcible way that we are suffering in the eyes of the French as to the extent of the effort we are making and preparing to make to win the war, because our effort is not sufficiently boomed. In fact is often decried by our own people. I am sure things would be much better if we got the Press more on our side. I am sure of this. My idea is that we ought to send out, on your invitation 4 or 5 of our big newspaper Proprietors e.g. Northcliffe, Burnham etc for a few days to some part of our front. If you can agree to something of the kind I'd be glad if you sent me a reply by return of post.

LHCMA, Robertson Mss, I/22/45

31

General Sir Douglas Haig to General Sir William Robertson

[Typescript with holograph additions]
Copy 3 June 1916

Replying to your letter of yesterday—it is by no means a convenient time to receive newspaper proprietors out here. There will be preparations in progress which it is essential to keep secret, and everyone will be extra busy.

At the same time, I wish to do anything I can to smooth away such difficulties as the Press may be causing at home, and if this visit is considered sufficiently important to over ride the disadvantages I have mentioned I am willing to receive the visitors you propose to send and to arrange for them to see something of our front.

Everything possible is being done to satisfy the Press representatives out here, and I believe with success. I am sending you an official letter on the subject, explaining the arrangements that have been made to furnish fuller information to the press, and making proposals as to the methods to be adopted to guide press policy.

I personally saw all the accredited correspondents last Thursday.[38] They all expressed themselves as thoroughly satisfied with the facilities given them for visiting the front & writing reports. The difficulties you complain of seem to come from the Editors.

NLS, Acc 3155, no. 106, Haig Mss

32

General Sir William Robertson to H. A. Gwynne

1765 Mayfair
4, South Street
Park Lane

[Holograph] 18 June 1916

Two points not without importance I forgot to mention this afternoon.

(a) Effect on the allies if they have cause to suspect (political) control of military operations. You well know how strong the *military* feeling prevails in regard to military matters in countries where national service has long prevailed.

(b) Effect on our own Commanders and armies in general of a similar result. I believe they now have confidence in the management of military affairs. If they have not, it is *my* fault, and not that of the system. Armies are very human in their nature, and like to feel they are being ordered to fight by one of their own kind who knows & understands them. Men object to being killed by amateur strategists.

I believe that the relations now established between the Imperial Headquarters & the Armies in the field are good and promising. To disturb them will react right through to the men in the front trenches.

IWM, Gwynne Mss, Pt. III, fol. 350

CHAPTER II

The Somme Campaign to the Fall of Asquith

The initial phase of the Somme battle was an unmitigated disaster. At 7:30 a.m. on 1 July eleven British divisions participated in an Anglo-French assault. At the end of the day the British had suffered 57,470 casualties. In contrast the German defenders on the British Somme suffered approximately 6,000 casualties.[1] The magnitude of this setback to British arms, however, was not at first immediately apparent to Haig at his advanced General Headquarters at the Château de Beauquesne. As late as 4 July, he 'thought the situation "most favourable" and called upon "God's help ... to turn it to account"'.[2]

Robertson, who had arrived at advanced General Headquarters on the day the offensive began, quickly perceived that something terrible had gone wrong. In secret correspondence with Haig's subordinates, he attempted to influence future tactics. At the same time, he felt it his duty to support Haig loyally at this critical juncture. He wrote encouraging words to the Commander-in-Chief of the BEF. In the War Committee, he gave the civilians no reason to question Haig's leadership of the greatest force that Britain had ever committed to battle. Haig's failure to keep him fully informed of either his plans or the course of the battle made Robertson's task doubly difficult. Another of Robertson's concerns was possible friction over the conduct of the battle between the French and British commanders-in-chief. As abundantly reflected in his personal correspondence, Robertson, like the vast majority of the senior British officer corps, was contemptuous of the French. But he recognised that Allied unity was essential to the defeat of the German Army. His private views consequently were not allowed to influence his relations with the French or other allies.

Robertson was able to contain criticism of Haig's conduct of the Somme battle within the War Committee. Even Lloyd George, the high command's most dangerous critic, gave his support to the continuation of the offensive.

Relations between Robertson and Lloyd George, however, were at the breaking point during the first half of October. Lloyd George's implied criticism of the BEF's generalship during a trip to the front in mid-September and his support of military intervention in Arabia created serious friction. But it was Robertson's unbending opposition—even to the point of threatening resignation—to Lloyd George's support for reinforcing the Allied force in the Balkans to prevent the defeat of Romania, Britain's newest ally, that brought matters to a head.[3] When Robertson mobilised his supporters, including the King and influential newsmen, Lloyd George made a strategic retreat, telling Asquith that he had 'implicit confidence in both Haig and Robertson and if either of them were to go he knew no one who could fill their places'.[4]

Robertson's uncompromising support of Haig had its price. The massive casualties on the Somme front, in conjunction with Russia's decline and the deterioration of the Allied position in southeastern Europe, eroded civilian support of the Imperial General Staff. Robertson had been careful never to suggest that the Germans could be defeated in 1916. Nor had he underestimated British losses.[5] Nevertheless, the War Committee expected more and was sympathetic to Lloyd George's suggestion on 3 November that a fresh look should be taken at the military situation.[6] Temporarily outmanoeuvred, Robertson came very close to having his strategical direction of the war curtailed by being sent to a military conference in Russia where he would be away from the War Office for a month or more.

As the third Christmas of military stalemate approached, the strain on the nation was great. There was a crisis of confidence. But the civilian rather than the military leadership underwent dramatic change. Lloyd George replaced Asquith. Robertson favoured the change of government. He believed that the new government would 'get a move on', especially in the area of mobilising the country for total war; and there would be no talk of compromise peace.

33

General Sir William Robertson to Major-General F. B. Maurice

General Headquarters
France

[Telegram] 2 July 1916

Following for His Majesty and War Committee: There was very hard fighting yesterday, and in many cases the Germans held out until their last man was killed. Their trenches and dugouts were more formidable than any yet encountered, while their guns, though not preponderating were well placed and effective. Evidently they had made careful preparations to receive an attack on the front north of FRICOURT and consequently this section of the attack was not so successful as had been hoped. To the south of FRICOURT our task was less difficult though there was heavy fighting for MAMETZ. The French had a very easy task as apparently the enemy expected no attack south of the Somme. The French in some cases took positions in parade formation as they express it and practically without any loss. The weather yesterday was hot and trying. Our artillery is reported to have done its work excellently and the Royal Flying Corps was especially good. Apparently some of our new divisions were a little too reckless and as was to be expected through want of adequate military experience they failed to meet unexpected situations correctly. All our troops, however, fought with the utmost gallantry and today all are in excellent spirits. I have seen several commanders and I am satisfied that the Germans have had very heavy losses though they are fighting hard.

Bodleian, Ms Asquith 128, fol. 26

34

Lieutenant-General Sir A. G. Hunter-Weston to General Sir William Robertson

Headquarters,
[Typescript] VIII Corps
Private 2 July 1916

Appropos of our conversation this morning I should much like to see you tomorrow if you have a spare moment. May I motor over to you after breakfast, at any hour you may appoint? The bearer will wait for your answer.

We were mistaken in supposing that two battalions had got through to Serre, but had been cut off by Germans getting up out of dug-outs behind them. Later and more accurate information established the fact that these battalions, and the majority of the other battalions all along this front, were defeated by the enemy's artillery barrage, and by his machine gun fire, which in many cases simply wiped out the battalions before they reached the German trenches.

The gallantry, discipline and devotion of our troops was beyond praise. But we had not knocked the German trenches about nearly enough to block their dug-outs and fill up their trenches in the way the German artillery does to our trenches, and so, as you will see on reading the enclosed interesting notes I have had typed, the German Infantry and Machine Gunners were able to come out of their deep dug-outs, and man their parapets, as soon as our men showed, and were thus able to prevent our men reaching their trenches.[7]

The reason of the lack of success of the Third Army and left of the Fourth Army is that the Germans here had better trenches, and a much more powerful artillery. It was at Gommecourt, Serre and Beaumont Hamel that they most feared attack.

A contributory cause was the inadequacy of the artillery and of the ammunition available. The Germans keep up a drum fire with heavy howitzers for many hours. For this we neither have the ammunition nor the howitzers, nor, indeed, could our howitzers stand such continuous fire. We always have to be saving our guns. Of ammunition we had only about 1⅓ heavy howitzer shells per yard run of fire trench, whereas we should have had about 10 per yard run. However, this latter reason is for your ear alone, it is inadvisable to give currency to such unpleasant and dangerous facts.

LHCMA, Robertson Mss, I/21/27/1

35

Notes as to the Battle West of Serre on the morning of 1st July 1916, by Brigadier General H. C. Rees, D. S. O., temporarily Commanding 94th Infantry Brigade, 31st Division

[Typescript with holograph additions enclosed in above]

General Rees, who was commanding the 94th Infantry Brigade, and who, from his post of Command in DUNMOW TRENCH which is about 600 yards behind the front line trenches and on a slight elevation, was able to have a perfect view of the advance of his Brigade, states that none of his Brigade, except perhaps a few individuals, reached SERRE.

He, who had only recently taken command of this Brigade, is enthusiastic over the behaviour of the men of this Brigade. They advanced in line after line, dressed as if on parade, and not a man shirked going through the extremely heavy barrage, or facing the machine gun and rifle fire that finally wiped them out.

***

The result of this very severe and well directed high explosive, shrapnel, machine gun and rifle fire of the enemy was, that hardly any of our men were able to reach the German Front Line trenches. He saw the lines which advanced in such admirable order melting away under the fire. Yet not a man wavered, broke the ranks, or attempted to come back. He has never seen, indeed could never have imagined, such a magnificent display of gallantry, discipline and determination. The reports that he has had from the very few survivors of this marvellous advance bear out what he saw with his own eyes, viz: that hardly a man of ours got to the German Front Line. The only exception to this is that a few of the 11th East Lancs on the right of the advance were successful in getting over the enemy's front line trenches, and certain of them, perhaps 100 in all, managed to reach the fourth line. From there it is possible that certain determined individuals got on into the village of SERRE, but he is quite sure that with the exception of these few individuals none of our men reached SERRE

***

LHCMA, Robertson Mss, I/21/27/2

36

General Sir William Robertson to Lieutenant-General Sir L. E. Kiggell

Dictated [typescript with holograph additions] — War Office
Private — 5 July 1916

The more I think of it the more I am convinced that at any rate until we get through the enemy's defences the road to success lies through deliberation. All last year I preached this doctrine. I maintained then, and still maintain, that nothing is to be gained but very much is to be lost by trying to push on too rapidly. Before the war our theory was that anybody who could make ground should make it. This is a dangerous theory until we get through the enemy's trenches. People who can and do push on in front of the general line seldom or ever stay there. They are usually cut off or at any rate driven back. The fact is that the whole line must go forward together. Parties pushing forward in front of the general line nearly always come to grief and have never yet on any occasion done any good, so far as I can remember.

If the above view is sound it follows that the objectives must be exceedingly limited. In fact limited to such a distance as there is reasonable prospect of the whole line being able to reach. This theory tends to what is absolutely necessary, namely, concentration of artillery fire. No nation in the world can turn out sufficient amunition to deal with a long front (which is an absolute necessity) and at the same time to deal with great depth. I conceive that a great amount of ammunition is needed for this effort, & if it fails, it is not possible to keep on providing ammunition to do the work over again. Take the case of two villages one in rear of the other. It is quite obvious that in most cases the second village cannot be taken until the first has been taken, and therefore everything should be turned on to the first in the first instance and make it a certainty. I cannot help thinking that there is a want of recognition as to the great amount of time the enemy requires to establish himself in new positions. Time is not nearly so important a factor as we used to think it—I am speaking of course of Trench Warfare. Troops which have been fighting all day cannot do very much digging at night, especially if they are plied well with shrapnel. Instead of continually urging the men to push on I think they should be absolutely forbidden to go beyond a certain line until they are told to do so. It is only a question of getting through the entrenchments. After that we can revert to our old theories perhaps, and I cannot help thinking that these theories are still misleading us and that they or something else are certainly causing us very heavy losses.

Similarly, I think we are inclined to attach too much importance to deceiving the enemy. There can in the nature of things be very little deception, and more than that, the enemy has not now any large amount of reserves to draw upon. What we have got to do is to plod on carefully, slowly, and deliberately until we get through, and we can only do this by powerful artillery action as a preliminary, and for this we want concentration and not dispersion of artillery fire. Every action by the artillery should give us additional ground. In cases where it does not we must repeat the action.

***

I do not wish you to show this letter to *anyone*, but I hope that you will bear in mind what I have said at the beginning. The thing is to advance along a wide front step by step to very limited and moderate objectives, and to forbid going beyond those objectives until all have been reached by the troops engaged. I feel sure that we have got the Germans in a difficult position now if we only proceed on a deliberate system. Once we get into the open country we can make our numbers tell. Until we get there it is of no use crowding in more men. It is not a question of men but of artillery until such time as we get through the defences.

LHCMA, Robertson Mss, I/35/65

37

General Sir William Robertson to General Sir Douglas Haig

Dictated [typescript with holograph additions]

War Office
5 July 1916

I enjoyed my trip and once more got in touch with the troops. Since my return I have seen several Cabinet Ministers and the first question has always been how you are getting on and what you propose to do next. As regards the first I have said that you are getting on very well, but that it would be a slow business. As regards the second I have been able to say that I do not know what you propose to do next, that being the truth. The position taken up by Joffre on Monday[8] is very tiresome and I hope that he will come to see that in the general interest he should not haggle as to which is getting on best but should endeavour to make the best of the situation. At any rate we have carried out our first object to a much greater extent than the French did at Loos[9] where they carried out nothing. It seems to me that the situation is full of favourable possibilities. The enemy's front has been thoroughly well broken on a front of some 12 miles to a depth in some cases of nearly 5 miles. This has all been done in less than a week and is extraordinary good as fighting goes. I cannot help thinking that the German is now feeling very hard put to it and all that we have to do is to keep up a deliberate and relentless pressure. Once we get properly through his defences on a sufficiently wide front we can then let the troops go more freely.

As regards Joffre's attitude, I may remind you that on every occasion that we have co-operated with the French in fighting important actions there has always been a considerable difference of opinion as to what should be done next, and I suppose this always has been the case with allies, and probably always must be the case when the whole of the operations are not definitely under one man. Different people are bound to have different ideas. The great thing to me seems to be that the French should not dawdle about waiting for you, but should push on and make the most of the advantage they have got, as I am sure you will do with those of your Corps which have now got well started.

Let me know of anything I can do to keep you supplied with what you want. I have had a long talk with Lloyd George and he says he will try to get more 9.2″ ammunition for you. As regards drafts we can of course only send what we have got. But as a matter of fact the pressing question at present is not men so much as artillery ammunition, so it seems to me. May the very best of Luck continue to attend your efforts.

NLS, Acc 3155, no. 107, Haig Mss

38

General Sir William Robertson to General Sir Douglas Haig

1765 Mayfair
4, South Street
Park Lane
7 July 1916

[In other hand]
Copy

My French liaison officer, who has recently returned from Chantilly, rather makes out that Joffre is annoyed with himself because of last Monday's explosion, and that he (Joffre) fears that relations with you are now a bit strained in consequence—just at a time when they should be the most cordial.

***

Good luck to you, and do not misunderstand my reason for sending the above which may be and I hope is valueless. But the present situation is so important that I must tell you what I have heard in case it may help to put right what may be wrong. Of course, as you will fully agree, the great thing is to make the most of the results already achieved, to regard the whole operation as one battle—not two. We may *never* have so good a chance again for inflicting decisive defeat, and in the General interest of the war it is, in very many important respects, most essential, perhaps vitally so, that we should make a real success of the splendid beginning of a week ago. If, therefore, there should still be any hesitation on Joffre's part to resume complete and harmonious relations, because of his recent error, you can well afford to be generous, now that you have told him your position, and by giving him a lead get things going in full swing. *We have these Germans this time for a certainty* if *we* take *the chances now offered. Good luck.*
P.S. I hope you will keep me informed of what you think as to your future prospects. This is really essential because of the many theatres and Allies which we here have to deal with. Our vast and complicated foreign policy necessitates the War Committee being kept fully informed of our prospects and doings in every theatre. I am not referring to detailed plans but to the General

situation. The Communiques also really do affect neutral and foreign opinion. If you could send me a short letter which I could read to the War Committee I am sure it would be to the General interest, and to *your* interest in particular.

LHCMA, Robertson Mss, I/22/51

39

General Sir Douglas Haig to General Sir William Robertson

General Headquarters
British Army in
the Field

[Holograph] 7 July 1916

Yours received—I'll send you a note on the situation. Meantime I scribble a line to let you know that in my opinion your French Liaison Officer has been talking rubbish! My relations with Joffre & Foch are excellent. I am afraid the Liaison Officers who visit you from Chantilly are nothing more than gossips! So I hope you'll disregard their nonsense ...

LHCMA, Robertson Mss, I/22/52

40

General Sir William Robertson to General Sir Douglas Haig

Dictated [typescript with holograph additions]
Private

War Office
10 July 1916

Many thanks for your recent letters. I hope I made clear that there was no idea of attributing to you anything in the nature of blame for the alleged awkward situation vis-a-vis the French. On the contrary what I wished to make clear was that the French Staff were annoyed at Joffre's outburst and that they feared you might, quite naturally, be a little stiff in consequence. This they wished to avoid. In fact they rather took the line of *apologising* for what had happened. I said nothing in reply—one way or the other—of course.

***

NLS, Acc 3155, no. 107, Haig Mss

41

General Sir William Robertson to General Sir A. J. Murray

Dictated [typescript with holograph additions]

War Office
10 July 1916

Before you get this you will probably have received a telegram informing you of some new Conclusions of the War Committee regarding Salonika. If Rumania definitely comes in then we shall probably be required to do something from Salonika, and of course if we can do anything we ought to do so, because it is no good sitting there doing nothing if and when something useful can be done.[10] At the present time nothing useful can be done, nor, I am sorry to say, can I persuade the French to reduce the garrison. We shall probably be sending some heavy artillery and other things to Salonika so as to be ready in case we are required to act. Later on if it is not required there it may come in for you. We ought not to regard the dispositions as between different theatres in too rigid a manner, but be ready and willing to transfer from one theatre to another according as the situation and the season requires. Next winter you may require a good deal of help. On the other hand you may not. We shall see later on. The great thing is to push on the El Arish railway as quickly as you can and if you find that the Egyptian people do not give you all the assistance you think they could I shall be glad if you will let me know. But I have no doubt McMahon will do all that he possibly can.

Good luck to you.

British Library, Add 52461, Murray-Robertson Mss

42

Lieutenant-General Sir L. E. Kiggell to General Sir William Robertson

[Holograph] G.H.Q.
Private 14 July 1916

Please forgive the long delay in answering your letter of the 5th, which I have treated as entirely personal in accordance with your wish.

The main point you wrote about has settled itself practically. We have not been able to push on very rapidly. If it had been possible to do so we should have dealt a more telling blow in the first few days as the Bosche was badly rattled on a good part of our front, & it is much to be regretted that we could not take further advantage of it. The 'green line' might really have been further forward on the southern front, where we reached & passed it. Though we did not reach it elsewhere its position as the objective to try for did no harm & some good. The efforts to reach it helped elsewhere.

***

Future critics will show conclusively that we could & should have gone faster! I wish we could go & hear the Staff College lectures on the subject to the next generation,—and have the lecturers here now to try their hand! If we could go faster I think there is no doubt it would increase the German losses & decrease ours. But we can't. He sticks too tight in strong places which can't be rushed & must be dealt with methodically. Today's success[11] has convinced any doubters left amongst the French as to the soundness of our general plan—& anyhow we are going on with that plan methodically & deliberately.

***

Sir D. H. never turns a hair & Rawly & staff have done excellently. The administrative work has been most satisfactory & as for the troops—all arms including the Flying Corps—none could have done better if any as well. I don't think the infantry will have much fault to find with the artillery preparation & support. If they do find fault I can only say they are impossible to satisfy because it has been most effective. Otherwise what has been done could not have succeeded.

LHCMA, Robertson Mss, I/22/56

43

General Sir William Robertson to General Sir H. S. Rawlinson

Dictated [Typescript] War Office
Personal 26 July 1916

Many thanks for the Notes you sent me on the recent fighting. They are very interesting. I am sorry you were not in when I called last Monday as I wished to have a talk with you, but probably

Montgomery will have told you what I said to him. If you keep hammering away in a methodical and careful manner the Boche may yet crack. The thing you have got to keep your eye on is that he does not beat you in having the better man-power policy. We never cease here giving our attention to this question, and do not omit thinking about black as well as white men. The general situation is now better than it has ever been before and all that is needed is the use of common-sense, careful methods, and not to be too hide-bound by the books we used to study before the war. As you know better than I do each war has its own peculiarities, but one would think that no war was ever so peculiar as the present one, and Field Service Regulations will require a tremendous amount of revising when we have finished with the Boche. Principles, as we used to call them, are good and cannot be disregarded, but their application is a very difficult business, and I think that we still take these principles too literally. I think you know what is in my mind. Good luck to you.

LHCMA, Robertson Mss, I/35/100

44
General Sir William R. Robertson to General Sir A. J. Murray

Dictated
[typescript]

War Office
1 August 1916

I hope the Turk will receive a sharp lesson for being so audacious as to present himself in front of your troops. From all the information I receive it seems impossible that he can have more than a comparatively small force for some weeks to come, and I do not suppose that he appreciates much more than we should being pushed out 100 miles in advance of his Base into a country like the Sinai Peninsula. The longer he stays where he is the stronger he will become, and therefore the sooner he is dealt with the better. But of course it is equally essential that you should not go for him before you are ready. It is a question of your balancing opposing factors. I am more convinced every day that his policy is a defensive and a deceptive one. He would never be so mad as to dream of attacking you in your prepared positions.[12]

I hope you are making full use of native labour in every respect. There should be no lack of it in Egypt and it should save your own troops enormously.

I am sorry not to receive a better account of the efficiency of the Territorial troops. Of course they were knocked about a good deal in Gallipoli but after leaving there had a considerable spell of decent weather before it became as hot as at present. The Territorial divisions in France have done their work as well as any other kind of division, and I can only think it is the fault of the commanders. You must harden your heart in connection with them. We cannot afford to have any doubt as to the competency of commanders, especially brigade and divisional commanders.

***

The general situation is more favourable to us now than at any time since the commencement of the war. Six weeks ago the Austrians were beginning to reach the Italian Plains and Italy was calling for assistance. Russia was on the front to which she was driven back last year. Verdun was on the point of falling. All this has now been changed, and thanks mainly to the Somme offensive. It has prevented a single German soldier being sent to the Eastern front, and therefore Russia is free to pursue her victorious way. During the Somme operations the Germans have brought up no less than 27 divisions, which is a proof of the success of our attack. The German losses must have been very heavy. The first few days their units and formations were pushed up to the front anyhow and were destroyed as fast as they arrived. In one case a whole battalion was brought up by train and shortly afterwards the greater part of it was captured and put into another train the same evening and sent off to Havre. We calculate that during the last 6 weeks the Germans and Austrians have lost at least 750,000 men, of whom 600,000 are a dead loss. Briefly put the German Main Army on the Western front now faces us and the French and time will show what the result will be. Our fellows are in splendid spirit and feel they are winning.

Smuts is doing well in East Africa and I hope he may finish off the job in the course of the next month. But on the other hand a good many of the enemy may get away further south and so get us into guerrilla operations which may last for another six months at least.[13]

All we want now is for you to give the Turks a good hiding in the Sinai Peninsula. The Grand Duke[14] has been punishing them severely in the Caucasus; the Sheriff[15] is causing them a good deal of trouble; it is not unlikely Rumania may after all join us within the next few weeks; and if on the top of these things you can deal the Turks a really smashing blow things will look very bright indeed. I do not imagine that they can have many guns and therefore will not worry you much in that respect. What they probably have is plenty of machine-guns and with these the Germans are very expert. No doubt you have a certain number of Germans in front of you to look after machine-gun work. It is no use launching infantry to attack machine-guns. They must be dealt with in some other way. But I do not suppose there are a great number, not like there are on the western front where there are many thousands of them. Remember me to Lawrence[16] and wish him Good Luck. It would be a good thing to remove this Egyptian bug-bear, for it is nothing more now and never has been, and it never should be if only the Grand Duke keeps going.

British Library, Add 52461, Murray-Robertson Mss

45

General Sir William Robertson to General Sir Douglas Haig

Dictated [typescript with additions in other hand] — War Office
Personal — 1 August 1916

The War Committee met to-day and passed off quite satisfactorily. Knowing that a certain amount of impatience prevailed I took advantage of the Meeting to review the results achieved by the Entente during the last 6 weeks.[17]

***

I also said that in my opinion you were correctly carrying out the instructions of the Government, and that generally speaking you could do no more and no less than you are now doing. As regards casualties I mentioned that during last week they amounted to only about 18,000, and that in normal times we would have some 5 or 6,000 during a week on that front. I said that we were now engaged in quite a new kind of warfare and that decisive results could not be expected in 24 hours nor 24 days, and that relentless pressure on all fronts was the proper course to pursue and was promising good results by the Winter. I estimated the total German and Austrian losses during the last 6 weeks at 750,000 men of whom 600,000 represented a dead loss.

Everyone who returns from the front speaks in the highest terms of the good work that is being done there. Being ignorant of what modern fighting means they are rather impatient and apt to attach too much importance to gaining ground and do not pay sufficient attention to the effect that is no doubt being produced on the enemy by the pressure to which he is now exposed.

No one of the War Committee made any comment on anything I said, and so far as they are concerned I should say that they are thoroughly satisfied. The trouble is with a few outsiders eg F E Smith & Winston.[18] L G is all right provided I can say *I* am satisfied, and to enable me to do this it is necessary you should keep me acquainted with your views. I don't want your plans and you can rely upon me acting discreetly. But if I have to depend almost entirely upon Press Communiques, my opinion is regarded as not much more valuable than that of anyone else, and indeed it is almost impossible to give an opinion. So if you could manage to send me your views—as briefly as you like say once a week, I think matters would be more satisfactory. Monday is a good day—as the War Committee usually meets on Tuesday. Kiggell could draft.

LHCMA, Robertson Mss, I/22/62

46

General Sir Douglas Haig to General Sir William Robertson

General Headquarters,
British Armies in
France

[Telegram] 3 August 1916

Replying to your letter of 1st August, I am very glad to hear that you have been able to satisfy the War Committee. Any weakening of purpose now would certainly have deplorable effects on our Allies' trust in us, on the general faith in our power to achieve victory, and even on the confidence of our own army.

I sent you, yesterday, a note of my views which I hope will satisfy the War Committee.

I shall be glad to send you a statement of my views as often as you may find it necessary to have them, but I cannot think that a weekly statement would be of any use to you as it would, ordinarily, only amount to 'views unchanged since last report'!

The telegrams sent to 'Chief' daily really give the situation accurately. If you think it would help you, however, I will have a weekly summary of progress drawn up in addition, for your information.

LHCMA, Robertson Mss, I/22/63

47
General Sir William Robertson to General Sir Douglas Haig

Dictated [typescript with additions in other hand]

War Office
5 August 1916

In reply to your letter O.A.D. 92 of the 3rd instant there will be no necessity for you to send a statement for Monday next as the one you recently sent fully meets the case. I read it to the War Committee this morning and it pleased them very much indeed. It is to be printed and circulated to the Cabinet as a rejoinder to a Memorandum recently put before the Cabinet by Winston Churchill. I shall not trouble you with his views but merely repeat that your Paper is an adequate reply to what he has said. As a matter of fact I had already told the War Committee practically everything you did say, and I reminded them this morning that your Memorandum had been written independently of what I had previously told them.[19]

I still think that it is necessary you should periodically send me a similar Paper during the progress of the present operations. The telegrams sent to me, which as a matter of a fact do not contain daily more than is in the Press Communique, do not meet the case like a periodical review by yourself. I will therefore leave it to you to send in such a statement when you think desirable, and not necessarily weekly, but if I feel the want of one I will send you a wire and then I hope you will understand my object.

NLS, Acc 3155, no. 107, Haig Mss

48

General Sir William Robertson to General Sir Douglas Haig

[Holograph] War Office
Very private 7 August 1916

Winston, French, Fitzgerald,[20] and various dégommméd people are trying to make mischief lately. W. C. has sent to the Cabinet a damnable paper. So far, however, they have not a friend in the War Committee or anywhere else amongst honest men. L. G. too is quite all right, & says he will record them if they put questions in the House. The *whole* object of my recent letters in this connection has been to give you a hint as to what is happening (it always *does* happen unfortunately in all wars) & to show you the necessity of giving me the necessary data with which to reply to the swines. You are doing quite the right thing in my judgment, and you have the full confidence, I can assure you of the War Committee. But they, alas, must have an answer to the insinuations.

L. G. will come round I think as regards Maxwell.[21] *I believe L. G. is all right. He merely requires to be made a fuss over, & put well into the limelight.*[22] Good luck to you. My heartfelt best wishes. We are winning all right, without doubt. Do keep me posted—in the general interest, & in your own.

NLS, Acc 3155, no. 107, Haig Mss

49

General Sir William Robertson to General Sir Douglas Haig

War Office
[Holograph] 8 August 1916

Winston & his like are in bad odour. Your position is quite all right—you need have no fear. It always has been. My desire was to keep it so—hence my request for an appreciation. I hope the War Committee conclusion sent you by this post will be proof of what I say. It was *not* inserted by my suggestion, but was spontaneous on the part of the Committee after I had read your paper and explained things.[23]

NLS, Acc 3155, no. 107, Haig Mss

50

General Sir William R. Robertson to Lord Esher

Dictated [typescript with holograph addition]

War Office
9 August 1916

***

The powers that be are quite strong enough with regard to the continuance of the war.[24] What worries me is the making of peace. I confess that I have anxiety when I think of the day on which we may be seated round the 'Council Table' discussing terms of peace. I am not thinking so much of the enemy as of the Allies. I do sincerely hope that we shall be very strongly represented when that day comes, but I do not see how we can be unless certain important changes take place.

As regards our increasing strength in France it is not possible for the French to have it both ways. The stronger we become the more predominant we become, I hope, and I certainly intend to make us as strong as possible. As I have said above my chief anxiety is that the efforts our Armies are making may be sacrificed, or at any rate not sufficiently rewarded when the day of reckoning comes. In council, as you say, the French will always prevail, unless we can get the same predominance there as I think we are acquiring on the field.

LHCMA, Robertson Mss I/34/7

51

General Sir William Robertson to Lord Stamfordham

War Office

[Holograph] 10 August 1916

The Prime Minister showed to me and the Secretary for State for War this morning a letter from you regarding the promotion of Sir D. Haig to the rank of Field Marshal. We both felt that such promotion was rather early in the day, as the battle of the Somme is not nearly finished yet. The Secretary of State will speak to the King on the subject when he comes to General Headquarters on Saturday. Like myself, he fully recognises that his Majesty's wishes must be complied with, and therefore he is rather disturbed in appearing to advise contrary to those wishes. I have therefore suggested to him that I should write to you beforehand, and say that, on the analogy of Jellicoe, who has finished *his* battle,[25] a similar reward, G.C.V.O.—would be preferable. The 1st Lord is not anxious that Jellicoe should be made an Admiral of the Fleet, and is inclined to think that for Haig to be rewarded in the same way as Jellicoe has been would be desirable. If Haig were made a Field Marshal it would seem to follow that Jellicoe should have been made an Admiral of the Fleet. He was not, and the 1st Lord does not wish him to be made. We have still a long way to go before we finish the war, & to defer the baton would be no hardship.

***

RA, Geo V, F. 983/3

52

General Sir William Robertson to General Sir Douglas Haig

Dictated [typescript with holograph additions]

War Office
14 August 1916

I am sorry it is impossible to send you Cobbe because he has just been given Command of an Army Corps in Mesopotamia in succession to Maude who is replacing Lake. Mesopotamia is in a very unsatisfactory condition, and causes me more trouble and worry than all the other theatres put together. It also has a very uncertain future and we must have two good commanders there.

I quite realise the difficulty you must find in selecting Corps Commanders, but I should have thought that you would have more than one divisional commander now equal to the job. The first few which come to my mind are Furse, Perceval, and Capper. Perhaps you do not agree but I should have thought that they were to be found. Of course finding them reduces the number of good divisional commanders, but as regards these I suggest that you should seriously consider employing in some of the divisions officers who may not yet have had much experience at the front. After all there is some advantage in introducing new and fresh blood. It is hard work commanding troops upon your front and officers are all the better for having had a rest. There are four at home now who occur to me—Gorringe, Forestier-Walker, Fanshawe, and Broadwood. On all sides I hear that Forestier-Walker is quite a different man now that he has had his lesson. He undoubtedly has great ability. As regards Gorringe he could not get on with Lake and apparently turned a little insubordinate. I had to support Lake and bring Gorringe home. But I am very much inclined to think that the fault did not by any means all lay on the side of Gorringe.[26]

***

LHCMA, Robertson Mss, I/22/68

53

General Sir William Robertson to General Sir Douglas Haig

Dictated [typescript with holograph additions]

War Office
25 August 1916

***

I have been busy to-day with the Adjutant General and his underlings with regard to drafts, and during the next fortnight we shall send to you every man we can lay hands on who is fit to go, but I am afraid that we shall not be able to bring you fully up to strength. We knew all along that we would be short during August and September. In October we shall be much better placed as the Military Service Act will then begin to have effect. However, I do not think you should be very short even before October. I am paying every attention to the Tanks.

I am sorry to say that it will not be possible to send you any further divisions at present. There are only ten in the Kingdom. Of these one is in Ireland and cannot be taken away and of the other nine five are composed entirely of Home Service men, and we have drawn heavily on the other four in order to keep you supplied with drafts.

I am sorry that I cannot come over just at present. The King has commanded me to go to Windsor Castle at the end of this week and next week I must take three or four days' leave for real rest. Moreover we are very much fussed about the Balkans just now. Our Ministers there send us the most alarming reports and I dare not turn my back on the people here for a day or they would be sending out another Expeditionary Force—if they could find it. It was seriously proposed a few days ago that we should send such a force to Athens, and it has also been proposed that we should send a larger force to Mesopotamia, and this quite regardless of the fact that we cannot feed properly the unfortunate fellows who are now there. It is a queer business for me to conduct here, but I am glad to say that I have no difficulty in getting my own way. But I dare not turn my back on them.

LHCMA, Robertson Mss, I/22/70

54

General Sir William Robertson to General Sir Douglas Haig

Dictated [typescript with holograph additions]

War Office
29 August 1916

Your letter of the 27th instant. The French are indeed very tiresome. I believe Castelnau is at the bottom of it all. Several hints have reached me (not by any means all through Clive) that Joffre and Company think you are going too slowly. I have always regarded Castelnau as very much against us, while old Joffre is I imagine pretty tired and querulous. I spoke to Lloyd George about this the other day, and he repeated what he has said many times lately that he thinks you are playing absolutely the right game, and doing your job in absolutely the right way. You can attach any importance you choose to his opinion, but it will be satisfactory to you to know that he at any rate thinks you are doing the right thing. All the War Committee think the same. Briand told Asquith last week that he was delighted with what you had done on the Somme. Of course we all know that for many reasons you should get going on a big scale as soon as you can, but we also know that it is useless going off before you are properly ready. In fact it is much more serious than being merely useless. My advice to you, for what it is worth, is do as you think best and do not be influenced by Joffre and Company. The gist of the information I get is that the French seem to think that the operations will necessarily soon come to a standstill because of the winter. I fail to see why this should be so. In 1914 we fought up to nearly

Christmas and this year the Germans attacked Verdun in February. I think you will agree with me that we must keep up the pressure without ceasing, winter or no winter, so far as the weather will admit. If we do not do this the Germans will be taking troops over to the Eastern Front and Alexeieff is already beginning to call out. As you know the equivalent of some 11 divisions have gone to the Eastern Front since June last, although most of them had gone when you began your operations on the Somme. Still some of the divisions have gone since you started. It seems to me ridiculous that the French should talk of Verdun falling. I imagine we have had quite as hard a task at Ypres as the French have had at Verdun, and Ypres has not fallen and will not fall. Such dissatisfaction as there may be is due to Joffre and Castelnau I believe. In any case you do what you think best and I will see that the support you now have here continues. I hope the Tanks will prove successful. It is rather a desperate innovation.

***

LHCMA, Robertson Mss, I/22/72

55

General Sir William Robertson to General Sir Douglas Haig

War Office

[Holograph] 7 September 1916

I have been away for 5 days. I find L. G. has got the Servian fit again, and maintains we have been wrong all along & the French have been right, as shown by Rumania's coming in. He thinks Hindenburg will now go for Rumania à la Servia & therefore we ought to be ready to assist Rumania with *more* troops. Of course I have an answer to this talk if he makes it when I see him. But as you may see him before he comes back I send this to let you know how his mind (?) is working.[27] I will write more fully later.

***

NLS, Acc 3155, no. 108, Haig Mss

56

Lieutenant-General Sir L. E. Kiggell to General Sir William Robertson

[Telegram] Advanced G.H.Q.
Secret and Personal 17 September 1916

Consider that the utility of the tanks has been proved. It has been established that the magnitude of the success on the 15th in certain localities was directly attributable to the employment of tanks.[28] Further there is no doubt that their employment minimises loss among the attacking troops. On the 15th, approximately 48 tanks deployed. Of these 30 started. Of these 21 did good work. Four were hit by artillery fire in movement. Of the remainder breakdowns were chiefly attributable to either mechanical trouble or to inexperience of drivers and the very difficult conditions. Butler, who will be in London on Tuesday, will have further details.

LHCMA, Robertson Mss, I/14/40

57

General Sir William Robertson to Brigadier-General W.H.-H. Waters

R [telegram]
Personal & War Office
Secret 28 September 1916

We are inclined to think Hindenburg will for various reasons attempt decisive defeat of Roumania this autumn. He wants a success badly. He cannot get it in west and on Russian front. Season and other circumstances are against him. But he might conceivably be able to collect from East front during autumn sufficient force with Bulgarians and perhaps Turks seriously to menace Roumania. The Russians and Roumanians constitute practically one front under Russian auspices and I am wondering if Alexieff is contemplating while necessarily tied by season to defensive on his own proper front sending more troops towards Roumania to oppose Hindenburg's possible plan and if latter does not mature to make heavy attacks on Bulgaria and so sever communications between Central Powers and Balkans. This would be a great achievement from every point of view and especially from Russian standpoint. It would not be appropriate for me to suggest any thing to Alexieff but wish you to take first opportunity of ascertaining in your own way his views on the matter.

LHCMA, Robertson Mss, I/14/43

58

General Sir William Robertson to Lieutenant-General Sir L. E. Kiggell

Dictated [typescript with additions in other hand]

War Office
29 September 1916

Clive tells me some story about your being dissatisfied with what the Press people at home say regarding your operations, the chief offender being 'The Morning Post'. If you will tell us exactly what we can do to help you we will try to do it. I understand the difficulty is that the Press at home draw too much attention to the French proceedings and not enough to ours. Until a short time ago I used to think that 'The Times' was the greatest offender in this respect, and that 'The Morning Post' always stood up for our army. There is of course a good deal of jealousy between the different papers and it is very necessary to treat them all exactly the same, otherwise there will be trouble. However, I understand that Gwynne is visiting Sir Douglas now and therefore the matter will probably be put right.

Taking the papers as a whole, and also the public, I think you may be congratulated on having established a very good reputation in regard to your official communiques. At one time they were considered to be much too short and bald, and it was thought that the most was not being done to tell the public what was happening, especially as regards bringing out the work of the different units. You have succeeded well in doing this and at the same time establishing a reputation for being thoroughly honest in your statements, claiming nothing to which you were not entitled and holding out no hopes which were not likely to be realised. This is a very good achievement I think and it has had a good effect in this country. I remember at one time when I was in France the public were frequently disappointed by hopes being held out to them in the communiques which were not realised. Whatever you do you must not *disappoint* the public. It is better to be curt and bald than to lead up to disappointments.

The reason I make these remarks is that during the last few days you have been adding to your communiques information obtained from the enemy as to the bad time he is getting and as to the splendid fellows our troops are. I think you would be well advised to be cautious how far you proceed with this rather new departure, or you may lead to the impression that the enemy is beaten and that you have got a soft thing on and therefore that you will achieve more great things, which after all may not be achieved. The public are always on the look-out for an indication that you have got a tremendously big thing or a breakthrough entirely and they are very easily disappointed. I hope you will not mind my giving you this hint, but I should be very sorry to see the fine reputation your communiques have recently established suffering any diminution. And of course I leave the matter entirely to your discretion, but with a National Army one has to remember the public, practically all of whom are personally concerned.[29]

LHCMA, Robertson Mss, I/35/66

59

General Sir William Robertson to General Sir Douglas Haig

Dictated [typescript with additions in other hand]

War Office
9 October 1916

I am very sorry that I forgot to tell you that Lord French was about to visit the French front. It was thought that there have been so many developments in regard to the employment of artillery in the last three months that the man at home who is responsible for training should know what these developments are.

***

I may add that the Secretary of State partly suggested to Lord French that he should also visit your front so as to get the whole story. For reasons that will occur to you Lord French did not much like the idea of visiting the British front.

The visit of Lord French has no connection with what happened during the visit of the Secretary of State[30] and he was merely directed to make himself acquainted with recent developments in the employment of artillery so as to assist him in the training of the men at home. He will make no report to us. At least he is not asked to do so. I am really sorry not to have explained all this before. I am having a rotten time. I don't want to make trouble, but I doubt if I can avoid it much longer.

LHCMA, Robertson Mss, I/22/80

60

General Sir William Robertson to David Lloyd George

[Typescript] War Office
SECRET 11 October 1916

About a month ago I laid before the War Committee a memorandum regarding the probability of a heavy attack being made on Rumania, and the Committee agreed with my view that our best assistance would be the prosecution of the offensive on the Western Front combined with vigorous action by the Salonika forces.[31]

I again brought the question before the Committee on the 9th instant and repeated the advice given before, and said that to attempt to assist Rumania by sending any further considerable body of troops to Salonika would be unsound and probably quite useless.

You felt it your duty to disagree with this advice[32] and recommended certain action being taken by the Committee with the object of inducing France and Italy to combine with us in sending to Salonika a reinforcement of some 8 additional divisions for the purpose of undertaking extensive offensive operations, directed on Sofia. After discussion I was directed by the Committee to ask General Joffre for his opinion on certain points regarding which I had already given my opinion. The meaning of these proceedings is:

(a) A plan of campaign was contemplated entirely contrary to the conclusions of the War Committee a month ago.

(b) My advice was set aside and the advice of a foreign General sought.

A short time ago the question of sending an expedition to Rabegh[33] was before the War Committee. At great length, verbally and in writing, I advised the Committee not to send it. I gathered they were inclined to accept my advice, but after I was called away from the Meeting it was decided, I understand mainly on your suggestion, that the advice of certain commanders subordinate to me should be obtained.

The above examples of want of confidence in my advice is causing me, not unnaturally I think, grave concern—not so much on my own account as on account of the efficient conduct of the war. You will I think agree with me that it is essential to the proper conduct of the war that the C.I.G.S. should be able to count upon the support of the Secretary of State for War in regard to the military plans which he puts forward for the consideration of the War Committee. If this support is not only not forthcoming but conflicting views are presented to the Committee the general cause must suffer. Further, I am compelled to point out that if it is decided by the War Committee, whether on the advice of General Joffre or not, to undertake the extensive operations proposed by you it will mean that I shall be committed to a military plan which I have stated to the Committee is in my judgement unsound. I could not be responsible for conducting this very difficult war under these conditions, nor would it be in the Country's interest that I should attempt to do so.

I am sending a copy of this letter to the Prime Minister, as the matter is one with which the War Committee is concerned.

LHCMA, Robertson Mss, I/19/7

61

General Sir William Robertson to Lord Northcliffe

War Office

[Holograph] 11 October 1916

I am touched by your letter. It *is* very hard work trying to win this war. The Boche gives me no trouble compared with what I meet in London. So any help you can give will be of Imperial value. I greatly regret I cannot see you this morning. I have to attend a meeting which will keep me all the morning. Perhaps I shall see Geoffrey Robinson later today.

P.S. I *think* I can keep things right but am not sure, & in any case the effort greatly encroaches on my valuable time.

British Library, Northcliffe Mss, 62334

62

H. A. Gwynne to General Sir William Robertson

Bath Club

[Holograph] 11 October 1916

I have had a talk with Bonar Law this morning. I expressed my alarm at various rumours I had heard about disagreements between you and L.G. and hoped they would not come to an acute crisis. His answer was that if they did come to that point he would certainly resign unless you had your way; and he said he was quite sure that the great majority of the War Council would be of his way of thinking. He always presumed that you would choose a good *military* ground for fighting.

IWM, Gwynne Mss, Pt. III, fol. 352

63

General Sir William Robertson to H. H. Asquith

War Office

[Holograph] 11 October 1916

I enclose the copy of a letter I have just sent to Mr. Lloyd George. I am, really, most sorry to add to your burdens, but the sense of duty to my country compelled me to write the letter.

Bodleian, Ms Asquith 30, fol. 254

64

General Sir William Robertson to Lieutenant-Colonel C. Wigram

War Office

[Holograph] 11 October 1916

I enclose some correspondence for such action as you think right. It is not merely a question of Salonika. It is the same with everything, and throws a significant light on the proposed mission to Russia. I have tried my best to get on. But I can't. Half my time is employed in considering how to deal with adroit manoeuvres to make me do something against which my judgment recoils.

P.S. I fancy L. G.'s French interpreter[34] went to Paris this morning. He is suspected of acting as liaison officer between L. G. and Paris [. . .] intrigues. I shall not be surprised if we shortly receive from the French Government a request for a conference re Salonika. I may be wrong.

RA, Geo V, Q. 1200/4

65

David Lloyd George to General Sir William Robertson

War Office
Whitehall, S.W.

[Holograph] 11 October 1916

In the course of the two conversations I had with you at the War Office since Monday's War Council you made no protest against my taking a line of my own on Roumania. Tonight's letter would therefore have caused me some surprise had not a leading newspaper proprietor[35] given me the pith of its contents 8 hours before it was despatched to me. He had clearly been taken into counsel by some one in your close confidence & by him acquainted with matters so confidential in their nature that they have not yet been imparted to the Cabinet & so dangerous in their character that their publication would materially assist the enemy. This great journalist even threatened publication unless I withdrew immediately from the position I had taken up. Had he done so my only defence would have been the public disclosure of equally secret & equally dangerous material essential to complete the story. Of course you could not have authorised such a breach of confidence & discipline. But unfortunately this kind of thing is of frequent occurrence in the service & must be stopped in the best interests of the Army. I have during my short sojourn at the War Office frequently encountered this grave subversion of discipline in high places. I have found complaints against action taken by the army council & myself lodged with the Press—even before they ever reached me. These complaints must have emanated from fairly exalted quarters for no one outside that circle had a right at that stage to know what was going on or any interest in protesting. In each of these cases I could not have defended myself against these press assaults without divulging information which in the interests of the army should remain secret. In any event the spectacle of a British Secretary of State engaged in a newspaper controversy with anonymous leaders of the Army of which under the Sovereign he is the civilian head would have been unseemly & mischievous.

I feel confident you must agree with me that this state of things is an outrage on all the best traditions of the service & must tend to impair discipline in all ranks of the Army & I am certain that I will receive your assistance & that of the Army Council in putting an end to these injurious practices. Privates have recently been courtmartialled for complaining direct to their MPs & to the Secretary of State & the Army Council have asked me to enforce discipline against MP officers who ventilate their grievances in Parliament. How can I do so when such an example of indiscipline is set by men in high places.

Although therefore I still think it would have been better had there been a straight talk between you & me before the Prime

Minister had been troubled with these misunderstandings I think there is a good deal to be said for talking out with him & if necessary with the War Council at once the whole position so that you & I should know exactly where we stand.

There are two questions which must be settled immediately in the interests of the harmonious working of the War Office—so essential to the conduct of the war.

One is the point of discipline I have raised. The present position is intolerable & full of peril to the efficiency & safety of the Army. This leakage to the press must percolate to the enemy.[36]

The second is the point you raise. There can be no doubt as to your supreme responsibility in all matters affecting strategy & the direction of military operations—subject of course to the War Council. I have never questioned your authority in this respect. But there seems to be some doubt I gather from your letter as to my position as a member of the War Council. It ought to be decided whether I have the same right—although I am War Secretary—to express an independent view on the war in the discussions that take place as any other member of the War Council—or whether as long as I am War Secretary I must choose between the position of a dummy or a pure advocate of all opinions expressed by my military advisers.

As to Roumania I never had an opportunity of discussing with you the paper you sent in & I could not attend the War Committee that approved it. But surely all military advice must be subject to the changing facts of the campaign. That is why General Joffre has changed his attitude.

You allude to the advice given by the General Staff about Salonica. They advised evacuation on the ground that the place could not be defended. Had not the War Committee overruled their advice Salonica would now have been German & the Bulgarians would have another 260,000 well equipped men available to crush Roumania.

I am perhaps overanxious that our prestige and honour should be saved in the East. The Servian blunder has damaged both badly. I know what will be said here if after bringing Roumania to aid us we look on whilst she is being butchered before our eyes without taking the most serious risks to rescue her.

I am glad that since Monday a good deal has been done to strengthen General Milne. The French ought to help.

You are misinformed as to the Rabegh incident.

Believe me there is no man who has more sincere admiration for your great gifts than I have & there is no one more anxious to cooperate with you so as to make the most of those gifts for the benefit of our Country but you must not ask me to play the part of a mere dummy. I am not in the least suited for the part.

LHCMA, Robertson Mss, I/19/6

66

General Sir William Robertson to General Sir A.J. Murray

Dictated
[typescript]

War Office
16 October 1916

I have been more than usually busy during the last few weeks and therefore have not had an opportunity of writing to you. I hope you will not mind. I had great difficulty in knocking out the Rabegh proposal. It gave me a great deal of trouble. It would undoubtedly have been strategy gone mad. I notice in the Sirdar's letter to you of the 1st instant that he says you are naturally concentrated on winning in Sinai and I on winning in the West. I wish you would endeavour to get him to hold a little broader view of the war. I am not intent on winning in any particular quarter of the globe. My sole object is to win the war and we shall not do that in the Hedjaz nor in the Sudan. It makes one despair to see the short-sighted views held by the Sirdar. Our military policy is perfectly clear and simple, and it has the approval of the Government, and we cannot change it every day in the week. The policy is offensive on the Western Front and therefore defensive everywhere else.

Last week I was worried by the French to send more divisions to Salonika, and it was with the greatest difficulty I managed to get my own way. I am handicapped greatly because as you know the Secretary of State for War is in favour of the Balkan operations. I eventually wrote a straight letter to him indicating that I could no longer carry on unless my advice were accepted. It was accepted but I know the same thing will occur again later.

I am much obliged to you for the way you always play up. I shall not unduly deplete you unless I feel it is necessary to do so, but I hope that it may be possible to take away a division next Spring. However we shall see. I hope you are keeping very fit.

LHCMA, Robertson Mss, I/32/48

67

General Sir William Robertson to Lieutenant-General G.F. Milne

R [telegram]
Personal and secret

War Office
25 October 1916

War Committee felt compelled to send the additional division and I wish you clearly to understand that I have no intention of adopting the Balkans as a main theatre. Russians are pressing us hard to do so and ask us to march on Uskub etc. We are winning on the West front undoubtedly and for innumerable reasons it would be folly to weaken our effort there in futile hope of gaining decisive results in Balkans. The French political authorities have throughout followed some scheme of policy which I have not yet fathomed and they succeed from time to time in getting Joffre to urge sending more reinforcements although he always maintains to me that the West is the decisive front. Result is we continue half and half measures by keeping unduly strong forces for defence and too weak forces for decisive offence. Keep these points in mind and let me have your views occasionally addressing them if necessary to me by name and personal. Note that all my R telegrams are entirely personal and should not be referred to except in telegrams sent to me for personal information.

LHCMA, Robertson Mss, I/14/47

68

General Sir William Robertson to General Sir Douglas Haig

Dictated [typescript with additions in other hand]

War Office

Private

25 October 1916

As I feared would be the case it has been decided to send another division to Salonika. The War Committee were very good about the matter and quite realised the uselessness of sending the division and also the great disadvantages with regard to your front. But tremendous pressure was brought to bear upon them by Poincaré, the Czar, and the French and Russian Governments, to say nothing of the Rumanians. Had they refused to send the division they would have been left in the position of being the one Ally who refused to give assistance. They carefully weighed the military disadvantages against the political and moral conditions and eventually with regret decided they would send the division. A condition has been made that it is to come back in the Spring if we think that necessary and desirable, though I doubt if this condition will prove to be of much value.[37]

***

I am writing a letter to Joffre on the question of the Balkans because the Russians are now urging us to regard it as a main theatre and I am sure we shall have great pressure in this respect put upon us at the Chantilly Conference and I want to get old Joffre definitely on my side. I need not tell you how futile and dangerous such a proposal is. Allies are a tiresome lot. I suppose the weather has interfered again today.

LHCMA. Robertson Mss, I/22/84

69

Lieutenant-General G.F. Milne to General Sir William Robertson

[Telegram]
Personal and secret

[Salonika]
27 October 1916

I fully realise the position and trust nothing I have said has led to the sending of the other division, the arrival of which makes me stronger for defence but is too insignificant a reinforcement for more than local offensive purposes. I am altogether opposed to half and half measures and have held consistently to the view that we can only hope to hold the Bulgarians and that any offensive is impracticable except on a scale which is, I realise, inconsistent with your policy on the Western Front. Of course if the Bulgarians were forced to retire owing to pressure elsewhere, the situation would be changed. I believe from what I hear that Briand is greatly under the influence of Sarrail, who is doing all he can for French interests in the Near East after the war. From very secret sources I gather that he sent in his resignation of this command unless reinforcements were sent, hence Joffre's anxiety. (This is for you only). The French Army here is very weak, probably only 25,000 to 30,000 rifles. I quite understand your telegram R (apparent omission). I shall be only too pleased to send my views fully by a (apparent omission) leaving in a day or two.

LHCMA, Robertson Mss, I/14/48

70
General Sir William Robertson to Charles à Court Repington

Dictated [typescript with holograph addition]

War Office
31 October 1916

With reference to our talk yesterday regarding policy and strategy, although I naturally acquiesced in the view that in this war at any rate there is much to be done in regard to policy or diplomacy or whatever it may be called, at the same time whatever is done must be in harmony with strategy. As you know there has been some discussion as to where the soldier ends and the politician begins, and therefore I hope you will be very careful as to how you deal with the subject in this respect. The crux of the thing appears to me to be that politicians and soldiers must each keep within their respective sphere, must work close together and in sympathy the one with the other, and remember that it has never been good policy to adopt bad strategy. Where the politician goes wrong is in wanting to know the why and the wherefore of the soldier's proposals, and of making the latter the subject of debate and argument across a table. You then have the man who knows but who cannot talk discussing important questions with the man who can talk but does not know, with the result that the man who knows usually gets defeated in argument and things are done which his instinct tells him are bad. The politician should select those whom he considers would be his best advisers, and having selected them should receive their advice and their advice alone. What sometimes happens is that if the politician cannot get from one soldier the advice he would like to have he is apt to look for it elsewhere, and unfortunately there is usually some soldier available who is prepared to give him the advice he wishes to have. I do not say that the second soldier does it from an evil reason. He probably does it because he is not responsible and does not know all the facts of the case. If I were not in my present position I daresay I could find half a dozen different ways of rapidly winning this war. Being in the position I am and knowing what I know I find it is not so easy to produce a scheme certain of winning in a short time. After all, the educated soldier should know something about policy and not put forward proposals which from the point of view of policy are objectionable. The great thing is for the two branches to work cordially, honestly and openly together giving each other credit for the desire to win the war. Chief of all is the necessity for the politician backing the soldier, not only in public but in private. As soon as he feels that he cannot do this he should at once change his soldier. Until he does that he should be guided by him in all military matters.

LHCMA, Robertson Mss, I/33/73

71

General Sir William Robertson to General Sir Douglas Haig

Dictated [typescript with holograph additions]

War Office
1 November 1916

The man Stern[38] who has something to do with the production of tanks has been telling Lloyd George that he can put in hand still another 1,000 tanks for you. Lloyd George is rather in favour of giving out this further order, but it seems to me that the 1,000 you have already asked for is as far as we should think of going at present having regard to the present experimental stage of these things and to the large number of personnel they absorb. I therefore told L. G. that I would like to communicate with you first. I should like to know whether you agree with me that we should at present limit our order to one thousand. Besides the men they absorb they also take up a great deal of steel, which is now rather scarce, and in general the tanks should not be ordered unless you think they are really necessary.

LHCMA, Robertson Mss, I/22/86

72

General Sir William Robertson to Lieutenant-General G. F. Milne

Dictated [typescript
with holograph additions] War Office
PERSONAL 7 November 1916

This is a 'Personal' letter and therefore is not 'Official'. I wish you to remember this in all my 'Personal' communications with you. I wired to you to-day in connection with 'R' telegrams and your appreciation of the situation. I think the mistake there arose through my fault in asking for your appreciation by an 'R' telegram, but as I had already asked you not to quote 'R' telegrams in official documents I thought you would tumble to what I wished done. However it does not matter. What I wish to point out is that I must have a little private and personal communication with you sometimes. I cannot see you, and letters may sometimes take too long. With Haig the matter is quite different as he can always be seen or our Staffs meet. The reason I use 'R' telegrams is that all other telegrams go to the Secretary of State and to a host of other people, and it so happens that the Secretary of State is all out for a Balkan Campaign. My personal opinion on the matter is that we shall never win this war in the Balkans. We can only win it by defeating the German Army. We shall never find any great number of German troops in the Balkans, and therefore nothing can please the Germans better than to see us being killed by the Bulgars and our killing the Bulgars. The fewer Englishmen and Bulgars there are about the better the Germans will be pleased. We have not enough men and artillery to fight in two main theatres, and if we had they would be much better employed in one. I know you have great difficulties with the French, but everyone has and always has had. You can only make the best of it.

***

P.S. I have just received your private letter of the 27th October. It confirms what you have told me before and I quite realise the difficulties you have to contend against. But you must remember that Haig has very similar difficulties in France. In fact I think his difficulties in some respects are greater than yours. You can only make the best of things. What I am concerned about is your statement that your Army will slowly waste away from disease next summer unless you get on the other side of the mountains. You must use all your energy to keep a sound spirit up in your Command, and you may depend upon me trying my best to give you all the rewards for your troops which you may ask for and to do everything I possibly can to let them see that their services are appreciated. You must be very careful about keeping up their spirit. Maude has a similar task in Mesopotamia and he is going very well. Also remember that events are happening in other parts of the world, and that your troubles in future may be less than you might at first imagine. I hope by next summer, if the Allies will only do the right thing, that a very material change for the better will take place and that it will react upon the theatre in which you are. I have already asked you to send me occasionally an official review of the situation. This I shall circulate to the War Committee, and you should write it accordingly. In addition to this I shall be glad if you would occasionally write me private letters. Also remember that I can only look to you to see that the health and spirit of the troops are maintained. I have four campaigns on my hands besides the one in France, and unless I am told what the situation is I cannot help you. Always let me have your proposals in good time so that I can get to work at this end and prevent your troops from being wasted any more than can possibly be helped either from the enemy or from the climate. Of course the whole story is the one I have often mentioned, namely, that we have too strong a force for defence and are not strong enough for offence. To make us stronger for a real offence would mean a serious depletion in the main theatre and we must try to avoid that. So I can only look to you to do your best and I will give you all the help I can. I do not wish to know very much about your tactical arrangements. In fact the less I know about them probably the better. What I want to know is how you propose in general to continue to carry out the instructions you have received, and any proposals you may have as to the desirability of modifying those instructions. I hope this is all clear and I wish you every Good Luck. It is a great boon that we have served together before. Keep up your pecker and put into the heads of your troops that they are as a matter of fact doing good work. Tell them so, say I say so. They are, though undoubtedly with better arrangements they could do more. Still I have no doubt that our men have done *everything* that can be expected of them.

***

LHCMA, Robertson Mss, I/34/10

73

General Sir William Robertson to General Sir Douglas Haig

[Holograph]

Strictly Secret — War Office

Private — 8 November 1916

I am going to tell you some of my worries. But treat them as an entertainment. They do not generally trouble me.

Did I tell you before that about 6 weeks ago L. G. tried to shove me over to Russia, saying I was such a splendid fellow to go & see Alexeieff & buck up Russia in general—about which we hear, still, rumours of a separate peace with Germany—which I *do* not believe.

I told him I *could* not go.[39] Also told the Prime Minister. The King took up matter strongly, & it was dropped. The idea was to let L. G. become top dog here & have his wicked way. Like he used to get rid of poor old K. I could not do the trip under a month, & he would keep me there for weeks more once he got me there. He has been a good deal with Winston & F E Smith, & French is also not far distant at times. Last Friday, in McKenna's absence (a friend of *ours*) he got up a War Committee at which were no *naval or military experts*.[40] He got together another yesterday. Result was a telegram to Briand saying L. G. & Prime Minister would come over on Tuesday next to discuss general matters & to arrange an Allied conference at *Russian* Headquarters, as the only useful way of securing real cooperation etc etc. Also that Chantilly Conference should be postponed for at least a week as it could not usefully meet until it had before it the decisions of the Tuesday (political) Conference. To represent *us* in Russia L. G. told me last night it was thought that Grey & *I* should go; *France*, Joffre (or Castelnau) & a minister; *Italy*, Cadorna (or Poroo[41]). Of course *Italy* will send no one. *France* may refuse the whole thing. On the other hand Briand may be in the plot, (he would welcome *my* absence from the helm) & agree to send representatives to Russia—including old Joffre, if he wants to be rid of him. No answer has yet come. Its reply depends upon whether Briand in the plot or not. If he is not, I imagine he will refuse the Russian idea & the Chantilly Conference may not be postponed for more than 1 or 2 days. If he *agrees* to Russia, I imagine there will be no Chantilly Conference at all, as it will be superceded by the Russian one.

But I am not concerned except as regards myself. I have no intention of going. The idea is absurd. The Prime Minister ought to have said so. But he is very weak. It is a devilish clever plot & L. G. has misled the War Committee. I have seen McKenna & he says he will stick to me. I have *no* intention of going. But it is a nice mess! And takes so much of my time. Of course I have told the King, & he is lying low, on my advice, for the time being—like myself. Salonika is at the bottom of it all. L. G. is always saying the West is a failure & will be so. He is egged on by Winston & F. E. Smith. There will be no peace till we have a row.

Good luck to you. What awful mud you are in. Such very bad fortune. Never mind. No answer. Will tell you *if* Chantilly is postponed. I have wired Joffre & am wondering what his reply will be.

NLS, Acc 3155, no. 109, Haig Mss

74

General Sir William Robertson to Lord Stamfordham

War Office

[Holograph] 9 November 1916

No further developments, except that I hear Joffre knows *nothing* of the subject—as yet. But I hear much about the general plot, & feel that if I went I would be left there for weeks & that French would come here to 'act' for me!

RA, Geo, V, Q. 1200/14

75

Lieutenant-Colonel Sir M. P. A. Hankey to General Sir William Robertson

[Typescript]

SECRET & PERSONAL

Copy 9 November 1916

I think it might be useful if I were to give for your strictly personal information a short summary of the general attitude of the War Committee, gathered largely from private conversations with individual members, towards the general military situation:—

1. Let me say at once that your position and Sir Douglas Haig's is as strong as ever. I should tell you so quite frankly if this were not the case. At the same time the members of the War Committee realise that the ultimate responsibility rests with them, and that they must feel absolutely sure before approving any particular policy or before discarding any alternative policy.

2. As regards the West there is a certain disappointment with the results of the Somme offensive. In the flush of the early successes hopes were probably raised too high. Among some, but

not all members there are doubts as to whether the enemy has lost as heavily as the Allies.

3. There is a general agreement (Ll. G. a possible dissentient, but I am not sure of this) that the offensive in the West must continue, both this winter, so far as is possible, and next year. But there is also a unanimous, or almost unanimous, feeling that this will not enable us to win the war in 1917 unless supplemented by greatly increased efforts elsewhere, and more especially in the east.

4. There is an intense desire to finish next year. This is due to a very real anxiety about the submarine danger, and a doubt as to whether after 1917 the shortage of shipping may not bring us to a stop. There is also felt grave doubt about the staying power of our finance after 1917.

5. Hence there is a strong desire to re-examine the situation in the east, not as a substitute for, but as a supplement to the great offensive in the West.

6. As regards the east I find no supporters of Ll. George's idea (if it is his idea) that additional *divisions* should be sent to Salonica. I believe it is recognised by everyone that an advance on Sofia is a chimera, unless the Bulgarians are drawn off to the Danube, and that the physical difficulties, lack of communications, cosmopolitan character of the allied force, and shipping difficulties are an absolute bar. Milne's appreciations will clinch this.

7. At the same time I believe there is a strong inclination to think that, with more heavy guns and more technical equipment, the Russians would do a great deal more than they have done hitherto to supplement our offensive in the west. In fact that we might get better value for our money by sending a larger proportion of our future output of heavy guns to the east.

8. I do not think that the members of the War Committee hold any views as to where the Russians offensive ought to take place. They recognise quite properly that to be a matter for the Allied Generals and in particular for Alexeieff. Some, though, would be glad if Alexeieff decided to attack Bulgaria, because they believe

it to be a cardinal object of our policy to cut Germany off from through communication with the east.

9. There is a real and almost unanimous desire (McKenna is a possible but doubtful exception) that you should visit Alexeieff. Different reasons for this are held by different members, but all the views may be summed up as follows:—

(a) It is desirable that you should see the situation in the east and talk things over with Alexeieff in order that you should be in a position to advise the Committee with full local knowledge as to how much help we can expect from the east, and as to how far it is desirable to send guns &c there.

(b)It is essential that someone with real and great authority should explain to Alexeieff the limitations placed on the allied offensive from Salonica, especially by shipping, which Alexeieff is said not in the least to realise. (Grey and the Prime Minister are very strong on this.)

(c) It is essential to make a demonstration in Russia in order to improve the morale of the Russian people and to combat pro-German propaganda. The visit of a great General will have far more effect than that of any politician.

This is all very private of course and I have been absolutely frank about everything.

Churchill College, Hankey Mss, 4/8

76

Lieutenant-Colonel Sir M. P. A. Hankey to General Sir William Robertson

[Typescript]
Secret &
Personal 10 November 1916

I burned your letter immediately. Lloyd George asked himself to lunch with me yesterday. I put it to him straight that his proposal that you should go to Russia was open to the suspicion of being the Lord K dodge, particularly owing to the clandestine manner in which it had been manoeuvred. He at once disclaimed the remotest intention of anything of the kind. He spoke most warmly of you, and I don't think he could have simulated such evident sincerity. Finally he said he would be willing to go too in order to remove all possible suspicion. The rest of the War Committee would, I know, be no party to anything of the nature of the Lord K dodge with you.

I would give almost anything to see you and he closer together. I believe that a permanent breach is an almost irremediable calamity to the nation just now. With all his faults Ll. G. does get things done—munitions, compulsory service &c. I believe he is the only man who is likely to bring about the re-awakening of national enthusiasm and effort which is now so necessary.

If the result of a row were for you to go, the effect on the army would be disastrous. If he were to go the political effect would be equally disastrous, for he would speak his mind openly, many people would rally to him, and the encouragement to the enemy would be prodigious. I suspect that Thomas and his adherents and possibly Bissolati[42] would do ditto.

Ll. G. is desperately keen on this Roumanian visit and will not listen to any argument against it. I think though it is quite likely to fall through. The French obviously don't want it, and the Italians are quite cold. You may find it will all be dropped after the Conference next week, or it may merely become a visit by someone like the Duke of Connaught with a Cabinet Minister and a really good Staff Officer.

Of course I realise your difficulty in going with so much on your hands. I hope though that you will not have a row before the Conference next week. I am rather uncomfortable about the Conference, but I think it will at any rate clear up this.

Churchill College, Hankey Mss, 4/8

77

General Sir William Robertson to Lord Stamfordham

War Office

[Holograph] 10 November 1916

I have again told L. G. I ought not to go away. He says there is no alternative but Haig. No other development except Briand's reply, which doubts if conference in Russia can be arranged. But I hear that he had wired to Petrograd & that Czar welcomes the mission.

L. G. told me if I would go, *he* would go, & Derby carry on. Of course this removes danger here, but it does *not* alter desirability of my not going. I ought *not* to go away. The Chantilly Conference holds good for next Wednesday. Perhaps the wretched Russian mission may peter out, but I doubt it doing so. However, we can await events I think.

RA, Geo. V, Q. 1200/16

78

General Sir Douglas Haig to General Sir William R. Robertson

General Headquarters,
British Armies in
France

[Holograph] 10 November 1916

Yours of 8th only arrived this morning as the Post was closed yesterday—I must send you a line to tell you how truly I sympathise with you in all your difficulties with L. G. I wrote & asked him to come here for a few days, thinking that it would be helpful and at any rate show him that soldiers had no grudge against him! I have not had a reply yet. Whatever happens you must *not* on any account go off to Russia or any distant theatre. As we decided long ago the war has to be won in London—so there you must stay. The French have a rumour that Field Marshal Viscount French is going to Salonika. Can that be also part of the plot? To get F & Winston there, and follow them up with the bulk of the Army from France!!..

If the Chantilly Conference takes place as arranged I shall stay in Paris because the Inn at Senlis is full of correspondents.

The weather seems better and I hope may continue fine for a few more days.

Looking forward to seeing you in Paris next week.

NLS, Acc 3155, no. 109, Haig Mss

79

General Sir William Robertson to General Sir Douglas Haig

[In other hand]

War Office
10 November 1916

***

He [Lloyd George] is greatly pleased at your invitation, and is replying he would like me to accompany him. This is excellent. He says he wants to talk whole thing out with us. This will give us a chance. I have not yet quite fathomed whether he really means to play a straight game or not. However a good frank talk will do good.

We shall want you over here for the War Committee after the Chantilly Conference to discuss possible reduction of cavalry establishment. They were much on the subject yesterday, and eventually agreed no reduction could be made before your story was heard. (This is irrespective of withdrawing a part of your Cavalry for the winter.)

I have been having a real bad time lately, but it will all come right. They are not so fond of me as at first—as I knew would be the case—for I am daily blocking some mad scheme or cheese-paring because they will not face the situation.

I have heard more than once lately that Wilson[43] is being wasted in the war! You can guess how that originates. Winston and F E Smith are very busy, but they are not really dangerous though a great nuisance.

Very good luck to you.

LHCMA, Robertson Mss, I/22/89

80

General Sir William Robertson to Lord Stamfordham

War Office

[Holograph] 11 November 1916

Many thanks for your letter. I am of course ready to do what the King desires. Every one seems to know my business except myself. The Army going into winter quarters in nowise lessens my work, but rather adds to it, as my work is, chiefly, to *prepare* for fighting rather than to fight.

RA, Geo. V, Q. 1200/18

81

General Sir William Robertson to H. H. Asquith

Hôtel de Crillon
Place de la Concorde
[In other hand] Paris
13 November 1916[44]

As I have not seen you this Evening, and will not be able to see you tomorrow before leaving for Chantilly I write this to say that I fear you were not convinced by what I said this afternoon as to the impossibility of my going to Russia. The more I think of it the more I feel it would be absolute folly for me to go. Alexieff refused to come here because he could not get away; Cadorna and Joffre I am sure will not go, and yet the work they have to do is not comparable with that which falls upon me. I have larger forces in Salonika than anyone else; and operations in Egypt, Mesopotamia and East Africa calling for daily attention, besides France. Further our Army is still very much in the making; we are in the midst of introducing conscription; and there are a multitude of questions regarding training and provision of officers, organisation, and preparation for next year to which I alone can attend. Further I have nothing to see Alexieff about. I have no questions of strategy to discuss with him, and I have no assistance to offer him, more than he already knows about.

The temporary cessation of fighting in France does not affect the question. My chief business is the general control of all operations, organisations, and the coordination of preparation for next spring. To go away now would be fatal to these matters I think, and so does Haig and my Staff.

I have told the Secretary of State for War practically all the above, when we have been discussing the question.

My desire is to meet your views in every possible way, but I must tell you quite plainly that it would be very prejudicial to the conduct of the war if I were sent away now, and these disadvantages would not be in any way counter-balanced by a visit to Russian Head Quarters. Nothing could counterbalance them. To put me for a month or so out of touch with the five commanders in the Field and several others and also with the War Office would involve such a loss of control as could never be regained.

In short I cannot do the work I ought to do as C.I.G.S. if I go away, and no one can do it for me. I hope most earnestly, you will not now ask me to go.

LHCMA, Robertson Mss, I/13/21

82

General Sir William Robertson to Lord Curzon

War Office

[Holograph] 28 November 1916

I am gratified to learn that the paper[45] meets with your approval. But we really need to *get on*. Don't forget my 3 war principles—courage, action, determination. We fall short of all. The War Committee is too big, and wastes much time in doing work that ought to be done inter-departmentally. The War Committee should give *orders*. Department chiefs should stay in their offices and obey orders. London should have the same organisation as there is in the Field.

India Office and Records, Mss Eur F112/117, Curzon Mss

83

General Sir William Robertson to H. A. Gwynne

War Office

[Holograph] 28 November 1916

On consideration I think it best to be absent on Thursday night.[46] It is very kind of you to ask me. I feel that I ought to keep clear of any particular sect or movement. They are all bad. The only difference is that some are worse than others. In any case, I need to keep on a straight and unbiassed road.

IWM, Gwynne Mss, Pt. III, fol. 353

84

General Sir William Robertson to Lieutenant-General Sir H. S. Rawlinson

War Office

[Holograph] 28 November 1916

I should not go to Gwynne's. It is necessary I should not become too familiar with any particular sect of politicians. I think you would be well advised to steer clear.

Churchill College, Rawlinson Mss, 1/8

85

General Sir William Robertson to Sir Edward Grey

Dictated [typescript with
holograph additions] War Office
Personal 29 November 1916

With reference to your Paper[47] of the 27th instant written in reply to the one I prepared last week, I would like to make a little explanation.

I had already fully reviewed the situation at the end of last month and I could not understand why I should be called upon to say anything more, unless a great change had taken place in the minds of the Government as to our future prospects.

With regard to the statement that diplomacy had failed to assist us, I said that I made that statement in no critical spirit. I might have added that possibly diplomacy could not have assisted us. I really do not know whether it could or could not. The fact is it did not, and that is all I intended to imply. As you say you might equally urge that the Army had not assisted diplomacy and you would be quite right. Until this year the Army has not given that assistance. It could not.

The statement that our policy was out of step with our military preparations might have been expressed differently. What I meant was that the two were not in step, and it would have met my point equally well if I had said that our military preparations were out of step with our diplomacy. My point was that the pre-war policy, which *I* think we could not have avoided, practically committed us to assist France in defeating Germany, but the bulk of our officers held the opinion that our military preparations were inadequate to carry out that policy. I do not know what advice the military advisers of the Government gave before the war, but I have papers in this office which I myself wrote some 15 years ago, when here, calling serious attention to the danger of Germany. I was not then military adviser to the Government, but in my subordinate capacity it was my duty to call attention to what was going on and I did so.

I hope the above makes it quite clear that I had no intention whatever of attacking the Foreign Office. I certainly had not. What I wished to drive home was that we had a very bad start; we are up against a most formidable rival; and to win we must have patience and courage. Please do not reply.

PRO, F. O. 800/102, Grey Mss

86

David Lloyd George to General Sir William Robertson

[Typescript. Minuted by Robertson[48]]

War Office
29 November 1916

I have no doubt that you have given full consideration to what might happen at Salonika if the Germans succeeded in disposing of the Rumanian Army, either by defeat or by liberal peace terms of peace which might tempt the Rumanian Government to go out of the war. The latter alternative is by no means impossible. The Central Powers want no Rumanian territory, and the Bulgarians would have to be satisfied with the restoration of the territory of which they were deprived a few years ago. Germany only wants corn and oil from Rumania: that she can offer to buy. If the Central Powers succeed in one or other of these projects, is it not probable that they will turn on the Salonika Army, drive them out of Monastir and lay siege to Salonika? Do you think that under those circumstances the Allied forces in that quarter are strong enough either in numbers or equipment to resist such an attack as has been hurled against Rumania? I am anxious about this possibility and I should be very much obliged if you would give me your views on the subject.

H. of Lords RO, Lloyd George Mss, F/1/5/4

87

General Sir William Robertson to General Sir A. J. Murray

Dictated — War Office
[typescript] — 1 December 1916

I have no particular news to send you except that I hope we shall soon make rather marked progress in organising the Nation as a whole for war. The Rumanian business has gone pretty badly thanks to particularly bad management by the Rumanians in every single direction. They have changed their orders and hustled their troops about from one quarter to another ever since they began operations, with the result that although the Russians and Rumanians are superior on the whole to the enemy they are always inferior at the place that matters.

Rabegh has been a perfect nuisance during the last few weeks but I have been as stubborn as a donkey and so far have succeeded in getting my way. The chief trouble has been the French, plus one or two of your so-called local authorities who look at matters from a very narrow point of view and not very intelligently at that.

I wish you success in what you are now undertaking and hope you will have a good show and give us something to cheer up these London pessimists a little. They have been very bad lately as though the world was coming to an end because Rumania has made a fool of herself. Obviously we here could not do anything to help her more than what we have tried to do from Salonika—another pretty bad show.

LHCMA, Robertson Mss, I/32/49

88

General Sir William Robertson to Lord Lansdowne

Dictated
[typescript]

War Office
1 December 1916

With reference to our recent Papers placed before the Cabinet, I am most anxious to disabuse you of any idea that the expression 'cranks, cowards, and philosophers' had the least reference to you. I can assure you that it had not. How could it have, seeing the great contribution you have made to the war, to say nothing of the respect due from me to you personally and to the great services which you have rendered to the State for so many years past? I trust you will accept this assurance.

As regards my Paper as a whole it was not intended to be in particular a reply to your's. In fact I read your's through but once, and merely to enable me to understand what was meant by the 'knock-out blow' to which you referred. My chief object was to combat unnecessary pessimism. I thought that it undoubtedly existed, otherwise I would not have been asked to express an opinion as to our prospects of winning the war, as I had already expressed my opinion on the subject frequently during the past year. On the 26th October last I made a comprehensive 'general review'[49] of the situation, and from a military point of view had no more to say. I think it probable that you had not seen this general review, or those furnished by other State Departments, when you wrote your Paper. But as I was asked to give my opinion and as I had already said all I had to say of a purely military nature, I could do little more than reproduce extracts from previous papers and add some observations on the general aspect of the situation. I stated that there were many other considerations to be taken into account besides the military ones and I considered it to be my duty to point out, what is common knowledge, that the Nation is not really at war as yet and that until it is we cannot expect to win. Not only do we conduct 'business as usual' but in many respects we are doing much more business than usual. Many of our business people and railway authorities tell us that there is more business of a non-war nature now being carried on than before the war commenced. I am glad to think that steps may shortly be taken to remedy this and to put forth the full strength of the Nation.

LHCMA, Robertson Mss, I/21/47

89

General Sir William Robertson to Lord Stamfordham

War Office

[Holograph] 4 December 1916

I have spoken to Whigham and am quite satisfied that he has had no dealings of any kind with the Press. The last Press man he and I saw was Donald of the 'Chronicle', & this was in the first week of October.

I have seen no one, & have had no communication with any one, for at least a week, except Northcliffe when I said 'good morning' to him Friday in the Secretary of State's room. This was the first time I had seen him.[50]

Bodleian, Ms Asquith 17, fol. 181

90

General Sir William Robertson to General Sir Douglas Haig

War Office

[Holograph] 4 December 1916

We are in a great political muddle here, and goodness knows what will happen. The Prime Minister has not kept his team in hand. They have now revolted. He has never 'commanded' them, and has been sadly lacking in decision and firmness. The trouble has arisen because certain members of the Cabinet objected to the industrial compulsion scheme we got through the War Committee on Thursday last, and the Prime Minister at once began to wobble, and once again the whole thing was thrown back into the talking pot.[51] It is impossible to do business so long as each of 23 claim the right to 'object' or to 'consent' in regard to War Committee decisions. I sincerely hope they will get rid of their grievances soon and settle down or the result may be very serious.

***

NLS, Acc 3155, no. 109, Haig Mss

CHAPTER III

Lloyd George Replaces Asquith: Strategic Crossroads

The Somme campaign, which cost the British almost half a million casualties (498,054), had undermined Robertson's influence within Asquith's government. He had been shut out of ministerial discussions of the military situation; and he had narrowly escaped being given the 'Kitchener dodge' by being packed off to Russia. Ironically the downfall of Asquith and the triumph of the most influential critic of the Imperial General Staff's strategy, Lloyd George, served to secure Robertson's position for at least another year. The survival of the new coalition government depended upon the support of the Conservative Party, which gave strong support to Haig and Robertson. Lloyd George had Conservative support because of his energy, determination to fight the war to a finish, and record of mobilising the nation's manpower and industry. His 'amateur' strategic appreciations, however, found little if any favour with his Conservative colleagues. To placate them Lloyd George followed Robertson's advice and appointed Lord Derby, the soldier's friend, as Secretary of State for War.

Not having the political support for a showdown with Robertson, Lloyd George tried outmanoeuvering the CIGS to redeploy British military resources away from the western front. He asked the secretary of the War Cabinet, Lieutenant-Colonel Hankey, for an appreciation of the military situation. Hankey's views[1] on pooling the resources of the allies and treating the many fronts as one were exactly what Lloyd George wanted to hear. At an Allied Conference in Rome in early January 1917, he proposed, in opposition to Robertson, the diversion of big guns from Haig's forces to the Austro-German front. The lack of French and especially Italian enthusiasm for this plan allowed Robertson to let others do his talking for him. When it came to strengthening the Allied army at Salonika, however, Robertson took an extraordinary position. He bluntly informed the Prime Minister that he would refuse to sign any order to send additional British divisions to the Balkans.

Lloyd George then seemed to do a complete about face and embraced the offensive plan of the new French Commander-in-Chief Robert G. Nivelle. Robertson, although satisfied with the focus on the principal front, was unhappy that the British were being assigned the secondary role in the offensive, taking over French trenches and launching a preliminary attack to draw off German reserves. He also expressed concern that cooperation with Nivelle's plan would undermine the proposed summer British campaign to clear the Belgian coast of U-boat bases, and correctly asserted that Nivelle was foolish to predict a breakthrough within twenty-four or forty-eight hours of the launching of his attack. Of immediate concern to him was conflict between Haig and Nivelle about the timing of British support operations.

To Robertson's dismay Haig requested that the civilians act as arbiters. This gave Lloyd George an opportunity to intrigue with the French against his generals at the Anglo-French conference at Calais on 26 February.[2] Over their opposition Lloyd George succeeded in getting Robertson's and Haig's signatures on a document that placed the BEF under Nivelle for the duration of the campaign. The resulting unity of command was flawed. Unlike Generalissimo Ferdinand Foch in 1918, who occupied a position above the national armies, Nivelle commanded the British forces while retaining control over the French army. He also was under the sole authority of the French government.

Back in London Robertson vigorously lobbied against this arrangement and succeeded in preventing any real amalgam of the two armies. Assisted by Nivelle's arrogant treatment of Haig in the aftermath of Calais, he also strengthened Haig's position, with the War Cabinet actually ordering Lloyd George to demonstrate the government's 'full confidence in Haig'.[3] With a measure of independence retained by Haig, Robertson then played the role of a peacemaker. He was especially concerned about repairing the rift between the British and French generals because of Calais. Nivelle was assured of his good will.

The first phase of the British offensive at Arras in early April went splendidly, surpassing anything that had been achieved during the Somme campaign. Continued attacks following the capture of Vimy Ridge, however, achieved little. Meanwhile Nivelle's attempt at a breakthrough achieved the opposite of what was intended. The French, not the Germans, were brought to the brink of collapse. Meanwhile, unrestricted German U-boat warfare brought the United States into the war, a considerable asset for the future, but the immediate result was to place immense strain on British shipping. In the East the March Revolution destroyed Tsarism but failed to regenerate the Russian nation.

Lloyd George's response to Russia's decline was to advocate detaching one or more of Germany's allies through military pressure. He was especially interested in 'a campaign to break up Turkey'.[4] Disappointed with Murray's conduct of the campaign in Palestine, especially his setback at Gaza, he wanted him replaced. Robertson defended Murray initially and opposed Lloyd George's strategy. Given the precarious Allied military and shipping situation, Robertson wanted to take no risks in the outer theatres. He argued that the British commitment in the East, especially in the Balkans, should be reduced rather than expanded.

The French after the failure of the Nivelle Offensive were of particular concern to Robertson. He feared that they were about to adopt what amounted to a defensive position. Haig's forces had by default become the cornerstone of the anti-German alliance. Haig wanted to continue pressing the Germans, a policy with which Robertson agreed. But here, too, he was cautious. He wanted no grandiose objectives. As he wrote Haig, 'In other words instead of aiming at breaking through the enemy's front, aim at breaking down the enemy's army, and that means inflicting heavier losses upon him than one suffers oneself'.[5]

91

General Sir William Robertson to David Lloyd George

War Office

[Holograph] 6 December 1916

I think Lord Derby. He knows the ropes of the office. The country believes in him as a good, honest man. The Army likes him. If you would think me a good enough representative, then Lord D. need not be on the War Council if by putting him on it would become too big. He could, of course, attend, like other ministers, when needed.

Supposing you became Prime Minister, then the War Council could be you and two others, who need not necessarily be either 1st Lord or Secretary of State for War, provided you were satisfied with myself & the 1st Sea Lord, as *advisers*. I don't think that either of us should be *members* of the War Council. I *do* think that the Foreign Secretary should be on the War Council if you can arrange it. He *must* [?usually] be there. You *must* get your *Cabinet* to efface itself and leave the *War Council* to run the war. Good luck. Keep your War Council to 3 if you can, & not more than 4.

H. of Lord RO, Lloyd George Mss, E/1/5/5

92

General Sir William Robertson to General Sir Douglas Haig

War Office

[Holograph] 10 December 1916

Many thanks for your letter. I quite agree we must visit a bit before seeing Joffre's successor.[6] Probably I need not come—if

Joffre really becomes a sort of CIGS in Paris—we must wait & see. The new War *Cabinet* assembled yesterday. (L. G. Curzon, Milner, Henderson, plus ½ dozen attending.) Talked from 1130 to 530! *Quite as bad as the old lot.* Practically decided to send a force to the Hejaz from Egypt. Apparently intend to decide *everything*, but I have not had my last word yet! I have to see Joffre this week about Salonika. My people are not keen on it now. Think I shall squash the wild French project.[7] Good luck.

NLS, Acc 3155, no. 109, Haig Mss

93

General Sir William Robertson to General Sir Douglas Haig

War Office

[Holograph] 12 December 1916

Our new Prime Minister is well on the move. He is at last convinced Salonika is crazy & is going to tell Briand so next week. He & I will come & see you first. Though he is off Salonika he is *on* Egypt, and wants to get to Jerusalem! For this he is hankering after 2 Divisions from France for the winter. He is also after lending some of your big guns to Italy for the winter. I have done my best with him, and in company with you I've no doubt we can keep him straight. I want him to get the Divisions from Salonika but that will be difficult & opposed by all the Allies.

I have told the whole story to Davidson, so please do not reply to this.

We shall manage it.

NLS, Acc 3155, no. 109, Haig Mss

94
General Sir William Robertson to Lord Milner

War Office
[Holograph] 18 December 1916

We must have no 'peace' yet.[8] We can bring Germany to her knees if only we persist. Peace now means an intolerable existence later. We can yet do much with our blockade, and also with our army. The 'army' is everything in Germany, & it is very necessary we should *beat* it. We can do so. The difficulty is France & the United States. I think we ought to be very firm with the U.S. We have more supporters in the U.S. than Germany has. Wilson is a poor creature. Let us treat him as Germany has hitherto done. As to France I doubt if she would throw over her ally, Russia. I quite agree that no conference is desirable to discuss the Identic Note but I feel it very necessary that we should *personally* see and strengthen the French ministers. They are having a bad time just now and need help. Further, we should ensure, on the spot, that France is with us in our aspirations & aims.

Please do not reply.

Bodleian, Milner Ms, dep. 44, fol. 270

95
General Sir William Robertson to General Sir Douglas Haig

Dictated [typescript
with holograph additions] War Office
Very Secret 18 December 1916

***

The Cabinet is solid and sensible in regard to the German Note. The chief difficulty seems likely to be France, because apparently Germany may be prepared to clear out of Belgium and France and even to give up Alsace and Lorraine. If she does this we might have trouble with France, who perhaps might not be sufficiently strong to stand by her Ally Russia. We have received nothing from Germany but the Note published in the newspapers which has been communicated to us by the United States Ambassador ...

LHCMA, Robertson MSS, I/22/95

96

General Sir William Robertson to General Sir Douglas Haig

Dictated [typescript with holograph additions]

War Office
24 December 1916

Both French and Russians are again bombarding us to send more troops to Salonika and the question is once more on the tapis. I do not exactly know what is in the mind of the Prime Minister or the other Members of the War Cabinet. They had a meeting yesterday on the subject at which I was requested *not* to be present. I understand that there is a desire to lend some of your big guns to Italy for the next few months in return for the despatch of Italian divisions to Salonika or Albania. I also understand that our Ambassador at Rome[9] has been summoned home with a view to conveying a message to the Italian Government in the above sense. I daresay that everything will come out right in the end but it is as well that you should know how things are proceeding. You know what my advice will be if and when I am referred to, and I shall see that I am, and I shall suggest that before anything is done you should be asked to what extent your operations etc. would be interferred with by such an arrangement. If you are asked for this opinion I hope you will not mince words. There is a very dangerous tendency becoming apparent for the War Cabinet to direct military operations. No reply.

LHCMA, Robertson Mss, I/22/97

97

General Sir William Robertson to Lieutenant-Colonel Sir M. P. A. Hankey

Dictated [typescript
with additions in other hand] War Office
Personal 24 December 1916

As I am frequently absent from the meetings or part of the meetings of the War Cabinet I think there should be a clear understanding between you and me that I know nothing about what takes place when I am absent, over and above what I may later see in the Minutes. Anything that you may tell me I shall regard as 'Private and unofficial' and on the other hand I think it is desirable you should say in my absence as little as possible about my views and opinions. It would never do for me to deal with the Cabinet by proxy or to take cognisance of what I may be told as to what passes at the Meetings. The abuse is in connection with our talk last night. I *must* have an answer to Joffre's letter early next week re Salonika.

LHCMA, Robertson Mss, I/33/28

98

General Sir William Robertson to Andrew Bonar Law[10]

Dictated [typescript with holograph additions]

War Office
27 December 1916

I do hope that the War Cabinet will decide that we cannot send two more divisions to Salonika. Irrespective of general strategy and other things, no amount of argument can possibly modify the two following factors:—

(a) If the divisions are sent I doubt if they will suffice to hold the present line if attacked by the estimated possible strength. (The French themselves have asked the Italians to send 2, 3, or 4 divisions in addition to our two.)

(b) If they are sent I feel that, according to information given by the Admiralty and by the Quarter-Master-General, the forces there cannot be properly maintained.

The French attitude in regard to the matter is exactly the same as it has always been when the question of sending further troops to Salonika has been under consideration. They paint everything in the most lurid colours, and seek to persuade us against our better judgment by veiled threats as to what will happen if we do not agree. The real reason of their attitude is to secure their own political position. My Deputy[11] and the Quartermaster-General[12] regard the proposal as 'madness'.

H. of Lords RO, Bonar Law Mss, 81/1/71

99

Lord Esher to General Sir William Robertson

Paris
[Holograph] 27 December 1916

***

I may tell you that for 48 hours Lyautey had resigned the Ministry of War. He refused point blank to allow any orders to be given to Nivelle or Sarrail, *except by him*. As he was adamant, the government was forced to give way.

He is now perfectly satisfied. If you could get into close touch with this man, you could direct the great main operations of the War; but I see no way of doing this, so long as L. G. and Company desire to keep military control in their hands.

LHCMA, Robertson Mss, I/21/48

100

General Sir William Robertson to Brigadier-General C. Delmé-Radcliffe

Dictated [typescript with additions in other hand]
War Office
Unofficial & Private
28 December 1916

***

Still the French Government are afraid of a German attack on Macedonia and of a further set-back there, and therefore though they must know that the sending of a few more divisions can produce no real effect they wish them to go. By great difficulty I have contrived to prevent our Government acceding to the French request. At the same time some of our Cabinet think that Italy should send divisions there though in my opinion they would be of no more use than British divisions, and I can quite understand General Cadorna refusing to send any.

The result of the consultations of the past few days is that Mr Lloyd George has proposed to the French that French, British, and Italian political and military representatives should meet somewhere in Southern France next week and disuss not only the Salonika question but the operations as a whole for the forthcoming year. You will probably hear of this shortly. The Prime Minister tells me that if the French will not agree to this Conference then he and I will probably go to Italy. Meanwhile you can make any use of this letter you think proper in respect to General Cadorna, but it must not be quoted officially or referred to except between ourselves. I therefore leave you a free hand to do as much or as little as you like with the letter, subject to the conditions stated. It is I believe proposed by the War Cabinet that we should offer to lend to Italy a certain number of heavy guns for a short time if she will send divisions to Macedonia. The two things seem to me to have no connection and I do not see how it is possible for us to spare the guns. Moreover it would take at least a month to get say 50 batteries from our front to the Italian front and it would take nearly two months if the motor lorries etc. have to proceed by road as I think would be the case. Our output of guns next year will be much smaller than we anticipated because we have had to consent to losing a very large number in order that guns may be provided for commerce ships.

P.S. Cadorna must not mention this letter to his political people. I do not ask you to acquaint even him with it unless you think that useful & safe. It is chiefly intended for your own information.

LHCMA, Robertson Mss, I/35/25

101

General Sir William Robertson to Brigadier-General C. Delmé-Radcliffe

[In other hand] War Office
Copy 29 December 1916

I wish to add to my typed letter of yesterday that the proposed conference is not merely to discuss the question mentioned, but also, and mainly to establish closer relations with Italy. On reconsideration I desire that you will treat my other letter and also this as personal & private and not say anything to Cadorna until he hears from his own people and only then if he asks you. I think this is best, wisest & safest. Treat both letters as intended to give you a line if & when he talks to you.

Don't discuss guns with him at all. And as regards Divisions, although I would not send them if I were he, he must fight his own battle & cannot expect me to fight it for him. I have enough to do to fight my own.

LHCMA, Robertson, I/35/26

102

General Sir William Robertson to David Lloyd George

Rome
[Holograph] 6 January 1917

I don't know what effect Mr. Briand's oratory may have upon you in regard to the wretched Salonika business, but it seems only right and fair to you that I should tell you *now* that I could never bring myself to sign an order for the despatch of further British Divisions to Salonika. I tell you this as a friend (I feel sure you will not mind) and I sincerely hope I may not be compelled to say it to you as Prime Minister. I don't *think* I will, but not being quite sure that you realise how strongly I feel on the matter I think it best to tell you before it may be too late.

H. of Lords RO, Lloyd George Mss, F/44/3/6

103
General Sir William Robertson to General Sir A. J. Murray

Dictated [typescript with holograph additions]

War Office
10 January 1917

By this mail I am sending you instructions as to your future career. Possibly it may be a little disappointing to you, but we must keep our efforts directed to the main theatre. You will see in the instructions and the accompanying memorandum that I have every intention of giving you a good show later on, and that is as far as I can go for the present. I wish to goodness you could get some of the troops from Salonika or that they could go somewhere else. Salonika is doing more to prevent us winning this war than anything else and we spend more than half our time over the wretched place. We had the French Government over here the week before last urging us to send still more troops to the place and last week we were in Italy engaged on the same mission. Fortunately I managed to get my way. But at the same time there is not much prospect at present of getting anyone away. I only hope that we shall not have serious trouble there.

You gave us a capital show at Magdhaba[13] and, as you say, everything helps. The winter is a bad time for us in general. The public become impatient and so does the War Cabinet. Your little success was therefore all the more welcome.

Rabegh is as good as a comedy. I washed my hands of it months ago and left it to the Foreign Office supported by Chamberlain[14] and Lord Curzon, and a nice muddle they are getting into. However all is well so far. The brigade has not gone and I am inclined to think it never will go. If it goes it will be against my distinct advice. I have been very firm and straight about it and if anything goes amiss it will not be my fault.

We have had many changes here lately owing to the change of Government but so far things go on much the same as ever. The desire was to get a business government and the result is I think that we have got one which mistakes bustle for business. However, these troubles always occur in war and somebody has got to bear them. On the whole there is not much to complain of though I confess that lately I have become a little irritated as well as tired.

I hope you will do all you can to upset the Hedjaz railway communication. Even if it is only an occasional bombing it will be better than nothing. Personally I have never been worried about the Hedjaz. There has been trouble in the Hedjaz for the last 20 years to my personal knowledge and I am quite sure there will be trouble there for the next 20 years.

I am looking forward to you reaching the Egyptian frontier and giving the Turks a jolly good fright as well as inflicting upon them a blow which they will not easily forget.

P.S. Just received your news about Rafa.[15] Splendid. Mounted troops are the thing. *Unofficially* I think you can do a great deal with them yet, and can give the old Turk a real good shaking. I am inclined to think it is a case of 'l'audace' for you.

British Library, Add 52462, Murray-Robertson Mss

104

General Sir William Robertson to Lieutenant-Colonel C. Wigram

Dictated [typescript with holograph additions] — War Office
Personal — 12 January 1917

On the whole the results of the Rome Conference were not unsatisfactory in so far as Salonika and Greece are concerned. The French are rather badly disappointed because they did not get more divisions out of us or the Italians. They had hoped that they would have them I think because when they came over here before we went to Rome they were told that we could not give a definite answer until we had discussed the matter with Italy. It would have been much better if we had given a definite negative reply then. While at Rome we talked of practically nothing else but Salonika and Greece, and at one time I began to fear that after all we should be sending two further divisions. The French and Russians both fought hard for them and Briand held forth very eloquently for three quarters of an hour. The Prime Minister told me about this and when I expressed the hope that he would decline to send more divisions he did not give me a very definite answer. I therefore thought it necessary to warn him quite plainly that I could never consent to signing the necessary order for sending more. He was rather annoyed at this and described it as holding a pistol at his head. I did it for his benefit as I did not wish for him to commit us in an International Conference to a promise which I myself had definitely decided that I could have nothing to do with.

On the first day the soldiers and the politicians all met, with a large number of other people. I dare say not less than twenty in all. Everybody began to talk and to put forward different plans, and therefore I suggested to the Prime Minister that the politicians should formulate their policy in regard to Salonika and then turn out the soldiers to formulate the means for meeting the policy. The suggestion was adopted with the exception that the politicians did not first make up their minds what they wanted to do at Salonika. Some wanted to do one thing and some another and therefore the soldiers went off separately to see what they could do. The result was that Cadorna and myself came to one conclusion and the French and Russians to another. The soldiers did not again take much part in the Proceedings. Cadorna and I were sent for once or twice during the remainder of the sittings, while Lyautey, being a Minister, was present throughout the Proceedings. Cadorna and I kicked our heels most of the time in an ante-room while the politicians spent their time discussing Strategy, so I understand. However, no harm was done.

The Prime Minister weighed in with a strategical Paper[16] of his own, the main idea of which was a suggestion that the French and ourselves should send divisions and artillery to help Italy to break through the Austrian front en route for Vienna. Cadorna is to prepare a plan for co-operation and then send it to the French and British military authorities to consider. We shall receive it later. Not much will come of it!

Briand brought up a proposal for placing Milne more definitely under Sarrail's orders, and the Prime Minister seemed to think this was necessary. I was sent for to give my opinion and I gave it pretty plainly. I told them that we could not possibly put British troops really under a foreign General. That the thing was not practicable because our general could not be forced to comply with the orders of a foreign general. There is no law behind such a proceeding, and moreover our Government could not possibly divest itself of its responsibility for our troops and they could only look to our General to see that the right thing is done. After a good deal of talk it was decided that Milne should be to Sarrail as Gouraud[17] was to Ian Hamilton,[18] and orders to that effect are being sent to him. As a matter of fact it makes practically no change in the present arrangement.

There is a very strong pro-German feeling at Rome but perhaps it is not a true index of the remainder of Italy. Turin is however another very pro-German place. There is a good deal of Italian money in Austria and Germany; the Italians and Austrians have intermarried a good deal and have estates in each other's countries; and religion also binds the Austrians and the Italians together a good deal.

You may have heard of the difficulty which has arisen between Nivelle and Haig with regard to the extension of our front. As usual the French wish us to take over a great deal more line and at the same time prepare for a big offensive. This happened on every occasion when I was in France, but Joffre and Lord French usually came to a satisfactory conclusion. On this occasion however Nivelle has appealed to the Prime Minister. He wired to us en route from Rome asking the Prime Minister to see him. He declined to do so unless Haig were present. Nivelle has again returned to the charge, and is coming over here on Monday to see the Prime Minister—Haig will be there also. I think it particularly bad form on Nivelle's part to do this, and also it introduces the politicians into military matters.

Lyautey, the new War Minister, is a dried up person of the Anglo-Indian type who has been in the colonies all his life and talks of nothing else. He talks a good deal. He has no grasp whatever of the war as yet and I should doubt if he remains long where he now is. He and Briand had a regular set-to between themselves at one of the meetings in Rome.

Kiggell met me on the train en route from Abbeville and had a talk with the Prime Minister. Some of the statements he made were not at all to the Prime Minister's liking, and I should say that he did not make a very good impression. Kiggell stuck out for sound strategical ideas and tried to explain something of the difficulties we have to contend against, which the Prime Minister neither understood nor would listen to.

Sarrail is a fine looking, handsome man of the swash-buckler type. He completely captivated the Prime Minister who has formed the opinion that he is an exceptionally good man. In my opinion he is a man who may one day pull off a good coup, but he is quite as likely, perhaps even more so, to do the reverse and land us into difficulties. I am quite sure that he means to have trouble with Greece if he can possibly create it, and I do not think he would regret having a few troops cut up if that would suffice to bring about a row. He was very keen to be given permission to sweep up the Greeks in front of him as far as Larissa but I persuaded our people to stick out against this. We do not want war with Greece if we can possibly avoid it. There is no very formidable or tangible Greek Army, but there are a good many men with rifles who would make matters extremely uncomfortable for us if we went after them into their hills. It would be as bad as going into Afghanistan. Sarrail cannot with the force he has dispose of the Greeks. It would be like attacking a swarm of wasps. Moreover to send troops after the Greeks would mean weakening his own front and then would come the enemy's turn for an attack. Further, Sarrail pays no attention to administrative matters such as transport, rations, and so forth. He considers them as mere matters of detail. Eventually it was agreed that if the King of Greece accepted the latest ultimatum no action should be taken whether he carries out the agreement or not without referring first to us. Our Foreign Office is very sound I am glad to say on the subject of Greece. We had much better leave Greece alone. Our dealings with the Country have been of the most ridiculous type and have put the King in an impossible position, however bad he himself may be.

Milne, looking well, young, and confident, was at the Conference. He gives a very good account of our troops and says they are very well trained and in excellent spirits. His constant fear is that Sarrail will one day try to split them up. Milne has only quite recently succeeded in getting them together. All the other nationalities are intermingled and in case of hard fighting the question of supply and administration in general would become very difficult. It is a great pity we ever went to Salonika.

Murray has done very well indeed. Maude also is stirring up the Turks in Mesopotamia, whilst on the Western front Haig's men have got the Germans very tame.

LHCMA, Robertson Mss, I/12/31

105

General Sir William Robertson to Field-Marshal Sir Douglas Haig

Dictated [typescript] War Office
Secret 19 January 1917

Until Nivelle arrived in London the Prime Minister in particular and the Cabinet in general were frightfully anxious that you should not go off until you were fully ready and all the Allies ready too. More than once he has expressed alarm lest you should go off prematurely. Nivelle's appearance has caused an entire change and on several ocasions since you attended the Conference the Prime Minister and Lord Curzon have emphasised the importance of your going off as soon as possible, and this is the cause of the official instructions which I enclose herein.[19] In fact I have heard so much about it that, although everything may work out more or less right in the end, I think it necessary to put a little stopper on them without loss of time otherwise we may be laying up trouble for ourselves in the future. I have thought over the matter a good deal as to whether it would be best to let sleeping dogs lie or not and I do not think it would. I have therefore prepared the enclosed Memorandum[20] regarding which I should be glad to receive any remarks you may wish to make and also any additions (but not matters of detail). I should like to feel that the Memorandum has your concurrence when it goes in.

You will see that I deal with two points—the 'subsequent operations' and the date of the first offensive. The date is the more important thing I consider, but I am not altogether sure of my ground in regard to the 'subsequent operations'. I feel that Nivelle's plan and the extension of your front do militate against the 'subsequent operations' but I do not seem to have much to go upon. Still if they injure them in the summer I fear I ought to tell the Cabinet so, first because they have given you instructions to carry out those operations, and secondly because next winter we may be in a very bad way in the Channel and it is as well to tell the Cabinet now what we think about things.

I cannot follow what the Prime Minister has now got in his mind, but he seems to have an idea that you and Nivelle are going to do something very effective in the course of three weeks, although he has always hitherto told me that he doubted if we would ever be able to do anything useful on the Western front. He talks a good deal about the value of a partial success, whereas it seems to me that a partial success will at this stage mean nothing less than failure ...

NLS, Acc 3155, no. 110, Haig Mss

106

David Lloyd George to General Sir William Robertson

10 Downing Street
Whitehall

[Typescript] 25 January 1917

When I was at the War Office I put before you a suggestion that the Commander-in-Chief should make a systematic effort to encourage suggestions from his subordinates who had actual experience in carrying out his orders in the field as to the best means of securing success in future operations. I suggested that it would be desirable to invite opinions not merely from Divisional and Brigade Generals, but from Regimental Officers.

You told me a short time ago that you were in the habit when you were Chief of Staff in France of taking special pains to find out what Officers thought about your plans. I cannot help thinking that this course of action ought to be taken even now. Out of the hundreds of proposals or criticisms that will be forthcoming there will no doubt be a good deal of rubbish; but Field Marshal Haig and General Kiggell will be able to separate the wheat from the chaff.

Unless you think it undesirable I shall bring the matter before the War Cabinet for a definite recommendation.[21]

H. of Lords RO, Lloyd George Mss, F/44/3/8

107

General Sir William Robertson to Lieutenant-General Sir L. E. Kiggell

War Office

[Holograph] 26 January 1917

I don't want to bother the Field Marshal, but will you tell me a little about Ypres. There are signs of hostile concentration as you know. Are you fairly comfortable? Plenty of big guns & good trenches there? What about the state of the ground? Tell me anything useful, with which I can appease the War Cabinet when next they revert to the subject.

LHCMA, Kiggell Mss, IV/6

108

General Sir William Robertson to General Sir C. C. Monro

Dictated [typescript with holograph addition]

War Office
31 January 1917

I must ask you to treat this letter as 'Private and Very Secret'.

We hope to do something good on the West front this year, and at any rate are going to try to the utmost of our power. The French have got a new Commander-in-Chief who seems to know what he wants but unfortunately has a good deal to learn in regard to the management of large armies. He is cocksure of success which is all to the good but is rather French as you well know. We have got the Germans pretty cold on our front at the present time and are entering their trenches whenever we wish. Desertions are very frequent and 150 men came in during the first three weeks of this month. This as you are aware is a new feature. Along the French front little or nothing is being done as usual.

Maude is doing very well I think in Mesopotamia and playing quite the correct game. He is punishing the Turks severely without incurring great losses himself, and I am hoping he will have the Turk out of Kut altogether in the course of a few weeks, although I do not attach any importance to the place as a place. Still it will be all to our good. Moral effect counts for more than usual at this stage of the war.

East Africa still drags on. It is a big country, difficult, and has a bad climate, but I hope to get a good many of the troops away during the next two or three months.

Salonika remains Salonika and that is all I can say about it. The French have been trying their best to get up a row with Greece but so far we have managed to prevent it. Of course we do not want to go to war with her and so have another enemy with no advantage in any respect.

If we do not get a big success in the West this year we shall have difficulty in retaining popular support of the war. Not so much in this country as amongst some of our Allies, and therefore it is very necessary that we should have a second string to our bow and be able to show that we still have a good kick left in us. This second string is Egypt where we can hope to do a great deal and can compete with the enemy's communications. In Europe his communications are far superior to ours. Besides the great distances we have to traverse on the sea shipping is limited and movement is very precarious and uncertain. Based on Egypt, however, we shall be on more equal terms at any rate as regards railways and my object is to have a real good big show there next autumn and winter if the war is still going on. Murray has shaken the Turk up well during the last month or two. Maude is doing the same. Baratoff[22] & Company will also soon be on the move and I hope will do something useful, while a little later I hope that the Grand Duke will add his quota. The Turks in general are fed up. If therefore we are still fighting next autumn and winter and could have a good thing based on Egypt we ought to get good value out of it, and moreover it is the only theatre where we can operate in winter time and so keep up public interest. It is for these reasons that I am anxious to get the infantry of the 13th Division into Egypt and as many of your Territorial battalions as you can send. These with some units I shall get from East Africa will with those already in Egypt, reinforced by the necessary auxiliary services and by other formations from either France or Salonika or both, will enable me to give Murray a good force, and one sufficient to achieve important results.

***

LHCMA, Robertson Mss, I/32/53

109

General Sir William Robertson to Field-Marshal Sir Douglas Haig

Dictated [typescript with holograph additions]

War Office
7 February 1917

We are still in trouble with regard to the supply of men, and what the result will be I do not yet know. You shall be told officially as soon as we have anything certain to tell you, but I hope that everything will yet come out right. Still it is doubtful, more so than usual.

I enclose a copy of a Paper[23] which explains itself and which we sent in with the object of bringing things to a head. We sent in one in April last and got Conscription. We sent in another in November and the result got a change of government. I am not so hopeful of the success of our third effort, although it is more or less a compilation of extracts from the first two, which were fully concurred in by the Prime Minister before he took up that position. His view is now somewhat different so far as I can gather and as you may imagine.

There have been several meetings of the Cabinet on the question and the chief remedy suggested by the Prime Minister is to reduce the divisions from 12 to 9 battalions and then he says there will be plenty of men for drafts. I was not present when this proposal was discussed but the Secretary of State did his best to explain that it meant a reduction of the Army by about a quarter. The Army Council have no intention of leaving the matter at rest, and in the course of a day or two will endeavour to obtain a definite statement as to the Government's intentions. There is no doubt that men are becoming scarce in this country, and equally there is no doubt that every effort must be made to get 'A'.[24] men into the front line. I am quite sure that much can be done in this respect. At the same time there are also new men who can be got out of this country with proper organisation and that we have not yet got. Neville Chamberlain has done well and has backed us up, but so far the Cabinet are afraid to do more than has hitherto been done. The result of what has been done is shown in the enclosed printed paper.

Please treat this letter as 'quite private'. I send it merely to let you know how things are going.

LHCMA, Robertson Mss, I/23/4

110

General Sir William Robertson to General Sir A. J. Murray

Dictated [typescript with holograph addition]

War Office
13 February 1917

***

From all accounts Germany is in a very bad state and we frequently hear that Austria and Bulgaria would like to throw in their hands. We cannot pay too much attention to this, but it serves to show which way the wind is blowing. I do not think that it will make much difference whether America comes in or not. What we want to do is to beat the German Armies, until we do that we shall not win the war. America will not help us much in that respect.

LHCMA, Robertson, I/32/56

111

General Sir William Robertson to Lieutenant-General G. F. Milne

Dictated [typescript]
Private

War Office
13 February 1917

***

The criticism made on your telegram which we received a few days ago with regard to the despatch of a brigade to Petra was that you ought to have asked Sarrail to see you and have ascertained from him the reasons for going to Petra and not merely have reported to us that he had not told you and therefore that you did not know. I greatly regret that the Government decided that the brigade must go. I recorded my objection but I could do no more. There are so many points of difference between myself and the

War Cabinet that I cannot contest to the last every one. The small things I have to allow to pass. It is some satisfaction to know that the War Cabinet decided to write to the French Government and insist upon your being kept better informed and also to express the hope that the brigade will rejoin its division.

LHCMA, Robertson Mss, I/34/14

112

General Sir William Robertson to Field-Marshal Sir Douglas Haig

Dictated [typescript
with holograph additions] War Office
Private 13 February 1917

With the assistance of Geddes I have prepared a Memorandum on the breakdown of the French railways,[25] and in it I included extracts from your last letter showing the probable effect of this breakdown so far as operations are concerned. It has been decided by the War Cabinet to send the Memorandum I have prepared, with a covering letter, to the French Government. I will send you a copy both of the Memorandum and the letter in the course of a day or two. Meanwhile you may like to know that the War Cabinet feel that they undertook a great responsibility in opposing your views and mine with regard to the projected operations and accepting the views of Nivelle. The French Government will be told something of this nature. I repeated them to the War Cabinet this morning, and it will be recorded in the Proceedings what you and I said during the Conference regarding the Nivelle plan and its possible consequences.

We are still very much exercised over the question of men and in strict privacy I may tell you now that an official letter will reach you in the course of two or three days telling you that we may not be able to supply you with drafts after April next and calling upon you for an opinion for the information of the War Cabinet as to the extent to which this will affect your operations. We have for long been trying to get men and we have at last insisted that we shall tell you what your prospects are. You of course would be justified, if you think such a course desirable, in informing Nivelle and he will no doubt tell his own Government, and then the fat will be in the fire. I enclose a copy of a Memorandum[26] we sent to the War Cabinet on the 10th instant. In the official letter we shall send you we shall probably ask you for an opinion with respect to the reduction of the number of battalions in a division. I do not suppose you will say anything different from what the Army Council have already said.

LHCMA, Robertson Mss, I/23/5

113

General Sir William Robertson to Field-Marshal Sir Douglas Haig

Dictated
[typescript]

War Office
14 February 1917

About the railways and the general plan of operations, I daresay that if you had known of the letter which is being written by the Government to the French Government, and if you had felt that you would be justified in re-opening the question of the projected operations with Nivelle without Government knowledge you would not perhaps have sent me the telegram you did to-day proposing a conference of Ministers etc. In the circumstances I think you were quite right to send the telegram, but I also think that I am right in having got the Cabinet to ask you to see Nivelle first. This seems to me our only chance of getting back to the lines upon which you used to work before Nivelle came on the scene. So long as Ministers take part in the discussion of plans of operations we shall always have trouble of the worst kind I am sure. Soldiers understand each other and I have some hope that Nivelle will see you and that the two of you will come to a satisfactory agreement. The problem seems perfectly simple. The railways have broken down and until we can get them right we ought not to go off. The sooner we can get them right and the sooner we can go off the better in my opinion, subject to the other Allies also going off at the same time more or less. This is our old idea and it is the right one. But we will never get an agreement of this kind with Ministers. They have so many axes to grind whereas if you and Nivelle can come to some sort of a settlement the two Governments will have to agree. Of course if you do not come to a settlement they will have to intervene I suppose.

I have been careful to rub in on several occasions during the last few weeks that we are now tied hand and foot to the French not only in Salonika but also in France, and that this being so you cannot be held responsible for the result. My efforts are now bearing fruit, and as usual when the politician begins to find himself in a corner with responsibility on his shoulders he becomes uncomfortable. The result is that the Prime Minister and others in the War Cabinet are now very much inclined to go easy and not to embark on operations to which they know that you and myself object. I think if we proceed warily and keep the responsibility in the right place we shall get our own way. The method we should adopt is to be ready to accept full responsibility if we are allowed, within reason, to have our own plan, whereas if we are not so allowed then the responsibility must be on other shoulders.

LHCMA, Robertson Mss, I/23/7

114

General Sir William Robertson to Lord Esher

Dictated [typescript with holograph addition]

War Office
21 February 1917

Many thanks for your letter of the 16th. I shall have nothing to do with the establishment of anything in the nature of an Allied General Staff at Paris. It could not work. Within a week the members would be out of touch with the countries they represent. It would only be a multiplication of machinery without any real advantage.

I am anxious to become more closely acquainted with Lyautey and shall probably take a trip over to Paris shortly, if I do not meet him elsewhere. I had a long talk with him on our Rome trip and I tried to induce him to get into close touch with me, but so far he has not responded very well. He continues to work through his own Foreign Office—that is through the British Ambassador—or through the French Military Attaché here. Both these systems are bad. He should work direct with me or with Lord Derby, but so far he does neither. I think that his plan should be to aim at making himself a C.I.G.S. and War Minister rolled into one, having a good deputy to look after administrative matters. The whole thing on the French side is rather in a muddle since Joffre left. Nivelle has nothing to do with exterior operations, and I cannot find out that anyone else has other than the French Ministers. Questions are constantly cropping with regard to Salonika and the only machinery is the round about way of the Foreign Offices, to say nothing of the absence of the great advantage to be gained by two soldiers working together.

LHCMA, Robertson Mss, I/34/15

115

General Sir William Robertson to Field-Marshal Sir Douglas Haig

Dictated [typescript]
Personal and secret

War Office
28 February 1917

I had great forebodings of the result of the recent Calais Conference and that was why I tried not to have it. Unfortunately you had asked for it and thus gave exactly the opportunity certain people desired to have. After all we made very little progress with respect to the railway question, which was intended by you to be the chief question, as it also was by me. The result however was quite different, although I hope that no real harm has been done. I know that certain harm has been done all the same, but we must forget it and try and avoid conferences in the future. They always lead to evil. The thing is that Geddes must try and get on the best way he can. No matter whether it is railways, operations, or anything else we always seem to come off second best—for reasons known to you. The chief point made by the French was that for a given number of men we required very many times more transport than they are taking—according to what they say. No doubt this could be explained, but unfortunately it was not explained. I do not for a moment wish to dispute our estimated requirements, because I know nothing about them, but I do wonder whether they represent the minimum, or whether they are surely the total of the detailed requirements sent in by the different Armies and different Departments of your Command. I cannot think that this is so, but at the same time I do not forget that subordinates have a way of putting forward outside figures, no matter what they may refer to, and everything is so tight in these days that outside figures are not only impracticable but are apt to defeat their own ends. Of course you have not the time to go into matters of this kind. Now that Quartermaster-General has been relieved of railway work I am wondering whether Geddes has sufficiently gone into various demands put forward. Please do not trouble to answer this letter, at any rate so far as the railway business is concerned.

LHCMA, Robertson Mss, I/23/8

116

General Sir William Robertson to Field-Marshal Sir Douglas Haig

War Office

[Holograph] 28 February 1917

He [Lloyd George] is an awful liar. His story at the War Cabinet gave quite the wrong impression this morning.[27] He accused the French of putting forward a monstrous proposal, & yet you and I know that he was at the bottom of it. I believe he equally misled the Cabinet last Saturday. Derby is telling Balfour the whole truth. The former talked of resigning last night. He was furious & *disgusted*. He spoke up like a man for you this morning, and insisted on a letter of confidence & appreciation being sent to you. This will come in a day or two. Meanwhile I pray you & Nivelle may hit it off. These things always happen in war. But they are worse now than ever. Still I cannot believe that a man such as he can for long remain head of any Government. Surely *some* honesty & truth are required.

NLS, Acc 3155, no. 110, Haig Mss

117

General Sir William Robertson to Field-Marshal Sir Douglas Haig

[Holograph] War Office
Personal 2 March 1917

It is a damnable shame that you should be worried like this at the present time or at any time. According to Peyton,[28] Nivelle is asking for Wilson (no doubt being so instigated by the people over here) and for other awkward things to be done. I am sure you will do all you can to smooth things over, but on the other hand it is bad to lay up *certain* trouble in the future, and if things seem really to have reached the breaking point it may be best to have it all out *now*. Try in all you do to lean on the Army Council. Don't carry all the burden yourself, we will support you.

I attach a paper of interest.

NLS, Acc 3155, no. 110, Haig Mss

118

General Sir William Robertson to Field-Marshal Sir Douglas Haig

[In other hand] War Office
Personal 3 March 1917

Since yesterday I have thought further over the matter and am rather anxious. I am bringing the question before the Cabinet. (See attached note[29]). I want to get along with the war without trouble, but I fear trouble in the future and therefore am wondering whether we ought not to thrash out the matter more now. We ought not to have *signed* the document. Still we did, and the only thing is to put it quite clear. We shall probably discuss on Tuesday. If, therefore, you have any representation to make on the subject (I do *not* suggest you should—just as you like) I would like to have it by Monday. I think you may have great difficulties in carrying out the hybrid arrangement.

I trusted Nivelle to play the game.

It all depends upon him and I hardly dare trust him.

LHCMA, Robertson Mss, I/23/10

119

General Sir William Robertson to Field-Marshal Sir Douglas Haig

Dictated [typescript with additions in other hand] — War Office

Private — 6 March 1917

***

I hoped this morning to have had something more to say about my note on the recent Agreement. The Prime Minister said that if I wished to bring the question before the Cabinet, as a result of the Note I sent in (a copy of which I sent you last week) I could do so. It was to be discussed this morning but time would not allow. I am not sure it will be discussed now for some days as I propose to go to Italy on Thursday or Friday next for a week. Milner has just returned[30] and he certainly does not like the idea of what has been done, while Curzon also is not very easy in his mind. The whole difficulty has arisen because the Cabinet took the decision without first obtaining military opinion, and then the proposal was sprung upon you and me at 10 o'clock at night. We have not heard the last of this yet by any means.

We discussed this morning your Appreciation of the Situation and the Prime Minister seemed to think that you had at the back of your mind the upsetting of the Calais Agreement. However no one else at the Meeting took that view, and of course I did not and eventually the Conclusion come to was that paragraph iii of the

Calais Agreement met your case for the time being, and that if after seeing Nivelle he does not agree with you as to giving you sufficient control over your reserves before this projected battle takes place (as it never will) then that you should refer to the Cabinet who will decide. But until you have discussed the thing with Nivelle the Cabinet do not see how they can intervene. I think that is the right view. They all agree, except the Prime Minister, that you have done perfectly right in making the representations you have.

With reference to Nivelle's letter to you asking for Wilson & Company[31] I am not saying anything in our official reply to you on the subject but you must bear in mind that Nivelle's proposals for taking over our Armies, and all the attendant proposals, including that of the staff machinery he proposed to set up at his Headquarters were rejected. That document is dead. Apparently Nivelle still has the original idea in his mind and you should fight it. All they agreed at the Conference was to improve liaison work by appointing a General of increased status and by adding a representative of the Quartermaster-General's Branch, the details were to be settled between you and Nivelle. No doubt he hopes to get hold of our Armies entirely, and it will be difficult to stop him now that he has once got in the thin end of the wedge but we must do our best ...

LHCMA, Robertson Mss, I/23/11

120

General Sir William Robertson to Lord Stamfordham

Dictated [typescript with holograph additions]

War Office
6 March 1917

I managed to bring in this morning at the War Cabinet the question of the Command of the British troops in France, in fact

Lord Curzon asked the Prime Minister to what extent our troops were to come under French orders. The Prime Minister gave a reply and allowed me to say a word. What I said was:—'that at the Calais Conference the Prime Minister asked me whether under paragraph iv of the Calais Agreement Sir Douglas Haig would be obliged to obey Nivelle's orders in regard to the movement of his troops in the same way as a French Commander would, say Foch. That was the question put to me by the Prime Minister for my opinion as a soldier. My reply to this was that the paragraph certainly did put Haig under Nivelle's orders to that extent. The Prime Minister subsequently repeated what I had said to Haig when we all three were present'.

This was the statement I made at the War Cabinet this morning. It was heard by all present. It was concurred in as accurate by the Prime Minister. This I think will answer your question this morning as to the extent to which Haig is to be under Nivelle. Of course there is a small proviso in regard to the tactical employment of his troops, but that is nothing like the substantial proviso it should be.

***

The whole of the Cabinet therefore know what the situation is. I mentioned that I could not understand how Nivelle should be responsible to the Government for the British Army and no one gave me any reply to this remark except Mr Bonar Law who said that he knew they had taken a great risk but they had decided to take it. Nivelle cannot, *of course*, be responsible to the Government, and for that matter Haig cannot be put under his orders, strictly speaking.

RA, Geo. V, Q. 1079/22

121

General Sir William Robertson to Lord Milner

War Office

[Holograph] 7 March 1917

If you have time, please read the recent Calais Conference Procès Verbal—second session—before tomorrow, vide Nivelle-Haig relations (circulated today).

Bodleian, Milner Ms, dep 45, fol. 8

122

General Sir William Robertson to Field-Marshal Sir Douglas Haig

Dictated [typescript with holograph additions]

War Office

8 March 1917

With reference to the official communication I send you under separate cover, the War Cabinet were much disturbed yesterday by the receipt of the communication from the French Government.[32] I proposed that the matter should be left to be settled between the Generals and that I should go over and attend the discussion and represent their views and get things straightened out. Certain Members of the Cabinet would not agree to this. They think that the situation as portrayed in your Appreciation is so serious that Ministers must again intervene. (I wish to goodness the Calais Conference had never been held. I always dreaded it). After a long discussion the only thing I could get was a preliminary discussion on the part of the Generals, the Ministers to follow the next day. There was much excitement yesterday and the usual amount of suspicions, but by to-day the atmosphere had cleared a good deal and I think that good may come out of evil perhaps after all. This time we must be very careful to sign nothing to which we do not agree. If they want to do anything with which we do not agree then we will say that we will do what we can but we must put our names to nothing. We must also try to regain control over our Armies.

***

Several Members of the War Cabinet referred to the dictatorial and impudent tone of Nivelle's letter to you immediately after the Calais Conference. I earnestly suggest to you that you raise no difficulties about the Wilson Mission affair. Assuming you get the right man there you can leave the rest to time. It would please the Cabinet if you would agree to Wilson going. After thinking matters over I would, if I were in your place, be prepared to agree to his going, but of course this is a matter best left to your own judgment.

***

As regards regaining control of our Armies I do not think that we shall make any progress until after the next battle. This is the view I have after having had a talk with a Member of the Cabinet since I dictated the first part of this letter. The point is that we have agreed to make the best of the Cabinet decision and we must abide by what we have agreed to do unless and until we find it impossible to carry on. I felt at that time that the whole thing depended upon Nivelle and that I could trust him. Possibly he may be all right but there is someone about him who is all wrong.

NLS, Acc 3155, no. 111, Haig Mss

123

General Sir William Robertson to General Robert Georges Nivelle

Dictated [typescript with holograph additions]

War Office
13 March 1917

***

I wish to take this opportunity of repeating what I said to you this morning that I shall do my best to give you every assistance in your responsible task that I can give. Recently we have considered and made many Agreements, but the most essential thing of all is that we should work cordially together and have full confidence in each other. This quality is worth more than any number of paper Agreements. The French and British Armies have now been fighting side by side for more than two years and a half and I confidently think that they have stood the stress of alliance better than any two countries have ever before stood it. We soldiers all know that it is difficult for allies to work together. I think and have often said to people that no two allies in any war have ever worked so well together as the French and the English. This is my firm belief. Of course difficulties will arise from time to time, but I am sure that they will as quickly disappear if only we really believe that each of us is trying to do his best for the general cause. I have no doubt that you and I both have this intention, and therefore I look forward to the future with confidence.

I wish you a safe return to France and the best of success in the forthcoming operations. We never had such a good chance of achieving valuable results as we have this year.

Both the English and French War Cabinets seem to realise that military matters are best settled by the soldiers, and our aim should be to endeavour to settle any difficulties which may arise without having to call in the intervention of the Ministers, who have much other work to do and at the same time feel it to be very difficult to decide between two conflicting military opinions.

Let me repeat once more that my sole aim is, as it has been

throughout the war, to work to the best advantage with the French Army and its Commander-in-Chief.

LHCMA, Robertson Mss, I/34/18

124
General Sir William Robertson to Lord Esher

Dictated [typescript with holograph additions]

War Office

Private

14 March 1917

Many thanks for your letter of the 10th March. I hope to be in Paris during the next week or two and then to see Lyautey. I have had a long talk with him here. I quite realise the dangers to which you refer and they have never been absent from my mind. At the same time there is a lot of wild gossip about, and everything that is said is by no means true. I am very sorry for Haig as he has a great responsibility on his shoulders and we know that he has not felt that he has been supported to the extent to which he is entitled. This has recently been greatly changed for the better, and there is no reason he should not be perfectly satisfied with the assurances which have been recently given to him as to the confidence he enjoys providing he will believe what he has been told by the authorities.

I am aware that the French are difficult people to do business with, and I daresay that they think we are too. The point everyone must bear in mind is that we must get on with them whether we like them or not and that it is impossible to get on with them unless they are trusted to some extent to play the game. No Agreement, no Conference, no anything is of the slightest use without some approach to mutual confidence. I daresay the French place little trust in us, but unfortunately it is true too that some of our people place no trust in the French. This wretched state of affairs must cease if anything is to be done, obviously. It is impossible for me to support my people in France if they will persist in thinking that no good can possibly come out of any Frenchman.

We here are perfectly prepared to leave Nivelle and D. H. to work out their differences between themselves, if they will but do so. The last Conference was the outcome of the preceding one at Calais, and the one at Calais was proposed by Haig himself much to my dismay at the time. I did my best to ride it off but was not successful. I knew we should have trouble, and if there had been no Calais Conference there would have been none of the recent trouble. The second Conference was also brought about by representations from France, one from Haig and one from Nivelle. They wrote to each other in place of going to see each other. You will think that I have become a politician, but you will be wrong. At the same time it is the soldiers and not the politicians who are responsible for the last Conference I regret to say. However, they have had their lesson and in future will probably try to avoid conferences, as I have always done.

Please burn this letter as soon as you have read it and forget all about it until you see me. I am anxious you should do this.

I am surprised that you indicate that I am 'resolved' to let the French assume control of our Armies; nothing is further from my mind. My resolution is all the other way and as we stand now I do not think that any particularly great harm has been done. To tell you the truth I am feeling a little weary of the stories I hear about the wicked French. It shows rather a small mind on the part of some of our people. I repeat they must get on with the French if we are to win this war and I have not yet arrived at the conclusion that it is impossible to get on with them by any means other than that of allowing them to have their own way. I am quite sure that the Cabinet do not intend for them to have their own way in everything, but when they are constantly hearing from their own people that they cannot get on with the French they naturally come to think in time that all the fault cannot be on one side.

LHCMA, Robertson Mss, I/34/20

125

General Sir William Robertson to General Sir A. J. Murray

War Office
Whitehall, S. W.
2 April 1917

R [telegram]
Personal & secret

Your first report of the fighting south of Gaza gave rise to somewhat extravagant hopes, both on the part of the Government and of the general public. This was followed by some anxiety when the very incorrect Turkish communiques were published. Your last telegram has, I hope, made the situation clear, but I suggest that it is desirable to be conservative in your first reports and to lead up to more complete details of your successes in your later communiques. This has a much better effect upon the public mind, which, at this stage of the war when everyone is feeling the strain, has to be considered. The fog on the 26th was bad luck.

LHCMA, Robertson Mss, I/14/69

126

David Lloyd George to General Sir William Robertson

10 Downing Street
Whitehall, S. W.
6 April 1917

[Typescript]
Copy

As there will be no War Cabinet for a day or two I should very much like to know what steps have been taken to fulfil the requirements of Sir Archibald Murray's force in Egypt as set out in his last telegram. Some of these things he has evidently been pressing for from time to time for some weeks.

I am anxious there should be no failure owing to lack of support from home.

LHCMA, Robertson Mss, I/19/11

127

General Sir William Robertson to Field-Marshal Sir Douglas Haig

[Holograph] War Office
Private 3 April 1917

Just a line to wish you luck. The weather is abominable for you, but no matter. I know you will do well. Glad to say that the troubles here regarding you a few weeks ago, are quite past, and all is now very well so far as you are concerned.

A fortnight ago an attack was made on Milne, and this I scotched.

Today they have been going for Murray. He may not be a flyer but he has so far done his job well I think. It is abominable these constant attacks on our generals. I have beaten them about Murray this morning. It may [?sate] for the time being.

The Prime Minister is the arch-conspirator. *No* general is good enough for him. He is always producing some story he hears from people who can talk & who come home from the various theatres. However, all is now well all round once more.

I have a suspicion that Germany may have made up her mind slowly to retire in [?forcing] pressure throughout the summer to the borders of France or even a little further, but possibly not moving her right back, making us pay dearly for attacking & conserving her own men. If at the end of the summer she had done this, meanwhile going on with the submarine, she might get a suitable peace, including Antwerp etc in Belgium. This is not an unlikely move, but you will know how to watch it & not to play her game. If she should adopt the course sketched you would be able to blast her out of her positions (which could not be very strong) mainly by your artillery, and so conserve *your* infantry. Also I think you may make it difficult for her to continue a methodical retreat. I am glad to hear you have got your eye on a switch to the north if the other thing does not promise well.

Good luck.

NLS, Acc 3155, no. 112, Haig Mss

128

Field-Marshal Sir Douglas Haig to General Sir William Robertson

General Headquarters
British Armies in
France

[Holograph] 8 April 1917

***

I hear Nivelle has had trouble. Some of the French government wished to forbid the French offensive altogether; but Nivelle has gained the day. I think this indicates the instability of purpose of our French Allies! and if anything goes wrong Nivelle will disappear!—

***

NLS, Acc 3155, no. 112, Haig Mss

129

General Sir William Robertson to Field-Marshal Sir Douglas Haig

Dictated [typescript
with holograph
additions]

War Office
10 April 1917

You may depend upon me doing the right thing so far as it is in my power to do it with respect to the despatch of troops to Italy.[33] Our people here are all right, but those curious French people are again jealous of us and are very anxious that we should not send troops unless and until they do. Painlevé came over yesterday and told the Prime Minister this, and he assured him he need have no anxiety in the matter. I have seen Painlevé to-day and he tells me that Nivelle had been 'thinking' that it would be a good thing to send one British and one French division now. I asked Painlevé if I understood him correctly and he said 'Yes'. I still have my doubts. However it does not much matter because Painlevé has to-day received a telegram from Foch, who is now with Cadorna, in which he says that Cadorna says he can hold his own unless the enemy is very strongly reinforced and at any rate he does not require reinforcements now. Upon this Painlevé said there seemed no use in sending any. What my answer to him was you can imagine. I need not tell you except that I impressed upon him that what we must do was to insist on the Italians taking the offensive and of defending their own frontier if attacked, and that there could be no question of sending divisions, either French or British, at present. It would be folly to send them.

You had a splendid success yesterday, and I cannot help thinking that you really have now got a moral superiority over the Germans. I was afraid that the effects of the Somme might have worn off, but I do not think they have or it is unlikely you would have made such a big bag of prisoners as you had yesterday. There is just a chance that this Russian revolution[34] will have a bad effect in Germany. I hope to goodness it has for it is certainly having a bad one in Russia. In the Fleet everything is disorganised, the sailors have shot their Admirals and Captains, and the discipline in the Army is also very bad. As we feared, it has spread to the Caucasus where there has been a mutiny, and the General commanding one of the detachments which would shortly be co-operating with Maude has resigned his Command because his men refuse to obey him. I am fairly convinced that we shall get nothing out of the Russians this year anywhere. Even if they had fought well in Asia we might have pretty well knocked out the Turk before the summer is over, but as they probably will not fight there neither Maude nor Murray may be able to do much.

As against this however we have got America and we shall have great assistance in the way of money and shipping, and I hope we shall get some men. We are going to try to get men as drafts for our own units and have already a recruiting party in Canada waiting for the word to go, but I doubt if the American Senate will stand it. I am also urging them to send some troops to France at once even if only a brigade. It would be a good thing to get some Americans killed and so get the country to take a real interest in the war. Although it will take many months to raise new divisions we hope it may be possible to get over an advance force of say 50,000 men picked from districts as likely to become fairly efficient in a short period of time. We might get these over perhaps by August. Americans can be made into soldiers much quicker than men of most other communities.

The difficulty with Russia is that no leader has as yet come to the front and unless he does come shortly we shall get nothing out of Russia this year, and probably never again. However, that event would shut out the Constantinople obstacle which has done more than anything to keep the Turks in the field.

NLS, Acc 3155, no. 112, Haig Mss

130

General Sir William R. Robertson to Field-Marshal Sir Douglas Haig

R [telegram]
SECRET War Office
CLEAR THE LINE 13 April 1917

Reference your private letter of 8th instant. I am strongly of opinion that War Cabinet should know of the state of affairs regarding attitude of French Government towards current operations and Nivelle, as it clearly proves their instability and necessity of our reassuming full control over our own Armies. Can you send me by post any details of what took place and who the members of the Government were.

LHCMA, Robertson Mss, I/14/74

131

General Sir William Robertson to Field-Marshal Sir Douglas Haig

Dictated [typescript with holograph additions] War Office
14 April 1917

Everything appears to be going splendidly with you, and no praise is too high for all concerned. Apart from the improvement in general fighting efficiency, tactics, administration and training it seems to me that your success is largely due to superiority in morale and in artillery. As regards morale you are now reaping the fruits of the hard fighting on the Somme, while as to artillery you have now not only practically unlimited ammunition but a few larger number of guns than you had last year, and apparently they are being used in a most efficient manner.[35] I am inclined to think too that the German artillery is less powerful than it was last year. For all we know he may be rather short of ammunition, or short of guns, or have inferior ammunition. We know that he has been depriving his munition works of a large number of men, and after all Poles, Belgians, and women are not likely to be as good munition workers as the ordinary skilled man. If it really is a fact that we have got the upper hand in artillery and in morale we may yet do great things. Of course you cannot do everything, and unfortunately poor Nivelle is going into action with a rope round his neck. It is a horrible predicament for a Commander, and the worst of it is that one of his Army Commanders in the attack is not in favour of it. However the French may do better than I fear they will, in these circumstances. They are certainly beginning the fight under great disadvantages because of the cold water that has been thrown on Nivelle's plans. No more foolish or cruel thing can be done than to crab a man's plans once they have been decided upon and approved. In fact no plan should ever be crabbed. It should either be accepted or rejected, and if accepted criticism should be practically silent.

I have had a tiresome week again. Painlevé came over full of sending divisions to Italy at once (which was successfully knocked out) and led us to believe that Ribot was coming to see Lloyd George on the same subject. Ribot and Lloyd George met accordingly at Folkestone on Wednesday, and Ribot in the usual French style sprang another bomb-shell upon us in the shape of giving Sarrail a free hand in Thessaly and practically going to war with Greece. The Greeks have done all we asked them to do and have removed all their troops to the rear and now the French would like to attack them. A most wicked proposal. This was before the War Cabinet yesterday and was I think successfully defeated. I gather that Lloyd George is more or less in agreement with Ribot. What he will do now I do not know. I understand the question is to be the subject of still another Conference as between the French, British, and Italians. Of course what I want to do is to get men away from Salonika. Sarrail is by way of having a biff shortly and if and when he fails to do much—as I feel confident he will—I shall then go bald-headed for a reduction of the forces in Salonika. The Admiralty are fully with me because apart from the million tons or so of shipping employed for Salonika the Navy have to provide a large amount of naval craft for escort purposes. This would be very useful in home waters to put a stop to the sinking of ships by submarines.

***

We here are inclined to think that Germany's plan is, or at any rate was, to fight slowly and stubbornly backwards, preserving her men as much as possible, and trusting to submarines to bring us to terms before the Americans can assist. Moreover American assistance will depend upon the results of the submarine warfare.

***

I am inclined to think that Germany will allow Russia to stew in her own juice and will bring over as many divisions as possible from the East Front. She could certainly bring as many as 20 unless something unexpectedly good happens in Russia. This is a sorry picture, but it has got to be faced. On the other side of it I adhere to the opinion that Germany is probably in a much worse plight than we imagine. We know she has got a lot of divisions, but I do not think she would have given up the ground she has given up if she had felt capable of holding it, and if that is so—as I believe it is—it is plain proof that we are on top. The only question is how far can she re-establish matters by reinforcements from the Russian front? At any rate we have done the right thing at the present moment, for if these reinforcements are to come the more vigorous we act before their arrival the better. Any other attitude would be fatal and I only hope that Nivelle will have a good success. If he does the situation will as I have said above probably settle itself. On the other hand he may not have a great success and in that case we must have a fresh look at things.

As regards gaining proper control over our own Armies I am preparing my arguments accordingly, and one strong point will be the recent disinclination of the French Government to proceed with the offensive about which they have been pestering us for months past. Smuts has come back from you full of good ideas and he is horrified to find how we are dancing attendance upon the French. He is a great asset here and I only hope we may get things more to our liking before he has to leave.[36]

I do not ask you to answer this letter. It is sent merely to tell you that I hope to be over soon, if circumstances require, in order to get the benefit of your advice. I am hoping that I am right in thinking that our artillery is greatly superior to the German. If it is we can blast him out of the country and preserve our infantry as he is apparently intent on preserving his, though not with much success during the last week I am glad to say! Everyone in England has nothing but good to say of the way in which the operations are going. This is satisfactory and opportune, but at the same time it leaves an unpleasant taste in my mouth because I know the people who are the most fulsome in their praise are just those who would be foremost amongst the critics if things had not gone so well. It is horrible to think that nothing but success will satisfy some of these people. However the present success is a great one and will last us for a considerable time even as it now stands, and I have every hope from the way in which you are being uniformly successful that much greater results will yet be obtained.

I am worrying at the man question practically all day and night. I cannot do any more than I am doing.

NLS, Acc. 3155, no. 112, Haig Mss

132

Field-Marshal Sir Douglas Haig to General Sir William Robertson

General Headquarters
British Armies in
France
15 April 1917

[Holograph]
Personal

In reply to your telegram R 134 of the 13th instant. I enclose copy of a letter giving you the information asked for.

I think Clive may be able to confirm this statement, and possibly add details if you think necessary.

I agree that the British Government should re-assume full control over the British Expeditionary Force in France on the first favourable opportunity. But the question to settle is when the moment is favourable! I think it would create unnecessary friction, and would therefore do more harm than good to the Allied cause to raise the question at the present time—All goes smoothly now.

While touching on the Error of the Calais Conference, it is well that you should indicate the serious results which have accrued to our cause through the War Cabinet's decision at London Conference of January by which I was ordered (against my better judgement and protest) to extend my right to the Roye Road. But for all that ill timed decision I should now have at my disposal a large Reserve of well trained divisions with which to exploit our recent successes! or go to Italy??

Will History ever forgive the members of the War Cabinet for declining in January 1917 to have any confidence in the power of the British Army to play its part with credit on the Western Front?

Almost every week gives us fresh indications of the *decisive* effect of the Somme Battle on the German Army and the German plans. But you & I have always agreed on this I think.

LHCMA, Robertson Mss, I/23/19

133

General Sir William Robertson to Field-Marshal Sir Douglas Haig

[Holograph]
Strictly private
<u>and personal</u>

War Office
15 April 1917

After the Gaza attempt there was a special meeting of the War Cabinet to discuss Murray's fitness to continue the Palestine campaign. You see it is not so much what he has done the last few months as the previous knowledge of the man which influences the Cabinet, and he sends rather unfortunate as well as unnecessary telegrams making too much of his difficulties. However on my advice he was left in command to see what happens next time. Of course he knows nothing of this. But I have been told to earmark a successor in case of need. The best man seems to be Cavan.[37] What do you say? You won't like losing him, but we must have a good man. I need not tell you what *I* think of him because you know him better than I do. Will you please give me your opinion. Horne[38] & Birdwood were mentioned. The latter was a silly suggestion! Horne you would not like to [?much]. So what do you say about Cavan? Please don't mention this to him or to anyone else.

NLS, Acc 3155, no. 112, Haig Mss

134

General Sir William Robertson to Field-Marshal Sir Douglas Haig

Dictated [typescript with additions in other hand]

War Office
17 April 1917

Many thanks for your letter of the 15th instant giving me the information regarding the recent French Conference with respect to the offensive. The story was not told the same way by Painlevé to Lloyd George. However we can forget all about it now and hope that Nivelle will get on well. He has been cruelly handicapped by having doubt thrown upon his plan by his Government. I have no intention of raising the question at the present moment of re-assuming complete control over our own forces, but I am putting in a short paper to the War Cabinet to emphasise the necessity of getting this control as soon as we can. I have to be beforehand with these matters because as you know bomb-shells are thrown upon us suddenly sometimes, either by the French Government or our own, or by both. By getting control of our Armies I mean that assuming the 'front' as we have hitherto known it remains a hard and fast front somewhere or other, that the French should take back from you some of it and so give you a larger reserve.

LHCMA, Robertson Mss, I/23/20

135

General Sir William Robertson to General Sir C. C. Monro

Dictated [typescript
with holograph
additions]

War Office
19 April 1917

...In France our people have done splendidly, and show a great improvement on last year both as regards artillery and infantry. We really are top at last, but of course we are not very numerous as compared with the enemy. Before you get this you will know what has happened. The French attack has not gone too well. Unfortunately Nivelle was far too optimistic in public about it and talked grandly of getting right through the German lines within 48 hours. I said at the time it was very stupid of him to do so. Why he did it I cannot conceive. Now that he has not done what he said he would do his politicians are naturally thinking he has failed, and I suppose we shall have more trouble with them. I am still hammering away trying to get our troops away from Salonika. There again we are tied to the tail of the French. The French Government make out that the French Nation attaches great importance to the Salonika Expedition, whereas I do not think they do anything of the kind. It has been a Government blunder from the start and I have no doubt it will be the end of the

Government. I do not think the French themselves believe in it at all.

It is good business the United States coming in as it relieves the financial situation greatly, and will also help shipping as they will start on a big scale to build new ships. We want them badly as the submarine attacks are not to be disregarded. We have sent over Bridges[39] and some other officers to help them to raise an Army, but the extent to which they will be able to use it, if they ever raise it, will depend as everything else does upon the shipping. Generally speaking we are in a position probably never foreseen. Ever since I can remember and years before then it has always been assumed that we would have command of the sea and everything was based upon that hypothesis, and if anybody had thought it should be based on any other hypothesis they would have been classed as fools. As a matter of fact we have not got command of the sea. In every theatre we are suffering from shipping shortage, and this is why I am still hammering away at the Salonika fiasco.

The Russian situation is bad as I felt it would be from the start . . . I had hoped however that the Russians would have been able to do enough this Summer to keep the enemy divisions on the Front which are now there and then perhaps we could have managed the remainder, but I do not think Russia will be able to do this now. The whole Army has fallen to pieces. . .

On the other side of the picture there is a good deal of trouble in the Central Powers. They are frightfully hungry, strikes and riots are common, and everyone is discontented. Things will still go all right notwithstanding the collapse of Russia if only our side will set their teeth. The worst of it is that they expect to win this war without any great strain being put upon us, and of course there is no such chance. We have got a splendid Army and so have the French, and our combined artillery is far superior to that of the German. If only our so-called leaders will but keep up their courage all will yet be well.

I must again thank you for the splendid assistance you have given us. I can assure you that matters have seemed entirely different since you went to India. I feel that you will always do your very best and give us all you can, and that you are taking in the whole situation.

I expect Maude will have a good many Turks on top of him before long, but I have every confidence in him. Although the Turks as a result of Russian inaction may be able to spare a good many men from the Caucasus I do not think they can maintain very many in front of Maude because of the transport and supply difficulties, at least no more than he can deal with. If the worst should come to the worst he must keep his freedom of movement. We must have no repetition of Kut. There is one thing in war which a Commander should practically never do and that is allow himself to be shut up. But I am far from thinking there will be any question of this. I think Maude has done splendidly, and, I know that his success is largely due to you. Everyone here is delighted with what had been done in Mesopotamia, and I am glad to say that your contribution has not been overlooked.

LHCMA, Robertson Mss, I/32/57

136

General Sir William Robertson to Field-Marshal Sir Douglas Haig

Dictated [typescript with holograph additions]

War Office
20 April 1917

***

To my mind no war has ever differe so much from previous wars as does the present one, and it is futile, to put it mildly, hanging on to old theories when facts shown them to be wrong. At one time audacity and determination to push on regardless of loss were the predominating factors, but that was before the days of machine guns and other modern armament. Of course there must still be audacity and determination to push on otherwise nothing would be done, but there is no doubt that in these days these qualities must be governed, and in practice they undoubtedly are governed, by the effects of modern fire and modern entrenchments. Your recent splendid operations are a proof of this so far as I at this distance am able to judge, for it seems to me that your success was mainly due to the most detailed and careful preparation, to thorough knowledge of the ground by battalions and batteries and the higher units, and to well observed artillery fire. It seems to me that these factors will continue to the end of the war to be vitally essential, and if they are not so regarded success will be rather in the nature of a fluke, and will probably entail heavier losses than will justify the few hundred yards of trench or additional village gained. I cannot help thinking that Nivelle has attached too much importance to what is called 'breaking the enemy's front'. The best plan seems to me to go back to one of the old principles, that of defeating the enemy's army. In other words instead of aiming at breaking through the enemy's front, aim at breaking down the enemy's army, and that means inflicting heavier losses upon him than one suffers oneself. If this old principle is kept in view and the object of breaking the enemy's army is achieved the front will look after itself, and the casualty bill will be less. I apologise for breaking out in this manner into a sort of Staff College lecture, but after all lookers on do see something of the game, and I believe that if Nivelle's mind had been working a little differently he would not have contemplated for a single moment getting right through the enemy's defences in a couple of days, or at any rate of saying that he would be able to decide at the end of two days whether his operations had been successful or not. I have just turned up a Paper I wrote in January with respect to his plan, a copy of which I sent you, and I find that I was rather a true prophet as to what might happen to his operations. I am sorry I was. You must not think I am taking a gloomy view of his prospects, because probably he has done as much (I really do not know what he has done) as could have been expected. What troubles me is that he has failed to do what he said he could do, or would try to do, and that may lead to further trouble. Goodness knows there is quite trouble enough in dealing with the Germans.

You will see from the telegram I sent you two days ago that the

Russian is no use to us this year. I was afraid that would be the case as soon as the Revolution began.

LHCMA, Robertson Mss, I/23/21

137
Lord Esher to General Sir William Robertson

Paris
[Holograph] 23 April 1917

I am wondering what impression you will have gleaned from General Maurice of the French mentality.

To me it appears as bad as possible. The Pétain-Painlevé waiting game can only lead to a lame peace, and that in a comparatively short time.

To pause until America can train equip send over and reinforce a million men seems idiotcy.

But it is this childish faith in the U.S. coupled with cold feet that weighs with that school of thought, reinforced as it is by many soldiers, who for various reasons adhere to Petain.

Short of a miracle, I should suppose that Nivelle will not survive this fortnight or three week's grace.

The re-assembling of this Chamber, with all the intrigue that immediately follows its meeting, will probably darken the situation still more.

However, if Lloyd George *wishes* to do so, he can carry his point; America or no America.

If the offensive is stopped, people will think that there is a Sturmer[40] somewhere in the background.

LHCMA, Robertson Mss, I/21/60

138

General Sir William Robertson to Field-Marshal Sir Douglas Haig

R [telegram] War Office
<u>CLEAR THE LINE</u> 26 April 1917

I agree with views in your telegram No: O.A.D. 414 of 25th, and wish Painlevé to know that, apart from considerable British losses uselessly incurred if French pressure is relaxed and apart from breach of faith involved by such relaxation, after we had fully accepted and carried out French plan in all its details and commitments it would be folly to relax now that enemy is feeling the strain more than at any time before. Further, it is futile, in view of situation on sea, to be influenced by what America can do on land many months hence if ever. War Cabinet spoke very strongly yesterday about French apparent relaxation and it is necessary you should represent what I have *said above*.

LHCMA, Robertson Mss, I/14/76

139

General Sir William Robertson to General Sir H. H. Wilson

Dictated [typescript with holograph additions] War Office
27 April 1917

The Prime Minister sent for me this afternoon regarding the general situation in France, and the general feeling in official circles, and he told me to say that he was a little disappointed that you had not found it possible to send us more information as to what your personal opinion is regarding what the French are really up to and what we may expect of them. A good deal of information has come in during the last few days to the effect that the French are not now really out for business, and the War Cabinet naturally like to check out what they hear by information from reliable sources. They regard you as knowing the Frenchman better than anyone else, they constantly say as much, and they are anxious for you to assist them. The war is at a critical stage, and their anxiety to get good information is natural.

***

LHCMA, Robertson Mss, I/34/26

140

General Sir William Robertson to Lord Stamfordham

Dictated [typescript with holograph additions]

War Office
7 May 1917

I returned from Paris last night. The Prime Minister is taking an extra day in France in order to see his Son. No doubt he will see the King on his return. In the meantime and without officially anticipating the Prime Minister's report, I enclose a Paper which shows what happened at Paris.

As regards the Western Front I am satisfied. I am also satisfied in regard to the withdrawal from Salonika, except that I fear that the arrangements in regard to Greece may prevent the withdrawal from Salonika to the extent desired. I told the Prime Minister this. But he had a very difficult task, and with me he hopes that once we begin, as we intend to do, on 1st June to withdraw our troops we shall in course of time be able to get them away. The great thing is to begin.

***

To go back to the Western Front, the Prime Minister was very firm indeed with the French Government and insisted that they should say really what they meant and that he would not have our men killed unless the French also fought and to the full extent. He spoke very well and very strongly on the necessity for our keeping up pressure on the Germans. Pétain told me that he never had the least idea of stopping fighting. His object only was not to aim at such distant and impossible objectives as Nivelle had done and in this he is quite right. I think he is a straightforward man. Whether he will be able to keep up his end against his Ministers I do not know, especially after fully agreeing with me for continuing to fight hard on the Western Front, for withdrawing from Salonika, and for not going into Greece. All these views are in opposition to what the French Ministers have at the bottom of their hearts.

On the whole I think it is about the best Conference we have had. There is no doubt that the French were very shaky when we went over and required to be taken in hand. The Prime Minister did his part well and I feel that we have once more pulled the French together and got them going. Of course the Greece business is very complicated and will cause a great deal of trouble in the French Chamber. But anyway the Prime Minister made it quite clear that we shall begin to bring away one division and two cavalry brigades on the 1st June unless Bulgaria has before been made to contemplate suing for peace, a most unlikely contingency, and that we must bring away the others as soon as we can and of course in accordance with the situation.

LHCMA, Robertson Mss, I/33/70

141

General Sir William Robertson to Lord Milne

Dictated [typescript with holograph additions]

War Office
8 May 1917

I was glad to hear this morning what you said about Palestine. I wish the Prime Minister would realise the changed conditions. As you rightly said our original intention was to go for the Turks in Palestine while the Russians went for them in Caucasia. But now the whole situation is changed and the number of troops the Turks can put into Palestine or into Mesopotamia is limited only by their means of supply. There is no doubt whatever that Palestine will now be a very difficult operation, and it is no good burking the fact. On the other hand it seems equally certain that our task in the West will as a result of the collapse of Russia be also much harder than we originally anticipated. The West remains the main theatre now just as much as ever it did—that is until the War Cabinet changes its policy—and therefore Palestine remains a secondary theatre and must be treated as such. I am about to see Smuts shortly, but what he will say I do not know, but I think it would certainly be foolish and it might be fatal for the Cabinet to give any kind of promise that the wants of Palestine shall be supplied to the full extent. What we can give to Palestine depends upon what we may have to employ on the Western Front.
P.S. Just seen Smuts. I have asked Hankey to arrange for him to come to the Cabinet tomorrow if the Prime Minister approves. Smuts has talked very good sense. He agrees with your views.

LHCMA, Robertson Mss, I/36/65

142

General Sir William Robertson to Admiral Sir J. R. Jellicoe

Dictated
[typescript]

War Office
11 May 1917

I am glad to get a copy of your Paper G. T. 688. The question of Palestine will probably come up on Monday next. The Prime Minister is very anxious Smuts should go. Smuts does not wish to go unless it is going to be a real thing, and he doubts the feasibility of this.[41] Smuts's idea is that the only way of doing the trick properly is to land a force of some hundred thousand men at Haifa. This I imagine you could not look at. But in any case Smuts would want to use some of the Syrian ports. I have told him that you would look at nothing of the kind. Will you please be prepared to give your views on the question when it comes up. Smuts is by no means an advocate of the Palestine Campaign, but at the same time if they insist upon taking it on he wishes to make quite clear to them what they are in for. In this he is of course quite right.

LHCMA, Robertson, Mss, I/36/45

143

General Sir William Robertson to Field-Marshal Sir Douglas Haig

Dictated [typescript
with holograph additions]
Secret

War Office
17 May 1917

I am afraid I have bombarded you rather with telegrams recently concerning your proposed discussion with the French Commander-in-Chief, whoever he may be, but the Cabinet are very anxious, and quite rightly so, about the matter. As you know

Petain and Nivelle both made out at our Conference that they intended to fight; they also seemed to agree so far as they were concerned to the relief of the French divisions on the coast; and they also agreed to study the question of taking over part of your line. There is no doubt about it that at the back of the French mind there is a strong desire to avoid casualties, and after all that is only another way of saying that they do not want to fight. The Cabinet are quite consistent in the desire to support our views as to the necessity for continuing a real offensive action but at the same time they are equally desirous of the French doing their share, because if they do not it is quite clear that you will have all the German divisions which can be scraped together on the top of you, and we shall find ourselves at the end of the year with depleted divisions and the French will not. This will not be good from many points of view.

It is a very difficult matter for you to deal with because of course you cannot guarantee that the French will do what they promise, but you can form a pretty good idea; and at any rate you should make your doubts known to the Cabinet if you have any. Whether you deal with Foch or Petain is for you to decide. The Cabinet seem to think that Foch is being put in merely in an advisory capacity and that Petain is really their man, and therefore they asked me to send you the telegram I sent yesterday on this subject. But you may have information which I have not got as to who is the supreme authority. On the face of it Petain seems to be your man as you had intended before he replaced Nivelle to see the latter.

***

LHCMA, Robertson Mss, I/23/26

144

General Sir H. H. Wilson to General Sir William Robertson

[? Compiègne]
[Holograph] 18 May 1917

. . . The situation here is much cleared & is much stronger & better in many way than it was when I last wrote to you. I have had long talks with both Foch and Petain. Petain is now in a position to deal with Sir Douglas on war issues, and, in fact, did so at a meeting this afternoon at Amiens as you will have learned by Sir Douglas' wire. The meeting went off well & the Commander in Chief was pleased, & he will, no doubt, give you his impressions by letter. We are more than fortunate in having Foch in Paris.[42] You know him well, & you also know what I think of him and it amuses me a good deal to see both French & English people acclaiming him as *the* man for the post when I remember how those same gentlemen used to say he was too old, and too tired, and too anti-English, and too loquacious & etc. etc.!

Yes, all these changes are very much for the good. Foch has many ideas about Russia, America, Salonica & the riflers action on the Western Front which you ought to hear as soon as you can arrange to come over & see him. Yes, the changes are all for the good, though, of course, we shall have to watch our friends all the time.

LHCMA, Robertson Mss, I/21/67

145

General Sir William Robertson to General Ferdinand Foch

Dictated [typescript with holograph additions]

War Office
23 May 1917

I am very glad again to have the pleasure of working with you, and I write to ask you to be good enough to meet me one day early next week to discuss the general situation, with special reference to outside theatres. I wish to learn your views in order that we may work in accord, because our Governments are placed in a difficult position if and when their respective military advisers do not agree, and we therefore should first endeavour to come to an agreement before questions are laid before our Governments.

As you no doubt are aware I do not interfere in any way with Field-Marshal Sir Douglas Haig in the execution of the policy approved by the War Cabinet. I am concerned only in regard to the establishment of that policy.

We need to consider what may be the developments of the Russian situation. I do not think that we shall derive any active assistance from Russia this year. The only question seems to be whether Russia can retain the whole or greater part of the enemy divisions now on her front, and if she cannot whether they are likely to be withdrawn and where employed. In this connexion there are the Western Front, Italy, and Macedonia to be considered.

The Macedonian question is still the most difficult and complicated one we have to consider, and I would like to point out that my Government, acting on the opinion of our Naval Authorities, were compelled at the recent Paris Conference to inform your Government that we cannot, owing to the shipping difficulty, possibly continue to maintain the large force now in Macedonia. Therefore I hope you will pardon me when I say that it is not within my power to discuss matters which merely show the difficulties and objections of reducing the Macedonian Force.

The hard fact is that the force *must* be reduced. I would like to add that the reduction of the British forces in Salonika has no direct connexion with operations in Palestine.[43] We are reducing our force simply because we are compelled to do so by the shipping situation. The two cavalry brigades are going to Egypt because we can there supply them from local resources or from India, and we can profitably employ them there. On the other hand we cannot employ them in France as we already have there more cavalry than are needed. The division which is being withdrawn from Salonika will also probably go to Egypt, because I must have a small reserve there to meet eventualities in India and the East generally, especially so as sea-communications are now so bad and precarious. At present I have no such reserve, and I may add that we are now just being compelled to undertake some punitive operations against certain tribes on the North-West Frontier of India. One can never tell what may happen on this frontier, and trouble in the near future is rendered the more probable because of much unrest and disturbance on the Russian frontier of Afghanistan in consequence of the Russian revolution.

Another question for our consideration is American assistance.

***

LHCMA, Robertson Mss, I/34/28

146

General Sir William Robertson to General Sir C. C. Monro

Dictated [typescript] — War Office
Personal & secret — 31 May 1917

... The Russian revolution has let us down very badly, and instead of finishing off the Turk this year we shall now have him on the top of us both in Palestine and in Mesopotamia, as well as have a good many more German divisions on the Western Front I daresay. As regards Palestine I will of course look after that to the best of my power. There will probably be a change of command there shortly. As regards Mesopotamia I think Maude should be all right notwithstanding what the Turk may attempt to do. We must quietly and gradually strengthen his force this summer in such ways as we can and leave him to do the remainder. The great thing for him is to have plenty of mobility, good communications, and avoid shutting himself up anywhere in case of a heavy hostile advance. I think we can trust him to drop upon the enemy if and when he begins to concentrate before he becomes dangerous. The enemy's line of communications is bad and will continue to be bad, and I do not quite see how he can oppose Maude with a force that is likely to be really dangerous.

***

LHCMA, Robertson Mss, I/32/59

CHAPTER IV

Passchendaele

On 21 November 1916, Asquith's government, concerned about U-boat attacks from German bases on the Belgian coast, had informed Robertson that, 'There is no operation of war to which the War Committee would attach greater importance than the successful occupation, or at least the deprivation to the enemy, of Ostend, and especially Zeebrugge'.[1] With the collapse of Nivelle's offensive, known as the Second Battle of Aisne, in April and early May, Haig naturally assumed that the way was now clear for the great Flanders offensive which he had been planning for months. Robertson, however, now had serious misgivings. Russia seemed finished for the war; the Italians were wavering; and mixed signals were being received about French willingness to support in strength a British offensive. Was this the time to launch a costly and prolonged British offensive with distant objectives, especially with the nation now facing growing manpower shortages on the home front as well as in the trenches? The differing views of Haig and Robertson were largely explained by their estimation of German staying power. Within the War Office, Charteris, Haig's chief source of intelligence on German strength, was considered 'a dangerous fool because of his ridiculous optimism'.[2] Robertson simply did not believe that Germany in the existing circumstances of the spring of 1917 could be defeated in 1917 or perhaps even in 1918.[3] A more prudent strategy might be the detachment of one or more of Germany's allies through a combination of military and diplomatic action. Meeting with Foch on 7 June, Robertson raised the question of concentrating on war-weary Austria-Hungary.[4] Two days later Robertson suggested to Haig that perhaps guns could be sent to assist Italy. Not surprisingly Haig was shocked that Robertson would even consider the deployment of military resources away from the western front.[5]

When Robertson returned to London from his visit to GHQ, he discovered a new challenge to his authority. On 8 June the War Cabinet, frightened by the collapse of Russia and rumours of mutinous action by some French troops, had established the War Policy Committee 'to investigate the facts of the Naval, Military, and Political situations, and present a full report to the War Cabinet'.[6] During the next weeks, this body, consisting of

Curzon, Milner, Smuts and Lloyd George,[7] held sixteen meetings before its final report was submitted to the War Cabinet on 20 July for approval.

Robertson apparently believed that he had no choice but to support Haig. If he did not, he feared that the civilians would exploit the disunity within the high command to redirect higher strategy. He thus opposed Lloyd George's proposal to divert artillery and perhaps even British divisions from the western front to support an Italian offensive. 'They will never go while I am C.I.G.S.', he wrote Haig on 13 June. In this same letter, he advised Haig: 'Don't argue that you can finish the war this year, or that the German is already beaten. Argue that your plan is the best plan—as it is—that no other would even be *safe* let alone decisive, and then leave them to reject your advice and mine. They dare not do that'.[8] Robertson succeeded in blocking proposals made in the War Policy Committee to detach Germany's allies through diplomacy supported by strong military pressure, not only against Austria-Hungary but also against Bulgaria and Turkey. On 20 July Haig's offensive was reluctantly approved by the civilian leadership.

The acrimonious debate leading up the the Third Battle of Ypres, popularly known as the Passchendaele campaign, cost Robertson dearly. He had vigorously deflected civilian criticisms of an offensive in Flanders concerning which he himself had serious reservations. Lloyd George and his supporters were now inclined to blame him even more than Haig if the offensive miscarried. On the other hand, his failure to share Haig's optimism about the state of the German Army and his opposition to distant offensive objectives, had seriously damaged his relationship with GHQ.

On 30 May Haig referred to Robertson in a most uncharacteristic and unfair way in a letter to his wife: 'Robertson CIGS seems to be tactless, wishing to be here during the Battle! It is all for his own advertisement, and no doubt he tells the War Cabinet that we here in France cannot get on without him'.[9] Three weeks later Haig supported an extraordinary proposal to move Robertson from the War Office to the Admiralty as head of the Board of

Admiralty. Haig may have been primarily motivated by the belief that Robertson would provide the navy with decisive leadership, but one suspects that he now believed that Robertson as CIGS had outlived his usefulness to GHQ.[10]

The next months were the most difficult period of the war for Robertson. Heavy rain turned Haig's battlefield into a quagmire and British progress was slow and costly. Long before the offensive ended in November, Robertson realised that the original and primary objective of the campaign—the Belgian U-boat bases—was unobtainable. Haig's optimism, however, was in no way blunted by his lack of success. On one occasion, Haig even had Robertson meet with his army commanders to determine whether they agreed with GHQ's view that the German soldier was near his breaking point. No army commander dissented with their commander-in-chief.[11] And Robertson never advised Lloyd George that the offensive should be terminated. Rather, he continued to fight Haig's battles for him in the political councils.

Lloyd George, depressed by the lack of progress and horrified by the mounting casualties of the BEF, seemed to want to change plans every week or so. Within the War Cabinet and War Policy Committee and at inter-Allied conferences, the Prime Minister sought to undercut Haig's offensive by continuing to advocate diverting British military resources to a campaign against Turkey or an offensive in the Austro-Italian theatre. On every occasion he encountered opposition from the CIGS. 'No plan is of any good unless carried out with confidence and resolution', Robertson told the wavering ministers.[12]

The Italians' lack of fighting spirit helped Robertson in late August and early September knock out Lloyd George's scheme to send British divisions and 300 guns south of the Alps. Deflecting plans to reinforce Allenby to enable the Egyptian Expeditionary Force to advance to Jerusalem and beyond proved more difficult. Robertson eventually had his way by 'cooking' the advice that Allenby forwarded to London. Coached by the CIGS, Allenby made an absurd request for an additional thirteen divisions 'to ensure decisive victory against the numbers which might possibly be concentrated against me by the enemy'.[13]

Lloyd George's frustration was now so great that he urged his colleagues to overrule the Imperial General Staff's strategical recommendations. Unable to get their support for this unprecedented step, Lloyd George then sought the advice of soldiers who might disagree with the Imperial General Staff. He told the War Policy Committee on 9 October, 'if a patient was very ill no one would limit themselves to taking the advice of a family doctor. They would call in a second opinion'.[14] The second opinion favored by the Prime Minister was a committee of Sir Henry Wilson and Lord French, both of whom Lloyd George knew had serious doubts about Haig's offensive.

Wilson's and French's critical comments concerning the Imperial General Staff's conduct of the war were eclipsed by news in late October of a surprise Austro-German offensive in Italy. The Italian army cracked at Caporetto; and Robertson now had no choice but to comply with Lloyd George's instructions to send immediately British troops to rescue Italy.

147

General Sir William Robertson to Field-Marshal Sir Douglas Haig

Dictated [typescript] War Office
Personal & secret 4 June 1917

I have arranged to meet Foch on Friday next at Abbeville. The same night I propose to go to the First Army, if you will kindly allow me to do so, so as to get a look at my boy and have a talk with anyone I see. On the Saturday I can continue this or meet you on the Saturday afternoon if you prefer. If this is too soon I could meet you on Sunday, but I must return to England that afternoon. I do not suppose you can say now whether Saturday or Sunday will be more convenient for you but I tell you my plans so that you may see what time I have available. If by any chance even Sunday is too soon for you then I must cross over again later in order to see you or you could come here if that would be convenient and agreeable. I am sorry I am not able to put off my visit to Foch any longer than Friday, but it is impossible to do so. I also think it necessary that I should see you in order to tell you something about the general situation, quite apart from operations on the Western front pure and simple. The general situation at present requires a great deal of watching. The strain everywhere is becoming great and we need to consider every move in all theatres very carefully.

LHCMA, Robertson Mss, I/23/31

148

General Sir William Robertson to Field-Marshal Sir Douglas Haig

Dictated [typescript
with additions in other hand] War Office
SECRET 30 June 1917

I had a satisfactory interview with Foch. He tells me that he adheres to the Paris Conference, that is to use all available forces in co-operation with us. The only question is what are the forces available? I think that he will impress upon his Government the necessity for giving all the help that can be given. In general, he said all that I think we could expect him to say in regard to future French assistance. I was quite satisfied with *him*.

On Friday morning I ran in to Petain's Headquarters to pay my respects to him, and with him I was disappointed. I could not quite make out what his line was. I went to see him with the full intention of showing that the German is now in a bad way, and that we have a good chance of finishing him off if only we will all stick to it. I felt that, the French being a little down on their luck, it would be a good thing if I showed myself to be fully satisfied and cheerful with respect to the present situation. But Petain would listen to nothing of this nature. When I talked about the internal condition of Germany; the probable shortage of ammunition and food; the weakness in effectives; and the burden of Germany's allies he simply dissented or attached no importance to what I said. In general I could make no headway in this matter. He insisted upon talking about Diplomacy, the necessity for detaching some of the enemy Powers, and the absence of any leader in France, and he drew sad pictures about the tired state of the French Army and more particularly the French Nation. In fact he talked like a man without a jot of confidence as to the future. As I have just said I did not quite know what his line was and why he put forward these views. I have not drawn any special conclusion from the few minutes talk I had with him because it was early in the day, and also he may have been worried by his Ministers lately for all I know.

***

LHCMA, Robertson Mss, I/23/33

149

General Sir William Robertson to Lord Curzon

Dictated [typescript
with additons in other hand] War Office
<u>SECRET</u> 4 July 1917

It would be valuable if you would kindly explain to the Prime Minister during the discussion of the Salonika question what the nature of the Balkan Country is. He seems quite unable to envisage it and to understand the difficulty of getting heavy artillery forward in an advance and in supplying an army. No one can explain the matter to him as well as yourself. Amongst other things he seems to think that there is a single range of hills between the Salonika Force and Sofia, whereas the whole country is a mass of mountains. The country is in short one in which a small army would be murdered and a large army would starve, and it is of a highly defensible nature. No amount of argument and no amount of heavy artillery will alter it.

You will understand that the above is in no way intended to influence the decision of the War Cabinet as to the policy they desire to adopt, but it is necessary that all Members of the War Cabinet should realise what the country is like. I am prepared to do my best to carry out any policy that may be laid down, but I feel quite sure that there is no reasonable prospect of a military success in the Balkans unless the Bulgars crumple up in a manner which at present we have no reason to suppose they will do, or unless the Russians put in a really big attack from the north, but that also we have no reason at present to suppose will happen.

LHCMA, Robertson Mss, I/36/19

150

General Sir William Robertson to Lord Curzon

Dictated [transcript
with additions in other hand] War Office
SECRET 6 July 1917

Many thanks for your slip this morning.

As regards Alexandretta I imagine we should need *at least* 100,000 men, and I do not see where they are to come from. We should also need the necessary ships and security on the sea, and I am sure that the Admiralty cannot provide either. Attacking an enemy from two different directions is very attractive. It is a scheme which has often been tried in war, and when successful is very effective. But with the exception of Waterloo and one or two other cases it has always failed. When attacking an enemy from two different directions it is necessary that each of the two forces should be capable of dealing with practically the whole of the enemy, who has the choice of going for either. Therefore it would be a very extravagant use of our men, as we should need most of all the forces now in Southern Palestine and a somewhat larger force at Alexandretta. The idea is quite impracticable.

As regards the Italian scheme I can say no more. If it is decided to go on with it I shall try my best to carry out the policy as long as I think I can be of use, but I am sure it would be a wrong policy. Guns alone would not suffice to do the trick, as I have already said, and there are many objections to sending other troops. Further, I am sure that the French would object to either guns, in large numbers, or troops. Also it would mean a lapse of several weeks before anything could be done and the Russians are daily expecting us to get on the move—not that they count for much perhaps. But I will not mention the various objections as I have already stated them. There is one small point, however, I may add and that is that Haig has been told to go on with his preparations. These will soon be complete, and if he is going to be stopped it ought to be done very soon. Further, as the French are arranging to co-operate with us it is necessary that they also should know.

From Hindenburg's speech the other day and from numerous other sources we know that the German aim is to down us by means of the submarine, and they mean to make it unpleasant for us in the air. Therefore, unless it is a dead certainty that the Italian trick will be completely successful it would seem to me to be the height of folly to change the present plan. The latter may not succeed—one cannot guarantee success in war—but at any rate we ought to try. I am thankful for your help and so would the Country be if it knew.

Napoleon said 'Councils of War never fight'. What he meant was that each member wishes to fight in another place, at another time, or in another way the result being nothing.

LHCMA, Robertson Mss, I/36/20

151

General Sir William Robertson to Field-Marshal Sir Douglas Haig

Dictated [typescript
with additions in other hand] War Office
SECRET 6 July 1917

As at present arranged it seems there will be a big Conference of Ministers and others at Paris on the 18th instant. You will remember that you were told to go on with your preparations and that the Prime Minister said he would see the French so as to

ascertain whether they really intended to co-operate. He had intended to see them early next week but I think he will not now go much if at all before the 18th. He is more keen than ever on the Italian plan, but I think it will right itself in time, because before long you will be on the point of going off and I cannot conceive that the French will listen to any such proposal as the transfer of the major operations to Italy and the practical stoppage of operations on the West Front. The Cabinet have been meeting by themselves on several occasions this week, but eventually they will bump up against me and then there will be trouble. I gather that while the Prime Minister is keen on Italy Smuts wants to land 150,000 men at Alexandretta (I do not know where he proposes to get them or the ships from). Milner is rather inclined to think that the Balkans will be a good place while Curzon sticks to our plan. It is pretty difficult doing business under these conditions. I will let you know as soon as the Conference is definitely fixed and tell you whether you will be required. I hope not although I expect you will be for at any rate one day.
P.S. By the way the Belgian Military attache told one of my people the other day that the Belgians were anxious as to the success of the 'landing operations'. Am afraid secrecy is a disappointment.[15]

LHCMA, Robertson Mss, I/23/34

152

Field-Marshal Sir Douglas Haig to General Sir William Robertson

General Headquarters,
British Armies in
France

[Holograph]
Personal

10 July 1917

***

Painlevé spent Sunday night here and left after lunch yesterday. Speaking generally, he seems to me quite sound in his views.

That is to say that he considers that all our efforts should be devoted to making my attack as powerful as possible. Until our efforts on the West front are over for the year, there should be no detachment of any kind made either to Italy or to take over more front from the French. (The same principles he applies to the French army viz no detachments to be made.) He assures me too that the French army will be able to assist us by attacking on its own front, and that the French government intend that it should do so.

LHCMA, Robertson Mss, I/23/36

153

General Sir William Robertson to Field-Marshal Sir Douglas Haig

Dictated [typescript with holograph additions] War Office
SECRET. Personal 18 July 1917

You will remember that when you left here the Cabinet had not definitely approved of your plans but said that you were to 'go on with your preparations'. The War Policy Committee of the Cabinet, whom you met, have been continuing their discussions ever since, when Mesopotamia has allowed them to do so, but up to the present no official approval of your plans has been given. I understand however that the War Cabinet are now in favour of your plans and I have daily been expecting that they would tell me so, but up to the present they have not done so. Apparently the Prime Minister is the only one who is sticking out against your plans and who continues to be in favour of the Italian venture. I have twice reminded him that time is running short and that your preparations will soon be completed. However, this is mainly to tell you what has been taking place and is in no way meant to interfere with what you are doing or what you propose to do. The order to go on with your preparations still holds the field, and as the War Cabinet know that your preparations will soon be complete there is no more to be said on the matter. I daresay that to-morrow or the next day I shall be told that your plans are approved.

The Prime Minister had the War Cabinet Members to dinner on Monday night when there was a long discussion, and apparently while all the Members except the Prime Minister were in favour of accepting our advice they all expressed, so I am told, at different times the fear that you might endeavour to push on further than you were justified pending further artillery preparation, because they have all got in their mind, and correctly so, that the greatest losses sometimes occur in trying to take and hold positions too far in advance. I had a talk with one of the Cabinet on this subject yesterday and impressed upon him that I thought they need have no fear as it is well understood that the extent of the advance must, roughly speaking, be limited by the assistance of the guns until such times as a real break through occurs. He replied that so long as this step by step system of advance was adhered to he would back your plan for all it was worth. I understand that the Prime Minister asked one of the Cabinet when your operations ought to be stopped, if they did not seem likely to achieve complete success—that is how many losses we ought to incur before stopping. The Cabinet Minister gave a good answer. He said that he could not answer the question merely with reference to losses, and that the time to stop would be when it appeared that our resources were not sufficient to justify a continuance of our effort.

***

LHCMA, Robertson Mss, I/23/38

154

Field-Marshal Sir Douglas Haig to General Sir William Robertson

General Headquarters,
British Armies in
France
21 July 1917

[Typescript with holograph additions]
Copy

With reference to your letter of the 18th instant:-

It is somewhat startling at this advanced stage of preparations to learn that the War Cabinet had not then yet determined whether my attack was to be permitted to proceed. The Members of the Cabinet evidently do not understand what is entailed by preparation for an attack under existing conditions, or what the effect—material and moral—would be of altering plans once preparations are in full swing. It may not be possible for the War Cabinet to realise it, but I hope you will be able to convey to them what a serious matter these preparations are, and how long beforehand they have to be commenced.

The importance of these operations was agreed to at the Conference held in your room at the War Office as long ago as the 23rd November, 1916. The project had been under examination by me, in communication with Admiral Bacon, for many months before that. The desire of the War Cabinet that the operation should be undertaken this year was communicated to me and to General Joffre on the 1st December, 1916. I was again reminded of the 'great importance' attached to this operation by the War Cabinet, on the 1st January, 1917 (your 0.1/68/210).

***

I note, however, that there is still a possibility of my being ordered to abandon the operation at some future stage; and that my judgment, on the spot and with a knowledge of conditions which a War Cabinet in London cannot have, is not trusted on this point, or even on the depth to which each advance should be pushed with due regard to the combination between Artillery and the other arms.

I very much regret to learn this, as in my opinion it is very important in the interests of the Country that such matters should be left to the Commander on the spot, and that he should have the confidence of his Government in his ability to judge on them. Otherwise, as has happened before, influences may be brought to bear, either directly or indirectly, which may interfere with the whole-hearted execution of the Commander's plan.

As regards my attending the Conference in Paris, I do not know what the terms of reference are, but I am very strongly of opinion that questions affecting the conduct of operations—present or future, the distribution of my troops, or similar matters relating to my command, should not be discussed with the French authorities in my absence, and I shall be glad if you will inform the War Cabinet that I hold this view.

As matters stand, it is unlikely to be possible for me to be present at the Conference on the date chosen for it, and I must therefore hope that such matters will not be discussed.

NLS, Acc 3155, no. 115, Haig Mss

155

General Sir William Robertson to Field-Marshal Sir Douglas Haig

Dictated [typescript with holograph additions] — War Office
Secret & Personal — 21 July 1917

I am sending you today a copy of the Draft Conclusions recently reached by the War Cabinet. We had a rough and tumble meeting yesterday. The fact is that the Prime Minister is still very averse from your offensive and talks as though he is hoping to switch off to Italy within a day or two after you begin. I told him that unless there were very great miscalculations on your part, and unless the first stage proved to be more or less a disastrous failure—which I certainly did not expect it would be—I did not think it would be possible to pronounce a verdict on the success of your operations for several weeks. He seemed to have in mind what the French said last spring when Nivelle told them that he would be able to say in one or two days whether his operations had been successful or not.

He is also very keen on capturing Jerusalem and this of course I also had to fight, and I intend continuing to do so. Altogether I had one of the worst afternoons I have ever had, but I find that after all I generally get more or less what I want. But it is very disturbing all the same to have these hankerings after other plans and mistrust in present ones.

I enclose for your information a copy of the Note I wrote regarding the West Front and one regarding Palestine.[16] They were both written when the *first* Draft Conclusions were circulated and therefore they do not in all respects hold good with respect to the Draft Conclusions I am sending you separately today. But they will suffice to show you the general arguments I have been using. You will probably think I might have said more about the necessity of getting every available man on the West Front from the outside theatres but I have said that ad nauseam and they just will not read or listen to it. I therefore have to depend more upon other arguments, the chief ones being shipping, the uncertainty of France and Russia, and the uselessness of Italy.

I am hoping that you will be able to allow Kiggell to meet me on Monday.

LHCMA, Robertson Mss, I/23/40

156

General Sir William Robertson to Lieutenant-General Sir L. E. Kiggell

Hôtel de Crillon
Place de la Concorde
Paris

[Holograph] 27 July 1917

Many thanks for your Note of the 25th, the contents of which have *not* been made known here. *Everybody* seems to know the zero date, down to the lift-man, and many enquiries have been made. The Belgian Minister asked me on what *day* we should get to Ostend!

This has been the *worst* conference I ever attended, & so you can imagine it has been a pretty bad one. 43 people were present! One day was taken up in Epirus; 2 in Salonika. Nothing was settled except to have another conference in London next Thursday!

The Russian debacle[17] has caused consternation, & the usual desire to change plans. Yesterday, to my great surprise—after the telegram I sent you from the War Cabinet on Wednesday—the Prime Minister proposed to the French & Italians a 'big blow'' of Allied forces in Italy, plus another by us & the French in Palestine. The French to land a Division at Tripoli. 'Wooden-footed & no imagination' had been our undoing in the past. *Now*, in the greatest crisis of the war, we must be prompt, vigorous, & courageous etc etc. This held the floor for 2 hours & was finally *knocked* out. But fancy it!

Good luck to your efforts. Petain has been here. He does not appeal to me. Foch has wanted to discuss your taking over more line. I declined to discuss without Haig & after the operations. So nothing has been done in that matter.

[P.S.] I have gathered recently that your people suspect me of not rubbing sufficiently into my 'colleagues' the impossibility of switching off from one plan to another. You put a good deal about this in your recent Memorandum to me, for the benefit of the War

Cabinet. I gave it to L. G. to read. Result, in less than 48 hours he is seen proposing to the Allies to go to Italy to fight! This will show you the kind of d_d madness I have to endure.

LHCMA, Kiggell Mss, IV/7

157

General Sir William Robertson to General Sir E. H. H. Allenby

Dictated [typescript
with holograph additions] War Office
Secret & Personal 1 August 1917

I received your letters of 11th and 19th July about two days ago. Many thanks for them. I shall do my best to send you out all I can spare in time for September as I quite realise the necessity of your being active then, with reference to your Arab bretheren. We passed four days at Paris last week arguing the point about getting you a division from Salonika, the only result being another Conference in London this week, which was to assemble to-morrow but as the French Government seems to be in prospect of falling perhaps the Conference will not take place. However, if you do not get the division in time for September I hope to send you a certain amount of heavy artillery and some more aircraft.

***

With you I think that our prospects in Southern Palestine are good provided we can give you what you ask for, or something like it. The Turk has never yet had a good shelling I imagine. At the same time, and with reference to the general situation we need to be careful as to the extent to which our commitments are increased. With Russia practically out of the war we have got to consider the necessity for economising shipping and men and also for being strong on the West front. Every day points to the probability of the war being prolonged to an indefinite date and as you can easily understand shipping is the vital factor. Therefore we must economise it. Extensive operations in distant theatres mean a great strain upon shipping, and we must guard against pushing forward to localities which would put an undue strain upon us in order to maintain our position. I am therefore taking the line at present that it will be a good thing to give the Turk in front of you a sound beating, but that the extent to which we shall be justified in following him by an advance into Northern and Central Palestine is a matter which for the moment must be left open. The further we go north the more Turks we shall meet; and the greater will be the strain upon our resources. Of course if we can so knock the Turk about that he throws his hand in, nothing would be better. On the other hand it is nearly 400 miles from where you are to Aleppo and the Turks' home lies beyond Aleppo. Do not take these remarks too definitely. They are only meant to show that for the moment we must keep an open mind as to the desirability of an extensive advance northwards. (Do not treat these private letters as official instructions. After I have written them I put them away and do not again refer to them.)

***

P.S.—I again ask you not to take too definitely what I have said about the advance into Palestine. As you know the Prime Minister is very much in favour of it and eventually the Government may decide to do it. The only point I wish to make is that in deciding to go forward we have to bear in mind what the situation will be after we have gone forward and whether we can, having regard to all the circumstances of the war, maintain ourselves after going forward *and to a useful purpose*. In short one has to look not only at the feasibility of going forward but what will happen after we have gone. This is especially necessary in Eastern countries because having gone forward it is usually very detrimental to have to come back. This is all I mean by what I have said.

LHCMA, Robertson Mss, I/32/66

158

General Sir William Robertson to Lieutenant-General Sir L. E. Kiggell

Dictated [transcript with holograph additions]
War Office
Secret
2 August 1917

I write to you because I am sure your Chief is very busy. I do not wish to be given any secrets you do not care to entrust to me, then I cannot give them to the Cabinet or to anyone else, but I would like to have a few lines occasionally giving your opinion as to how matters are progressing—of course with the knowledge of the Commander-in-Chief. Not unnaturally the Cabinet ask me my opinion every morning as to how matters are going and it is rather difficult for me to say much as I have nothing to rely upon but the Communiqué and the slight additions you occasionally send to me. It would well be worth while for you to drop me a line once or twice a week during the operations and give me such information as will enable me to show that things are going on satisfactorily. The Allies are causing us a great deal of trouble now and Russia's defection is an awkward blow, and therefore our Ministers have a good deal of anxiety to carry and it is all for the good of the war that I should be able to give them a good account of what is taking place in France. They asked me for my opinion this morning as to how matters were going and my answer was 'Very well'. So far as I know they are, but this is just one of those points I have in my mind when I ask you to send me occasionally any information that you think will be of assistance. Apparently there has been some very hard fighting, as I expected there would be, and no doubt there will be more, but I imagine that your task will be easier now you have got the Pilckem Ridge and have more elbow room in general. The first day's work appears to have been splendid. The rain is a great nuisance. Of course if the Chief would like to send me a short official statement occasionally I have no objection. All I want is some interesting information that I can properly give to these people, to which I think you will agree they are entitled. Good luck to you all.

LHCMA, Kiggell Mss, IV/8

159
General Sir William Robertson to Lord Milner

War Office

Dictated [typescript] 7 August 1917

The answer General Foch and I will give to the question put to us this afternoon of sending more heavy artillery to Italy in time for use in September next will be in the negative. I would like to invite your attention to Haig's letter of the 22nd July, a copy of which was forwarded to Members of the War Cabinet, regarding the doubt he felt as to his receiving the whole-hearted support of the War Cabinet in the important operations in which he is now engaged. In reply to that letter I was ordered to inform him that he might depend upon the whole-hearted support of the Cabinet, and that the plan would not be changed without first obtaining his views. In that letter he told us that it would take several weeks before he got the first main objective, Clercken Ridge. The bad weather will make the time longer. In these circumstances it is quite impossible to send guns to Italy in time for work next month.

Bodleian, Milner Ms, dep 45, fol. 247

160

General Sir William Robertson to Lieutenant-General Sir L. E. Kiggell

Dictated [typescript with holograph additions]

War Office
9 August 1917

Many thanks for your letter of the 8th instant. I am writing to Sir Douglas by this mail about the Conference which is just over. I have had some bad times during the last eighteen months, but this Conference was about the worst of all. I have not told Sir Douglas all that passed, as he has quite enough anxiety as it is, but you can imagine what passed when I say that the Prime Minister was about twice as bad as on the morning you had a discussion with him in the train.[18] He is an under-bred swine. Don't be hurt if I don't always answer your letters, as it will usually be best I write to Haig, who no doubt shows you what I send. Good luck to you.

LHCMA, Kiggell Mss, IV/9

161

General Sir William Robertson to General Sir E. H. H. Allenby

Dictated [typescript with holograph additions]
Secret & Personal

War Office
10 August 1917

I have done my best to give you the reinforcements you asked for in order to take on the Turk. As I told you last month it is not possible to give you everything by September but I hope you will agree that we have done pretty well and I trust that you will get the balance by November. We will do our best to give you the balance before. I hope you will find the War Cabinet Instructions sufficient and clear, and if not that you will refer any doubtful point. You see it is impossible to say now what we may hope to do because so much depends upon your communications, upon the Russians, and for that matter upon the Turk, and I cannot help thinking that the latter is in a pretty bad plight so far as Administration is conerned. The War Cabinet saw the draft Instructions and the result was rather amusing. Lloyd George did not think they went far enough and that I did not press you sufficiently to take advantage of any success you might gain. Others thought that I went too far and was trying to induce you to launch out into operations which we could not sustain. However, I managed to pacify both sides. I think the Instructions will be clear to you. They simply amount to doing the best you can with what you have got; to giving the Turk as hard a knock as you can; and at the same time avoiding going too far forward and getting into a position from which you can neither advance nor go back and which might involve us in commitments which we could not properly meet having regard to other places and to our resources. The paragraph about pressing the Turk early in September is intended to mean that you should be as active as you can in order to take advantage of your Arabs and also to assist Maude, while it is not intended to mean that you should make your big and deliberate attack until you are ready for it. Perhaps I had better say no more or I may confuse you. I wish you Good Luck and good weather.

LHCMA, Robertson Mss, I/32/68

162

Field-Marshal Sir Douglas Haig to General Sir William Robertson

General Headquarters
British Armies in
France
13 August 1917

[Holograph]
Personal

Very many thanks for your letter of 9th[19] instant telling me of the doings of the recent London Conference.

You already know my views. Briefly, this being the decisive point, the only *sound* policy is for the Government to support me *whole heartedly*, and concentrate all possible resources here. And do it *now* while there is time, instead of continuing to discuss other enterprises.

In this army we are convinced we can beat the enemy provided units are kept up to strength in men & material. Our opinion is based on actual *facts* viz: the poor state of German troops, high standard of efficiency of our own, power of our artillery to dominate enemy's guns, etc etc. An occasional glance at our daily intelligence summaries would convince even the most sceptical of the truth of what I write. Moreover I have been in the field now for 3 years & know what I am writing about. The Foreigners have constantly misled our Government. Yet, from what you say I see the Prime Minister prefers the advice they tender to your & my opinions.

The views which I have always held & expressed as to the decisive effect on the enemy of a blow North of the Lys are daily shewn to be sound. 'We must hold our positions between the sea & the Lys, or we shall lose the war entirely. The fate of Germany is now being decided in Flanders'. So write the German newspapers with the approval of their Government.

In my opinion the war can only be won here in Flanders. Even if the Austrians were driven from Trieste, the Germans will still hold the Belgian Coast & Antwerp!

As to the paper of Foch's which you send me I can hardly

believe *he* could have produced such an utterly stupid document ... [20] I fear the old man is done; but in any case the idea of organising an Allied Staff in Paris is quite unsound, even if a really good French Staff Officer were in existence.—

I am in complete agreement with your views on that head, as on all the main military questions. The only point I am not in accord with you on is the desirability of issuing such pessimistic estimates from your Intelligence Branch. They do, I feel sure, much harm and cause many in authority to take a pessimistic outlook when a contrary view, based on equally good information would go far to help the nation on to victory. Personally I feel we have every reason to be optimistic; and if the war were to end tomorrow, Great Britain would find herself not merely the Greatest Power in Europe, but in the world. The chief people to suffer would be the Socialists, who are trying to rule us all, at a time when the right minded of the Nation are so engaged on the country's battles that they (the Socialists) are left free to work mischief.[21] But whatever views may be held on the Social problems, there is only one possible plan to win the war & that is to go on attacking in Flanders until we have driven the German Armies out of it. If we relax our determination to do this then Germany will attain her ends in this war.

Please accept my hearty thanks for the way you supported the sound policy at the recent Conference & my heartfelt wishes for your continued success.

LHCMA, Robertson Mss, I/23/44

163

General Sir William Robertson to Field-Marshal Sir Douglas Haig

Dictated [typescript] War Office
Secret & Personal 17 August 1917

I am having a meeting with Adjutant-General's people tomorrow to see if we can scrape you up any more drafts than those we have already in view, and you can depend upon our sending you every man we can. I feel that the extent of your ultimate success will be governed mainly by your condition after you have taken the Passchendaele Ridge. I think so because you will not take that Ridge until you have pretty well beaten the German, and having done that future results must largely be governed by the condition of your divisions at the time. It is for this reason that I quite realise the necessity of giving you every man and gun we can.[22]

But I suggest it is equally necessary that your Staff should *immediately* take steps to scrape up all the men they can in France, and if not trained already put them under training so that they may later strengthen your divisions as much as possible. You will remember that I spoke to you about the possibility of combing out some men and collecting those probably and quite naturally hidden away in various places. I attach some figures which are rather instructive. I also spoke to Kiggell, and he rather seemed to regard it as a matter to be attended to after the fight. But I feel very strongly that it ought to be done at once, and I think you will agree. I repeat that all that we can do at home will be done. In this connexion I would like to disabuse you of the idea which seems to prevail in France, namely, that a lot of men who might be sent out are kept at home.[23] I have just been through the classification of the men in Home Service divisions and brigades, and I find there are less than 8,000 'A.1' men. (This is exclusive of the 67th Division which as you know is being drawn upon). These 8,000 men are men who have become 'A.1' from lower categories. We always have a certain number of them coming on and we are always taking them as they mature. You will probably have these

8,000 in less than a month, as you have all others as they become 'A.1' men. I may say that the Home Service divisions and brigades are now largely made up of 18-year old boys. We have scores of battalions of them and they constitute the main part of the Home Defence Force. There are of course other 'A.1' men in the country besides those in divisions and brigades but they are nearly all being trained to be sent out to you in due course. I am afraid that only about half of them are infantry. The remainder are in those very numerous categories which add up enormously such as heavy artillery, tanks, machine-gun companies, signals, Royal Engineers, Royal Flying Corps, etc. etc.

The Prime Minister sent for me this afternoon soon after I returned and I had a satisfactory talk with him. He again repeated that he hoped you felt that you fully enjoyed the confidence of the War Cabinet. Bonar Law was present and said ditto. I see the German is lying well to-day in his communique about yesterday's fighting.[24]

P.S. When I speak of combing out I am thinking not only of *permanent* reductions but equally of temporary expedients which will assist you in the battle. Some things must go short at a time like this, and the last thing to go short should be the Division. After all we are not likely to get to the Rhine this year, and the great thing is first to concentrate on well beating the Boche, and release every possible man for that purpose.

I shall send you tomorrow the last weekly report on the Labour situation, as a sample of what we get most weeks.

NLS, Acc 3155, no. 116, Haig Mss

164

General Sir E. H. H. Allenby to General Sir William Robertson

General Headquarters
Egyptian Expeditionary
Force

[Holograph] 26 August 1917

I have received your letters of the 1st and 16th instant.

The War Cabinet's instructions are sufficient and clear: and, with your explanatory remarks, I feel that I understand exactly.

I know that you are doing everything possible to supply our needs, and I thank you.

LHCMA, Robertson Mss, I/32/70

165

David Lloyd George to General Sir William Robertson

10, Downing Street
Whitehall, S.W.

[Typescript]
COPY

26 August 1917

The Italian attack seems to me to be developing well, and judging by the reports that come from Delme Ratcliffe,[25] there are great possibilities in it if fully and promptly exploited. I can of course only judge by what he says, but his account of the Austrian demoralisation and of their lack of reserves—both confirmed by the number of prisoners and guns captured and the extent of the ground occupied—seems to me to indicate immediate prospects of a signal military victory on that front.[26] I need hardly point out that the overthrow of the Austrian Army might produce in the present condition of Austrian public opinion decisive results on the whole campaign. I was therefore very distressed to find from one of Delme Ratcliffe's reports that Cadorna apprehended that these brilliant possibilities might be rendered unattainable owing to the imminent exhaustion of the Italian reserves of ammunition. Do you not think that a new situation has arisen there which requires immediate action on the part of the Allies to support the Italian attack, make up their deficiencies and enable them to convert the Austrian retreat into a rout? It would indeed be a severe reflection upon us all if later on it were discovered that we missed a great chance of achieving a signal and far-reaching military success for the Allied cause, through lack of readiness to take advantage of an opening made for us by the Italian Army.

I feel confident that you are watching events with anxious scrutiny. If you think that the Italian victory is capable of being pressed to important conclusions would it not be worth while your paying an immediate visit to that front to judge for yourself and to form an independent opinion as to what might be accomplished if the French and ourselves were to make sacrifices which would enable Cadorna to press on until the Austrian Army completely breaks?

Once more I would impress upon you and the War Cabinet the enormous responsibility that rests upon us not to allow the most promising opening which events have thrown in our way in any western theatre to come to nought for want of opportune support.

I should be obliged if you would mention this communication to the Cabinet this morning.[27] I am writing to Mr. Bonar Law on the same subject.

H. of Lords RO, Lloyd George Mss, F/44/3/19

166

General William Robertson to Major-General F. B. Maurice

War Office

[Holograph] 31 August 1917

***

I am very puzzled still about the 25 heavy batteries you have told Davidson to pull out. I can't see *how* you have done it, or even why you should. I explained to Prime Minister that if Haig was *not* told there might be more delay & he accepted that.

I think Italy would be a useful trip for you, but not congenial to your family I suppose. I do *not* see however what it can have to do with the Italian 'plan'. Every *hour* is of importance if guns etc are to go there, whereas you will not be *there* for nearly another fortnight. The chief thing to do is, if Cadorna's reply leads to the consideration of sending anything, to get Haig over at once to tell us not only what *he* thinks of his own chances but when he can make available what is to be sent. *We* don't know how long it will take him to give what is wanted. We can only guess. Then there is the question of railway transport, which we can't get on with because we may not tell anyone. The whole thing is muddled rot.

I want a short paper prepared by you & Director of Military Intelligence on the country & feasibility of operations on the Italian front. We seem to be forgetting that it is mainly a mass of mountains & narrow valleys. I think we can get help from this paper. *Of course* I would love to see Austria knocked out, but can we do it? I don't think so. I believe the country is too defensible & Italians too useless. I still think Cadorna has stacks of men & ammunition for anything short of a big & deliberate attack, & if this is a necessary preliminary to the Austrian debâcle then there is not time to mount such an attack. Of course he will try to get our big guns. But remember my points:—

(a) Get Haig here at once if & when the project is really considered.

(b) Get out a paper on what such operations mean as regards the nature of country.

(c) Have ready as much information as you can as to time needed.

If Germany does not soon help Austria I shall conclude (a) that she thinks Austria needs no help to hold her own, or at any rate that she is satisfied a setback will not mean Austria ratting; or (b) she can't send help. Either of these alternatives means that we should not waste time & power *now* in sending guns etc.

I like the telegram sent to Italy less every day.[28] It is bound to lead to trouble. Further Prime Minister & Milner will swear I agreed to it. I did not. I said if it represented their policy I saw no harm in it, but that there was much to be said against the policy, which to my mind was impracticable. But I fear I did not put my case sufficiently explicit. I ought to have made it clear that the telegram was *their's*, not mine in any way.

LHCMA, Robertson Mss, I/25/4

167

General Sir William Robertson to Lieutenant-General Sir C. Barter

R [telegram] War Office
PERSONAL & SECRET 6 September 1917

Reference last sentence of your 1229 of 4th instant. War Cabinet are closely following developments and will not fail to act in manner they deem most expedient, but as you can imagine many factors have to be considered.[29] Knox[30] is here and will give them his views. He thinks there are only two useful alternatives in present situation (a) Bring over some Japanese Divisions in hope that they will be able to restore situation (b) Deliver a strong joint Note to Kerensky insisting upon strong action. (a) seems to me unlikely of realisation and if realised of doubtful utility. (b) would bring matters to a head but perhaps that would not be altogether to our advantage. Knox apparently thinks the majority simply wish to stop fighting and if this is so the case seems hopeless. If they were bent on fighting there would be hope of some sort of assistance.

***

LHCMA, Robertson Mss, I/14/86

168
General Sir William Robertson to Field-Marshal Sir Douglas Haig

Dictated [typescript
with holograph additions] War Office
<u>SECRET</u> 15 September 1917

I am glad that the Conference regarding the guns passed off satisfactorily. I did not know that the Prime Minister had sent you a telegram on the subject. I will convey your gratitude to him when I see him. I have been round the Tank School and Machine Gun School this week. Both seem to be doing good work. I am inclined to think that we may get good things out of the tanks. Of course the difficulty is the ground in Flanders. It will never be very good for tanks I am afraid, but at the same time the more experienced in their use the men become the better will the tanks be handled. It seems to me that the tactical situation has become rather difficult. A year ago we thought that victory lay in having a large amount of heavy artillery. We have got a large amount now, but the enemy's machine-guns are still a difficulty not yet surmounted. Our hope is, I gather, that the artillery will knock out the hostile machine-guns, but unfortunately this entails the entire destruction of the surface of the ground and renders it almost impassable, especially in Flanders. We would therefore seem to be confronted with the problem that unless we use a great deal of artillery fire we cannot get on, and if we do use it the ground is destroyed. Of course this is a very crude way of stating the case, but it approaches accuracy so far as I can understand matters.

Therefore, the problem to be solved is how to get forward without too much destruction of the ground. For this the tanks seem to offer the best prospect, but goodness knows if they will furnish a sufficient answer.

I know little more about the Russian situation than you see in the papers. One thing seems fairly certain, that is that we shall get no more very effective assistance from Russia during the war. The best we can hope for is I think that Russia will not make a separate peace and will continue to be in such a chaotic mess as, whether she makes peace or not, to keep a considerable number of German troops tied up on that side.

***

Neither Korniloff, Kerensky, nor anyone else can do much good for us simply because the Russian soldier does not intend to fight any more than he can help, and there is nothing to cause enthusiasm or to arouse enthusiasm. In a word there is nothing to fight for and he knows it, and therefore he does not propose to fight.

In this country, too, it is necessary that the people should be got more in hand. They have recently become very restive and our people are afraid to tackle them. There are gradually accumulating in the country a great many wounded and crippled men who are not of a very cheery disposition; there are others who are mere wasters and without patriotism; and finally, there are the various Labour Unions etc. On the whole there is a fairly formidable body of discontented or half-hearted people. On the other hand the majority are quite sound. But the minority is increasing and will go on increasing unless our people will be more firm and steadfast with them. In fact, to sum up, everything depends, as I have been saying for months past, upon the solidarity and determination of the Nation as a whole, without which the Army and the Navy can do little.

LHCMA, Robertson Mss, I/23/51

169

General Sir William Robertson to Field-Marshal Sir Douglas Haig

Dictated [typescript with holograph additions] War Office
SECRET. Private 24 September 1917.

The Prime Minister has been away during the last fortnight,[31] and his mind has consequently been very active. I have recently had to knock-out a scheme for operations in the Aden hinterland involving the employment of not less than a division. I have also had to destroy one for landing *ten* divisions at Alexandretta, all of which would have had to come from you. Further, I have had to fight against sending now more divisions to Mesopotamia. Generally, all round, I have been quite successful, although the expenditure of energy which ought otherwise to be employed has been a little greater than usual. The whole Cabinet are very anxious to give the Turk as hard a knock as possible this winter; they have heard he is very sick of the whole business and they think if we gave him a hard knock and at the same time treated him liberally, at the expense of Russia who has let us down so badly, it might be possible to arrange matters with him. Of course this would be an enormous gain. But there is an 'IF' in the matter. Another thing that has been under consideration is Germany's intentions in Asia generally. Falkenhayn[32] went there some months ago, and there is no doubt that he has been given orders to do what he can to make things unpleasant for us in that part of the world. The Russian collapse is leaving the Turks free to act against Maude, and most of them are now in Asia and all of them might be sent there. Further, there is no doubt that Germany is getting one or two divisions ready for use in Asia, and we know for certain that she has sent a considerable stiffening in the way of experts, machine-guns, and artillery. India is also somewhat excited because Persia is likely to give trouble, and we have drained India nearly dry of troops lately. It is thought that the Turks and Germans combined may make things very unpleasant in Persia and possibly for Maude, who has not got a very large force and certainly not a particularly good one, as it is largely native and to a great extent consists of new units raised in India. Of course we shall not win the war merely by holding on to Baghdad, but at the same time its loss would shake the reserves of our nervous people.

On the whole the situation in the East requires careful watching during the winter months. After then it will become safer. As I have already said, I have succeeded in knocking out the various projects put forward, but at the same time there is no available reserve in the East, and as there are so many uncertain factors in the situation there our position is not altogether comfortable. This I have kept to myself, however, as much as possible but the whole of the Cabinet are unanimously of opinion that there must be some small reserve put into Egypt ready to go to Maude if necessary, and it is on this matter chiefly that the Prime Minister is coming to see you to-morrow. His intention in seeing you was, originally, to get you to 'concur' in the despatch of the Alexandretta force! There really is not much for him to see you about now, but a talk will be useful, as they have all been very unsteady lately, & he does as he likes with the War Cabinet. He has no intention of taking one or two divisions from you until you have proceeded further with your operations (which I may say have given the Cabinet much gratification during the last few days), but it is thought that during three or four of the winter months one or two divisions would be just as well in Egypt as in France. Of course this is not quite the case. But on the other hand it is practically intolerable to have *no* reserve available to meet probable Eastern developments. In order to improve sea-communications the Shipping Controller[33] has been ordered to place shipping for two divisions permanently at our disposal in the Mediterranean and if and when one or two divisions are sent from you to Egypt I do not anticipate any great difficulty in getting them back to you fairly quickly in the Spring. You will be pleased to hear that as Cadorna has said he must go on the defensive the Cabinet are awfully sick with him, and I think also with themselves! I do not anticipate that we shall ever hear any more

about your sending divisions to the Italian Front. I send this to let you know what the Prime Minister is coming to see you about[34] and of course you will tell him your own story with regard to the one or two divisions. I feel myself that I must have one, and as it cannot start for several weeks yet I am hoping by that time Allenby will have made himself so felt that there will be no necessity to think of sending the second. We are hoping to get the Greek Army organised so as to liberate divisions from Salonika, and that I hope will be to your advantage.
P.S. I have been finishing this on the boat.

NLS, Acc 3155, no. 117, Haig Mss

170

General Sir William Robertson to Lieutenant-General Sir S. Maude

R [telegram] War Office
Personal and Secret 24 September 1917

My 41847 of to-day is intentionally lengthy because I am somewhat puzzled regarding your X.3750 of 21st instant. What I am chiefly in doubt about is whether you demand reinforcements at once or are merely looking a few months ahead as I have for long been doing. The Russians are indeed very disappointing but so are many others of our Allies and we must make best of them. The enemy has similar difficulties. I would greatly dislike your not giving your views freely and boldly but you should remember your official telegrams are seen by War Cabinet and others who naturally cannot always put correct military interpretation upon them and are apt to become unduly anxious and therefore prone to expect me to take action giving complete security everywhere which is impossible. I dislike any general use of personal telegrams on official matters as they tend to confusion but if reference to them is rigorously barred in official telegrams they may on occasion I think be useful to you for expressing your personal views to me.

LHCMA, Robertson Mss, I/14/89

171

General Sir William Robertson to Field-Marshal Sir Douglas Haig

Dictated [typescript with holograph additions] War Office
SECRET. Personal 27 September 1917

With reference to the Paper you are preparing on the Military Outlook, assuming that Russia ceases to take an active part in the war, I am not sure that I made really clear to you on leaving yesterday what I meant with respect to the peace terms you heard discussed. There is no doubt that Germany is much more anxious at the present time for peace than she has ever been before. Information showing this comes before me in some form or other, and sometimes from very good sources, nearly every hour of the day. But at the same time the terms stated to you yesterday were I think probably greatly exaggerated. If such terms were offered we should do very well to consider them, but I do not think they will be offered until the German Armies have been further defeated.

As regards the collapse of Russia I enclose some rough notes recently prepared for me with which I generally concur. They may be useful to you.

The view taken, and quite naturally, by certain people here is that the collapse of Russia would make our task very much greater, and no doubt it would. Germany has some 90 divisions on the Russian Front while Austria has between 30 and 40. I do not think that the latter would be likely to come to the West Front but the heavy artillery might, and the Austrian divisions might be sent to the Italian Front. Of the 90 German divisions some would no doubt have to stay in and about Russia for a long time to come but the withdrawal to the West Front during the winter of even 30 divisions would make a considerable difference. There is also the question of the large number of German and Austrian prisoners that would be released. Against these things is the entry of America into the war and the effect of that you are as well able to judge as I am.

But the result of it all is that certain people here think it would be exceedingly difficult to bring about a decision on the West Front if the German troops there are materially reinforced, and therefore they are frequently looking about for means of detaching some of the hostile Powers. To detach them they maintain that more punishment is first required, and that naturally takes away from our concentration on the West.

My views are known to you. They have always been 'defensive' in all theatres but the West. But the difficulty is to *prove* the wisdom of this now that Russia is out. I confess I stick to it more because I see nothing better, and because my instinct prompts me to stick to it, than to any convincing argument by which I can support it. Germany may be much nearer the end of her staying power than available evidence shows, but on the other hand France and Italy are not much to depend upon, and America will require a long time. Further, it is agreed that stagnation will destroy the Nation's determination. It is not an easy business to see through the problem when present resources of both sides and hostile gains are considered.

LHCMA, Robertson Mss, I/23/54

172

General Sir William Robertson to Lord Milner

War Office

[Holograph] 27 September 1917

I do hope the Cabinet will stand firm about these further demands of the Labour people.[35] Whatever our proper strategy may be, it will certainly prove useless in practice unless men for the armies are forthcoming. 'Resolution', 'determination', 'sticking it out' etc are worthless if not put into practice. The war *is* a question of sticking it out, but we are not doing this. It is grotesque a minority should be achieving what it is, and yet it is most serious this should be allowed.

A minor point in the matter. I ask your attention to decision no 7 of Cabinet meeting of 20th July. No information has yet been given by the Admiralty. No identification of any kind has ever yet been made of the men the Admiralty have. I am told on good authority that there are in Naval employ many 1000's of men who could be taken for the Army, if replaced by other categories, women, etc. At any rate, Naval personnel should surely be subjected to the same scrutiny as Army personnel.

Please do not reply.

Bodleian, Milner Ms, dep 45, fol. 259

173

General Sir William Robertson to Field-Marshal Sir Douglas Haig

Dictated [typescript with holograph additions]
SECRET

War Office
3 October 1917

Thanks to you I hope that the bombing arrangements we made yesterday with the Cabinet will suffice to keep them quiet and also the public. As you know I have been fighting this diversion of air force for weeks past, but the cry has recently got so great that it did not seem politic to refuse any longer to take action, though I quite agree with you that the action we are about to take will not affect the bombing of London. I am inclined to think that it will greatly increase it. Trenchard spoke very well, and the Cabinet were quite satisfied with what it is proposed to do. I hope that they will continue to be satisfied, but the danger is that when the German redoubles his efforts we shall be asked to redouble ours and then we may get into trouble. However, it is no good meeting troubles half way. I have explained to Trenchard that the great thing is to send us *flaming* communiques on the French system. I am quite satisfied that the French are doing exceedingly little but the Cabinet and the newspapers all swear that they are doing a tremendous amount and with the best effect, as Paris is not being bombed while London is. They forget about Dunkirk and other places which are being bombed as you know. I have also asked Trenchard to send in, subject to your approval, a short account of what our Air Service has done during the last few weeks or month. The cumulative result must be very great indeed and I do not think the Cabinet have any idea of what we have done, and I feel pretty certain that they have even less idea of what we ourselves have suffered behind your lines. Lloyd George went yesterday to see the place where some of the bombs had dropped and he came back with a most harrowing description of the destruction of the house and the sight of blood on the walls! They have really lost all sense of proportion. I have told them that they may reckon upon London being bombed, and a great deal more than it now is, until the war stops unless it should be possible to discover some means of defence, which is most unlikely, or destroy the enemy aircraft entirely, which is equally unlikely. I have told told them that we are in the air zone and will have to put up with the consequences.

***

LHCMA, Robertson Mss, I/23/55

174

General Sir William Robertson to General Sir E. H. H. Allenby

R [telegram] War Office
Personal and Secret 5 October 1917

You will understand that my 42625 of today does not originate with me because apart from the strategy I do not believe that the policy if successfully executed would have the anticipated result.[36] However you are concerned only with framing your reply and, in it you should take no chances because of the many uncertain factors. You should also remember that transport, supply, water, time and space are imperfectly realised here and therefore they may need emphasising. I find it impossible to convincingly prove the great difference between the needs and facilities of Turkish and British troops in these and similar matters.

LHCMA, Robertson Mss, I/14/95

175

General Sir William Robertson to Field-Marshal Sir Douglas Haig

War Office

[Holograph] 6 October 1917

You are getting on splendidly, and your forecasts as to the cumulative effect of your efforts are proving well founded. One would think that the fine successes you are winning would suffice to satisfy even the people with whom I live, but it is not so apparently or they would drop the Palestine rot. On the contrary they are more full of it than ever. The War Policy Committee (Prime Minister (1) Bonar-Law (2), Curzon (3), Milner (4), Smuts (5)) resumed their labours yesterday. 1, 2, 4 are for Palestine. 3 I think not. 5 has really no definite view. He talks one day one way, another the other way. The idea is to give the Turk such a blow as will make him come to terms. When I try to show it is neither likely nor possible, I am accused of being a hide-bound west fronter with no imagination. The usual arguments are adduced against the possibility of decision in the West. The condition of France is ignored. Naturally I insist that Palestine must be considered with the whole question, and that troops sent there must be lost to you next year. The answer is (1) A few less troops to you will make no difference. (2) They will be back in time to resume with you. (3) That you wont want them as the Americans will be a great addition next year & the French will fight next year, etc. Time, space, human strength, concentration at decisive point are all ignored. However, I am, I hope, making my arguments in a direct and clear way and will avoid being jockeyed by degrees into a wrong course. I shall, I hope, keep the issue and consequences clear, & so have a good field of battle on which to fight these people. There I can beat them, or have a row. But of course the politician's cunning has shown itself. L. G. says if I will send Allenby sufficient troops—probably 5 or 6 divisions more— he will fight the French against your taking over more line. Alternatively, I *know* he will *not* fight them if I refuse—as I shall—to agree to his plan. You shall hear more later.

Once more, best congratulations. It is a hard war—not because of the Boche but because of these people here.

NLS, Acc 3155, no. 118, Haig Mss

176

General Sir William Robertson to Field-Marshal Sir Douglas Haig

War Office

[Holograph] 9 October 1917

Your memorandum is splendid, and I hope, greatly, that you will credit me with saying the right thing in my memorandum,[37] which, luckily, went in before your's arrived. I could have made mine much longer, but I have said all there is to say 1000 times already. I gather from Lord R Cecil that perhaps you are a little disappointed with me in the way I have stood up for correct principles, but you must let me do my job in my own way. I have never yet given in on *important* matters & never shall. In any case whatever happens you & I must stand solid together. I know we are both trying to do so. The Palestine thing will *not* come off. The Prime Minister dare not go against us. But what I fear is that he will sulk & pay us off indirectly; get the French military people against us; drag in political considerations, etc etc. Still we shall win through all right. Your news today, so far, is again splendid. If only you can continue to get successes we shall beat him hands down.[38]

He is out for my blood very much these days. Milner, Carson, Curzon, Cecil, Balfour have each in turn expressly spoken to me, separately, about his intolerable conduct, during the last week or two and have said they are behind us. Curzon was very good today in what he privately said to me after a bitter & unjustifiable attack the Prime Minister made upon me in Cabinet because of an 'Air' paper[39] I had written. (Copy enclosed) The Prime Minister called it a monstrous attack on the Cabinet & tried to get them to support him. But he quite failed. They all stood up for me & said I was merely doing my duty. Since then he has got my Future policy paper and your Memorandum. A Cabinet is now sitting. He will be furious, & probably matters will come to a head. I rather hope so. I am sick of this d__d life.

I can't help thinking *he* has got Painleve & Company here, in his rushing way so as to carry me off my feet.[40] But I have big feet! The great thing is to keep on good firm tactical ground. This is difficult for he is a skillful tactician. But I shall manage him. You will notice how I rubbed in, in my paper, the same points as you did—many of them. I am *very pleased* you are now doing so well. It is splendid. Yet the great War Cabinet has not sent a word of congratulations to you! They never have in the past, except when I suggested it so far as I can recollect. But I shall not suggest it again. If not spontaneous you would rather not have it, I am sure.

Continuance of good luck to you.

NLS, Acc 3155, no. 118, Haig Mss

177

General Sir William Robertson to Field-Marshal Sir Douglas Haig

Dictated [typescript with additions in other hand]

War Office

Secret & Personal

11 October 1917

The War Cabinet met this morning and discussed general policy, French and Wilson being present.[41] The Prime Minister made a speech for an hour on the lines with which you are familiar. He said much the same as he said to you when he last saw you. French and Wilson are to prepare their advice and they hope to have it ready for a meeting on Monday when it will be considered by the War Cabinet, if you can be present. Painleve and some other Ministers are here and very insistent upon a decision being come to regarding the taking over of line. I myself have not seen them and therefore I do not know to what extent they do insist. I had a talk with Foch yesterday and he agreed that it was impossible to talk now about taking over any line, but apparently his Ministers think otherwise. He has just been in again on the same subject, apparently sent by Painlevé. I refused to discuss. He says they want us to extend to Cemy (near Craonne)!

Your Paper seems to have had a curious effect on some of the Cabinet, as Carson and Barnes both remarked that it conveyed a very *pessimistic* outlook. It is really rather hopeless trying to do business with these people.

The questions put to French and Wilson are to consider three alternatives:-

(a) Continuance of offensive on the West front.

(b) Adoption of defensive on that front until the Russian Army is re-organised and the Americans have got their full strength in the field.

(c) Knock-out the German props, i.e. Turkey or Austria.

I do not much care what advice is rendered by French and Wilson as I shall not budge an inch from my Paper and I do not suppose you will budge from yours.

I have just heard from Whigham that I am to do nothing till he returns.[42] I have done nothing. But I have thought a lot. The fact is it is a *very* weak-kneed craven-hearted Cabinet, and L. G. hypnotises them and is allowed to run riot. We shall see what we see.

NLS, Acc 3155, no. 118, Haig mss

178

General Sir William Robertson to Field-Marshal Sir Douglas Haig

Dictated [typescript with holograph additions] War Office
SECRET & PERSONAL 12 October 1917

The French Ministers and Foch & Company are I understand returning to France on Sunday, and therefore I hope we shall hear no more about taking over more line for the present. As I told you at the time I have no knowledge as to why they had come here, and I have not yet discovered any reason. There has been no conference and no formal talks of any kind. The Ministers no doubt have had talks with ours and I have seen Foch twice, but there has been nothing of a formal nature. I talked to Foch pretty straight about the taking over of line and all the objections to an extension of our part. He seems to have become a more driveling old man than ever, and has no sound ideas on the war of any kind.

As regards the other business which has recently been occupying our attention French and Wilson say that they will not be ready to present the result of their cogitations before the middle of next week, and therefore you have been asked not to come until again sent for. It looks as if the thing will die a natural death. It depends upon what French and Wilson produce. We made a little advance this morning in that the Cabinet decided that the French-Wilson product should be sent to me in the first instance to be dealt with before it went to the Cabinet. This is how it should be if the thing has got to be done at all. The whole atmosphere is quite different to-day from what it was two or three days ago and I think the Prime Minister has found out that he has not got the Cabinet with him after all. I am only sorry that you should have been troubled with the matter in any way, but it was so important that I thought you ought not to be kept in the dark as to what was happening. That was really the reason I sent Whigham over as I did not know what developments there were likely to be. Many thanks for your letter. I am following your advice. Bad luck in the weather again.

NLS, Acc 3155, no. 118, Haig Mss

179

General Sir William Robertson to Field-Marshal Sir Douglas Haig

Dictated [typescript with holograph additions] War Office
SECRET and PERSONAL 24 October 1917

I hope the reply I am sending you by this post regarding your negotiations with Pétain will be satisfactory to you. It definitely puts off the question of taking over any line till your present operations are concluded, and it lays down as a condition that the taking over of line must depend upon next year's plan. This condition you have always strongly urged and I have always fully agreed with you, and that being so it seems inconsistent to decide anything now as to what front if any you will take over. I explained the case very fully to the Cabinet this morning, from start to finish, and the only reason they have not definitely supported your refusal to take over more than a four-division front is that they feel that nothing can or should be decided until next year's plan is fixed up. I think that my reply will be satisfactory to you because it at any rate puts the whole thing off for some weeks and leaves it entirely open.

I am sorry to say we have got no further with our meditations as to next year's plan. As you know Wilson and French were told to give their opinion and they sent it in on Saturday last, in separate papers. Originally they had intended to send in a joint Paper, but I fancy Wilson was not prepared to subscribe to the Paper sent in by French. I have not seen either yet as they went to Lord Derby, and he has told me that he was thinking of getting French to alter his

Paper, not so much because of what he says but of the way he says it and the recriminations he expresses as to the past. I have practically no idea as to what French has said as Derby will not tell me. However I shall see the Papers in due course, amended or otherwise. Meanwhile I gather that both are opposed to Eastern enterprises and that Wilson is inclined to wait for the Americans, while apparently French is not very definite as to what he would do. It would all be rather amusing if it were not so serious and did not involve such a waste of time. But I have no intention of wasting much time over it myself. The War Cabinet left to my discretion at the time whether I should send copies to you for your observations and of course I shall decide that when I see the Papers. I shall hope not to have to trouble you with them, for I do not suppose you will alter anything you have already said and I am sure I shall not.

Apparently you contemplate withdrawing Rawlinson's divisions, & the French to take over on the coast. Some of the Cabinet wondered why, because we made a point of getting there for tactical reasons, & also it would otherwise seem best to have our divisions there in place of [?further] [?events]. Perhaps you would tell me something about this, in case I am again asked.

NLS, Acc 3155, no. 118, Haig Mss

180

General Sir William Robertson to David Lloyd George

Dictated [typescript with holograph additions]
SECRET

War Office
27 October 1917

I enclose copies of some telegrams sent and received to-day regarding Italy.[43] Italy really has stacks of men of her own and there is no *military* necessity to send troops to her provided the

Italian troops fight reasonably well. There have been no new developments of importance in Italy since I saw you yesterday. I call your attention to the telegram sent by the French Government and ask for instructions as to whether you wish a similar telegram sent by us. If so I will send one in the name of the Government to Cadorna. But of course if we offer troops he is bound to accept them and it is really *very* hard on our men after what they have recently gone through to send them to Italy. But then everything is hard in war. Personally I am in favoir of waiting until Cadorna asks for them, unless you think that for political reasons we ought not to be outdone by the French. We must not get rattled over this business, but of course we must stop the rot if we can.

H. of Lords RO, Lloyd George Mss, F/44/3/27

181

David Lloyd George to General Sir William Robertson

Walton Heath Golf Club,
Walton-on-the Hill
Tadworth, Surrey
27 October 1917

[Typescript]
COPY

I have no doubt we ought to follow up the French telegram at once by a proffer of assistance. The loss of 650 guns is in itself a serious blow to the Alliance and unless the Italian morale is restored this movement may well end in an overwhelming disaster. If we mean to exercise a dominant influence in directing the course of the War we must do so in the way the Germans have secured control i.e. by helping to extricate Allies in trouble. We cannot do so merely by lecturing them at Conferences. We must help them, then we will have earned a right to dictate to them.

H. of Lords RO, Lloyd George Mss, F/44/3/28

182

General Sir William Robertson to David Lloyd George

Dictated [typescript with holograph additions] War Office
SECRET 27 October 1917

Orders have been given for the despatch of the two divisions as early as possible.[44] How soon they can go will depend upon the railway arrangements made by the French who of course have to undertake this part of the operation. The French are sending four divisions. It will probably take at least ten days from now before the six divisions have all left, and we shall before then be able to see whether we ought to send any further divisions. Foch just says his 4 Divisions will be *there* in 13 days.

***

H. of Lords RO, Lloyd George Mss, F/44/3/29

CHAPTER V

Command of the General Reserve and the Fall of Robertson

With the Italians in full flight, Robertson hurriedly left for Italy to assess the military situation. His absence from the War Cabinet deliberations made it easier for Lloyd George to gain support for the creation of an inter-Allied war council with its own advisory general staff.[1] Lloyd George marched under the banner of unity of command, but his primary objective was to diminish Robertson's influence over future British strategy.

At Rapallo on 7 November, the Allies agreed to establish the Supreme War Council, located at Versailles, to coordinate Allied military policy. Outmanoeuvred by the politicians, Robertson was furious. When the creation of the Supreme War Council was first broached by the Allied ministers, Robertson rose from his seat and left the proceedings, telling Hankey, 'I wash my hands of this business'.[2] The appointment of Sir Henry Wilson, who had just served as the Prime Minister's instrument to undermine Robertson's position, as the British Permanent Military Representative on the Allied general staff only served to deepen Robertson's distrust of Lloyd George's motives. Moreover, if Wilson were allowed to take an independent position in the military advice he gave, Robertson might be held responsible for the execution of military plans which he thought unsound and had played no role in formulating.

Robertson's precise relationship to Wilson immediately became the focus of the debate over the creation of the Supreme War Council. Rather than unity of command, Robertson and his supporters argued, there was now duality of military counsel. 'The Genesis of an Unworkable Scheme. The Disestablishment of The General Staff', a leader in the *Globe* warned.[3] On 19 November Lloyd George attempted to mollify the CIGS and his supporters, telling Parliament that his support of the Supreme War Council was to co-ordinate Allied plans, not to reduce Robertson's authority or place Haig under a generalissimo.[4] Whatever Lloyd George might tell Parliament, his primary motive was to wrest strategical control of the war from Robertson. Lloyd George and his allies were convinced that Britain would lose the war if Robertson and Haig continued to have their way. Given the dismal results of the Passchendaele offensive, the mutiny within the French Army, and the collapse of Russia, they thought it mad to continue assaulting the strong German defences in the west in 1918. Yet that was exactly what Robertson and Haig advocated.[5]

Events on the battlefield served to strengthen Lloyd George's hand. The Battle of Cambrai, which initially seemed an unqualified British success, turned into an embarrassing defeat when the Germans counterattacked. Away from the western front, Allenby conquered the Holy City on 9 December. The 'westerners' were on the defensive as never before. An emboldened Lloyd George considered replacing Robertson with Sir Henry Wilson. When consulted, Wilson demurred, suggesting that the Prime Minister enhance the influence of the Allied military advisers at Versailles, thereby reducing Robertson 'from the position of a master to that of a servant'.[6]

Lloyd George followed Wilson's advice. Bypassing the Imperial General Staff, Lloyd George worked through Wilson at Versailles to redirect British strategy. This led to a public break between the Prime Minister and Robertson on 1 February. When the Supreme War Council discussed a proposed British offensive against Turkey, which had been initiated by Wilson at Versailles, Robertson, despite the presence of his civilian superior, did not mince words. The Turkish offensive recommended by the Permanent Military Representatives at Versailles, he asserted, was not 'a practical plan, and that to attempt it would be very dangerous and detrimental to our prospects of winning the war'.[7] Rebuked by an angry Lloyd George following this meeting, Robertson feared that the Prime Minister contemplated '"taking action" against me before long'.[8]

An issue potentially more explosive than Robertson's disagreement with Lloyd George over a Turkish offensive was the Supreme War Council's decision concerning the creation and command of a general or strategic reserve in 1918. Robertson had no doubt that a general reserve was essential to parry the German blows he expected in 1918. He correctly believed, and never missed an opportunity to warn the War Cabinet, that the enemy would have for the first time since 1914 a numerical superiority on the western front. If the Allies were unable to coordinate their limited reserve divisions in response to an all-out German attack, France might be conquered and the British driven into the sea.

That a general reserve was sound military policy was, then, never in question insofar as Robertson was concerned. The command of these reserves, however, was another matter. There is some evidence that Robertson considered Joffre as generalissimo with himself as 'Chief of Staff & American & Italian staff officers under them'.[9] Haig, as Robertson well knew, was militantly opposed to the creation of a supreme Allied commander in any form. Robertson consequently proposed that the general reserve be controlled by the chiefs of the general staff of the French and British war offices. Lloyd George, on the other hand, was determined to undermine Robertson's influence by keeping the general reserve free from the CIGS's direct control. Encouraged by Sir Henry Wilson, Lloyd George engineered the creation of the Executive War Board, located at Versailles, to command the Allied general reserve. Chaired by Foch it was composed of the Permanent Military Representatives. Robertson immediately raised difficulties. How could Foch, a foreign general, override the British constitution and issue orders to British soldiers? The correct chain of command was through the CIGS. Put Robertson on the Executive War Board and this problem would be resolved.

Lloyd George's refusal to accept Robertson's formula sparked a national debate that threatened his Ministry. Robertson dug in his heels despite intense pressure from former allies such as George V, Lord Derby and Haig, because he knew that much more was at stake than how Haig received his orders: Robertson's ability to influence strategy would be determined by the outcome of his conflict with the Prime Minister. There followed tortuous and byzantine negotiations. Letters flew back and forth; questions were raised in Parliament; complicated discussions moved from room to room; the King's support was sought by both sides; Haig was called to London twice; and in the background a press war raged between supporters of Robertson and Lloyd George.

Since the controversy did not directly involve 'amateur' civilians overruling 'professional' soldiers on questions of higher strategy, Lloyd George, a master politician, held the advantage over Robertson. The CIGS was doomed when Lloyd George on 9 February persuaded Haig to break ranks and accept a plan that involved Robertson and Wilson exchanging places. As the British Permanent Military Representative at Versailles, Robertson would be isolated from the War Office and his supporters in London. Lloyd George and Wilson would dominate strategy and pay him no heed. On the other hand, as Lloyd George told Milner, this plan 'was much the easiest scheme to carry without serious opposition, as it offered a good position to Robertson'. If Robertson refused to go to Versailles, 'he would put himself in the wrong and nobody would have any sympathy with him'.[10]

On 14 February at a meeting of the War Cabinet, Robertson indeed appeared in a bad light. Robertson proposed making Wilson his deputy at Versailles: hence Wilson could speak for the CIGS when the latter was unable to attend meetings dealing with the general reserve. Lloyd George then cleverly asked Robertson if he would agree to go to Versailles as Wilson's deputy. Caught off balance Robertson emphasised that Wilson was 'only a temporary general'—hardly a convincing argument to those present.[11] Increasingly Robertson was being made to appear obstinate rather than as a man of principle. What was being left unsaid in the debate was that the control of future British strategy was much more the issue for Lloyd George and Robertson than the relationship between the CIGS and the PMR at Versailles.

There were a few more anxious days for Lloyd George's Ministry, but when it became apparent that Haig would not resign if Robertson were cast aside with Wilson becoming CIGS, Lloyd George knew that his government had weathered the severe political storm. On 18 February Bonar Law announced in Parliament that Robertson had accepted a home command in southeast England, the Eastern Command.

In June 1918 Robertson replaced Lord French at the Horse Guards as Commander-in-Chief of the Home Forces. In 1919 he took command of the British Army of Occupation on the Rhine; he was also created a Baronet and voted a grant of £10,000 by Parliament. After being promoted to field-marshal in 1920, he retired from the army the following year. He died in 1933.

183

Major-General Sir F. B. Maurice to Brigadier-General C. Deimé-Radcliffe

R [telegram] War Office
SECRET 31 October 1917
CLEAR THE LINE

Following for Sir W. Robertson; personal and secret. At to-day's War Cabinet Prime Minister announced that he had seen Painlevé and told him that War Cabinet refused to discuss question of line until next year's plans had been agreed upon. He also said that he had some weeks ago written to President Wilson to propose Allied Supreme Council and Wilson had just replied agreeing. Prime Minister announced he had made a similar proposal in writing to Painlevé and has sent his letter to the King. The King and Painlevé have both agreed in principle. Briefly proposal is that there shall be a permanent military allied staff charged with co-ordinating information and plans received from the Allied General Staffs and with presenting proposals for combined allied action to the Supreme Council composed of Prime Ministers each with one other Minister of their Cabinets. Military representatives not to be Members of Council and functions to be advisory only. Chiefs of the General Staffs of each nation to remain responsible for military advice to their Governments and for execution of plans by their Armies. War Cabinet has decided that you are to have choice of becoming Military Representative or of remaining C.I.G.S., subject to this H. Henry Wilson will be Military Representative. Prime Minister considers he must bring matter up to-morrow as sop to Painlevé for refusal about line, so that principle will probably be settled at once. If you wire me when you reach Paris I will send officer with all papers and information I can collect on this matter.

LHCMA, Robertson Mss, 1/14/96

184

Major-General Sir F. B. Maurice to Brigadier-General C. Delmé-Radcliffe

R [telegram] War Office
SECRET 2 November 1917
CLEAR THE LINE

Following for Sir W. Robertson begins Pétain has put up proposal for redistribution of command. Haig to command from Channel to neighbourhood of VERDUN Pétain to command from VERDUN to Italian front inclusive. War Cabinet much bitten with idea. Prime Minister and Painlevé leave London tomorrow to go to Italy to force this on Italians. He wishes you to accompany him. Think it well you should come to Paris to get papers I am sending over. War Cabinet propose to appoint Wilson military representative at once and he will accompany Prime Minister to Italy. Have ordered Cavan to concentrate about LODI.

LHCMA, Robertson Mss, I/14/97

185

Major-General Sir F. B. Maurice to Brigadier-General C. Delmé-Radcliffe

[R Telegram] War Office
SECRET 3 November 1917

Following for Sir W. Robertson. BEGINS. Latest development is that Prime Minister anxious to ensure British Supremacy in Italy is going to try to persuade Haig to take supreme command there, and if he accepts will try to force this on French and Italians. He meets Haig Paris tonight. I go over to Paris with him, returning here Monday, and will wire you from Paris. If you do not come Paris I will send Arthur on to Italian Conference with papers giving full story of recent events.

LHCMA, Robertson Mss, I/14/98

186

General Sir William Robertson to Field-Marshal Sir Douglas Haig

Rome

[Holograph] 4 November 1917

A good deal has happened during last week. The Prime Minister has wired me a new idea every day, all of which have been nonsense. I meet him tomorrow for the Conference. I am wondering if you have yet seen the French Wilson reports & what you have replied, if at all. I do wonder what you think of the new Allied Council System & of our representative. It has all happened in my absence, & I think Derby has let the Army down badly, as I shall tell him. I daresay I can make it more or less all right. Here the situation is much as in Russia. I told Director of Military Operations to report to you my reports sent in. I hope he has. Of course the Italians have lost their heads & so have our own people, evidently. Foch is playing the game correctly & takes the line that Italy must defend itself, though we will help. Twice I have been asked by War Cabinet to send more Divisions & twice I have declined. Foch thinks that certainly not more than 2 others should go & not there till we see later how things go. So [?their] view will help me. A more disgraceful sight than the returning Italians, without arms & equipment, was never seen. They are not for it. I shall hope to see you en route home but cannot promise. If I can't I shall ask you to let Kiggell sight my train somewhere unless you care to come. Good luck to you and believe me.

NLS, Acc 3155. no. 119, Haig Mss

187

General Sir William Robertson to Lord Derby

[Typescript] War Office
SECRET 15 November 1917

You have asked for my views as to the best way of working the Supreme War Council as far as concerns its military side. I am afraid I cannot usefully express any views until the position of the Military Representative is more clearly defined than at present. The reply to the Army Council's recent question[12] should enable me to do so, and if necessary I will then at once comply with your instructions.

Meanwhile, and without prejudice to what I may think when the Army Council receives its reply, I may say that I agree generally with the views of the Master-General of the Ordnance,[13] which have I understand been submitted to you. The only modifications I would make appear below.

Instead of an Inter-Allied Staff (a misnomer without an Inter-Allied Commander in Chief) I would establish a Military Secretariat to the Supreme War Council, on the same lines as the War Cabinet Secretariat. This could be made valuable. Roughly, its functions would be to co-ordinate information as to the military resources of the Allies, to summarise the military plans received from the High Commands of the Allies, noting any disagreements, discrepancies, or lack of co-ordination, and to prepare agenda for the meetings of the Supreme War Council, bringing forward such matters as require decision in order to ensure co-ordination of plans and harmonious working.

Beyond this all military advice to the Supreme Council should remain in the hands of the responsible military advisers of the respective Governments. Dual advice can only lead to delay, friction, weakening of responsibility and lack of confidence amongst the troops.

This system will not prevent the Government from obtaining on special occasions—such as the recent papers written by Lord

French and Sir H. Wilson—any special advice on military questions which they may desire to have, it merely ensures that all advice on the conduct of the war goes through the responsible military adviser. He alone has the machinery and information by which a military plan can be adequately examined and tested, and it is not humanly feasible, however good the intention to transfer this information to a second party.

LHCMA, Robertson Mss, I/20/11

188

General Sir William Robertson to Lord Esher

Dictated War Office
[typescript] 15 November 1917

Many thanks for your letter of the 10th instant. I have no intention of spiking the guns of Lloyd George or of anyone else. All I want to do is to win the war. As I told you in Paris, as the Scheme has been approved by the Government there is nothing for the soldiers to do but to try to carry it out. At the same time they will fall short of their duty if they do not represent their views as to the difficulties and dangers of trying to carry out a scheme which might be dangerous. I do not say that this Scheme is. It depends upon various matters of detail not yet decided. As usual, details are not the least in importance.

LHCMA, Robertson Mss, I/34/35

189

General Sir William Robertson to Field-Marshal Sir Douglas Haig

Dictated [typescript with holograph additions]

War Office
15 November 1917

Many thanks for the new railway programme, which you have sent us today. There will never be any friction between your Staff and mine if I can possibly help it. That would be the end of all things. The reason you got the War Office wires was that the French were wiring two or three times a day and saying that we were not using the trains they had allotted to us, and as you know the War Cabinet are most desirous that the divisions shall be got off as quickly as possible.
P.S. Thank you for your letter re the new Soviet. I will attend to the points you mention, but everything is as yet topsy turvy.

LHCMA, Robertson Mss, I/23/66

190

General Sir William Robertson to Field-Marshal Sir Douglas Haig

Dictated [typescript with additions in other hand]
SECRET

War Office
22 November 1917

You may like to know that there is to be an Allied Conference next week in Paris commencing on the 29th. I have not heard that your presence is likely to be desired and I suppose you have no particular wish to be present unless you are needed. What we are going to talk about I do not know, but as the Americans are to be there I suppose we shall devote most of our time to them and what they can do. I will keep you informed. I have not heard anything more about your taking over French line. If that or any other question specially affecting you should arise you may depend upon not being committed without being heard. It is just possible however that I may want some detailed up-to-date information with respect to your front, and if so I will let you know and if I find it necessary to ask for one of your Staff to run down to explain personally I hope you will be able to spare him. But I do not think I shall want him or the information.

You will have seen in the papers that there has been a great disturbance about this Inter-Allied Council. Lloyd George has been in a dilemma. When talking in France he was great on it having 'supreme' control, whereas in England he had to say that it would have practically no power at all. The Army Council have sent in their protest with respect to the status and duties of the Military Representative and have insisted that the recognised Military Adviser to the British Government should be the C.I.G.S. This has been accepted, and although there is doubtless trouble ahead I hope we shall get over it.

Your recent operations have been more than splendid, very opportune, and reflect great credit on everybody concerned.[14] I was glad to be able to assist in getting Byng promoted as recommended by you ...

LHCMA, Robertson Mss, 1/23/67

191

General Sir William Robertson to General Sir E. H. H. Allenby

Dictated
[typescript]
<u>SECRET</u>

War Office
23 November 1917

***

I cannot yet say how this new Supreme War Council is going to work. There is nothing new in the idea of establishing central control. That has been talked about for practically the whole of the war. The difficulty has been to set up machinery that can be depended upon and which will be useful. On paper central control seems obviously easy and necessary. In practice it looks rather impracticable because no one country is prepared to hand itself over body and soul to the dictation of another, and quite rightly so. Further, political aims and interests are somewhat divergent and this strikes at the bottom of everything. The Military Representatives appointed to the Council seem likely to lead to dual advice, and as the Council can have no executive authority it means that so far as military advice is concerned advice will be separate from responsibility for execution, which is always an exceedingly bad principle. It is quite easy to advise. It is sometimes very difficult to execute, and therefore the man who advises should feel the responsibility of having to carry out his advice. If he has not this responsibility he is liable to put forward impracticable schemes. However, I am hoping that all may go well. So far as I am concerned I shall attend the Supreme War Council as the British Representative and by that means will be able to keep things on right lines I hope. It is a great pity that the control has not been acquired by ourselves.

A good many Americans have been over here lately and are getting to work. Like ourselves they have been rather slow in starting but matters are improving now. Of course they have everything to learn. The burning question is to find transport to bring them over and maintain them in France. As you can imagine they require a terrific amount.

This question of tonnage and man-power still causes the chief anxiety. We have to pay our Allies and find them in a good deal of war material. This means that we must keep a good number of men in industries and employ them in making war material, and that being so it is not an easy matter to find all the men we want for Army purposes. In addition to this we ourselves are still expending at a great rate, both as regards artillery and aviation.

Your recent successes have been splendid,[15] and have come at an opportune time. Italy upset everybody here and made certain people look round for scapegoats, or for anything else affording shelter. The defection of Italy, the collapse of Russia, and the system of economising shipping, all make me wish to reduce your Force in the spring, and I hope this may be possible. As you know there is only one way to win this war and that is by beating the Germans. Everything seems to have gone splendidly in your operations and I imagine that you have had some difficult transport and supply problems to solve. I congratulate you heartily on what you have achieved and I hope that you are satisfied with those who helped you.

LHCMA, Robertson Mss, 1/32/77

192

General Sir William Robertson to Lieutenant-General Sir H. C. O. Plumer

Dictated [typescript with holograph additions]
SECRET. Personal

War Office
26 November 1917

I am sorry it has been found necessary for you to ask for as many as six divisions. I had hoped that four would suffice, but as you were told to ask for what you considered necessary, and as you told the French and the Italians that six would come, I had no case before the War Cabinet who said that under the circumstances six must go. I do not care so much about six going just now, what I feel is that we shall never get them back. We never have got divisions back once during the war from wherever they have been sent. I hope therefore that you will invariably take the line in dealing with the French and the Italians that these six divisions are not to be regarded as a permanency, but very much as a temporary measure only, and that you will later on as and when the Italians settle down report that a reduction can be made. We can never take a big offensive through in Italy in my opinion and I shall never advocate one.

***

Tomorrow I go to Paris to attend another big Conference and waste another week in talking. I have no objection to your keeping Radcliffe although my opinion regarding him remains unchanged, but so long as you desire to keep him you can of course retain him. I can quite understand him being very useful to you, at any rate for the present. I hope you will not forget to get out of the Italians any labour you require. We are going to suggest at the Conference that they should send 100,000 or 150,000 men to our Armies in France for labour purposes. It is preposterous that they should have all the millions of able-bodied men that they have and that we should be called upon to send 150,000 to 200,000 of our good soldiers to look after their wretched country. The least they can do is to give us some labour in return, but goodness knows if we shall get it. In trying to help our Allies we shall ruin ourselves if we are not careful.

Haig had a very good show last week and he gave a further proof of our ability to beat the Germans, but in order to beat them he must of course have adequate troops. As a result of the detachment to Italy Haig has had to close down practically everything.

***

I cannot account for her failure to exploit her advantage in Italy and to continue the prosecution of the attack upon Rumania except on the grounds of inability. I believe that her military power is less than we have thought and that the Austrians are in a much worse condition than we have thought. Now that the winter is coming on the Trentino flank should soon be quite safe, and I should hope that the Piave line will be held. There is no reason that it should not be.

You know my views on the general policy, namely, to fight the Germans on the West front, nearest to our own base, and where Germans can be killed. Every day I am more convinced that this course is the right one. I am also convinced that anything in the nature of a big offensive in Italy would not only be unsound for the above reasons but that communications render it impracticable. I will trust to you therefore not to send at any future date, at any rate officially in the first instance, anything tending to imply that you think that the war can easily and properly be won by sending more troops from the West front to Italy.

LHCMA, Robertson Mss, I/34/38

193

General Sir William Robertson to Major-General Sir F. B. Maurice

[Paris]

[Holograph] 30 November 1917

Assuming that I get back on Sunday in time I would like to see you about an hour after I arrive, which I hope may be about 4 pm.

The Supreme War Council is developing into a farce. The Yanks don't seem to care about it. Cadorna is here more or less alone. Clemenceau[16] would not let Foch go, & the latter seems to have tried to get his control by sending Weygand! And yet you make Wilson a general! Wilson's large staff, with Milner, have been at Versailles all the week, opening their shop & waiting for customers! And no one taking any notice of them! Tomorrow is the first sitting, and some 40 of us go to Versailles, where we find Wilson. What a farce!

LHCMA, Robertson Mss, I/25/9

194

General Sir H. H. Wilson to General Sir William Robertson

British Military Representative,
Supreme War Council
British Section,
Versailles

[Holograph] 2 December 1917

I was sorry not to see you last night. I waited 3 hours & then, as you had not returned, I came away. I asked Lucas to tell you the object of my visit. It was simply to say that there appear to be many people whose chief business seems to be concerned with making mischief between you & me, between Haig & me, between Haig & you. If we listen to their silly, & sometimes venomous, stories we are simply playing into their hands and, which is worse, into the hands of the Boches. I certainly am not going to be a party to so miserable, so suspicious, a game and I ran into Paris just to tell you this. I am confident that with good will & with mutual trust we can afford to laugh at these vermin.

IWM, Wilson Mss, 2/1A/1

195

General Sir William Robertson to General Sir H. H. Wilson

War Office

[Holograph] 6 December 1917

Got your letter *today*! Very sorry I missed you at Paris. I was kept at the d__d meeting till after 7:30 pm. I have not come across any one yet who appears to be trying to make mischief between us, and I can assure you that they will have no influence over me. At the same time the new arrangement will be difficult to work. I have already told you I shall honestly try to make it work, though I dislike the scheme. I do not see how, in our case, duality of advice (the politicians' aim) is to be avoided. You have your responsibility, & I have mine, and *more* than you have because you are free of *execution* which I am not, and after all, it is execution which matters most. The only real safeguard is to keep closely in touch, and the hope that we may not differ in essentials. I don't think we will. With the French & Italians the case is different. Italy counts for nothing & Cadorna is a nonentity. Weygand is of course Foch's man. You, on the contrary, were at first deliberately separated from me as far as was legally possible, though this has fortunately been improved by my attending the meetings of the Council.

There has been a Cabinet discussion here as to 'procedure' in your getting the information you want, and you will shortly get a War Office letter on the subject. It would never do for you to deal with your War Office (your chief helper) through Hankey. Delay alone is an effective bar.

I hope you are getting settled down all right. And you may rely upon my good will & confidence in you. Many thanks for your letter.

IWM, Wilson Mss, 2/1A/2

196

General Sir E. H. H. Allenby to General Sir William Robertson

General Headquarters
Egyptian Expeditionary
Force
7 December 1917

[R Telegram]
<u>Secret and Personal</u>

I quite understand your views[17] and I recognise that outside commitments must be cut down and reasonable risks be faced by me here.

According to the instructions given me when I was appointed Egypt Command I have conducted this campaign with a view to the defence that country entailing the defeat of Turkish army and the occupation to Beer Sheba and Gaza. That line is difficult if not impossible to hold and the only line that I can hold with reasonable security is the line Jerusalem—Jaffa with my flanks on the Dead Sea and the Mediterranean.

If I can get Jerusalem—Jaffa line I ought to be able to hold it with the force I now have if my establishments are maintained.

It will not be necessary to advance further north than the consolidation of that line requires, but it will be essential to maintain that line.

Any retirement would alienate the Arabs and result in disaster.

I consider that it would not be feasible to hold that line with a less force than that under my command and I would point out that for political as well as military reasons the majority of the troops in this country should be British.

LHCMA, Robertson Mss, I/14/109

197

General Sir William Robertson to General Sir E. H. H. Allenby

R [telegram] War Office
Secret & Personal 8 December 1917

I note your views and if and when I send you instructions contrary to them you will have an opportunity of repeating them officially and should do so if desired. I should hope no retirement will become necessary but even if it did the disaster you fear might well be far less than one in Europe. The force you may eventually need should of course be fixed by the strength of the possible opposition rather than by the length of any given line while your fine mounted force should be a very great asset. As regards the Arabs I confess I am so far somewhat disappointed at their contribution.

LHCMA, Robertson Mss, I/14/113

198

General Sir H. H. Wilson to General Sir William Robertson

Supreme War Council
British Section
Versailles
[Typescript] 10 December 1917

I am glad you have not met any of the mischief makers. I have been less fortunate, and some of them work within the bray of an 'ass' of your room. I am not so nervous of the 'duality of advice', as you call it, as you are and simply because I give no advice—as Wilson. The advice put up by the Military Representatives is signed by the soldiers of four countries. It is not the individual advice of any one man. I see the same thought as yourself and the same fear in an Army Council letter I received last night, in which a proposal is made that I should first send my advice to the Army Council before submitting it to the Supreme Council, but, then, I (Wilson) do not give any advice to the Supreme Council, and I do not suppose that Weygand, Cadorna and Bliss want to have their joint opinion submitted to the War Office any more than Cadorna, Bliss and I want to have ours sent to Paris, or the other combinations want to have their papers sent to Rome and Washington. I think all fear of duality, therefore, disappears. Cadorna is pressing very hard for unity of command in Italy. This demand has arisen from considerable friction between Diaz and Fayolle. I have asked for copies of instructions issued by you to Plumer and Milne, but it seems to me that men of that rank might be given the right of appeal in the case of being given orders which, in their opinion, needlessly endangers their forces.

IWM, Wilson Mss, 2/1A/3

199

General Sir William Robertson to Lieutenant-General Sir H. C. O. Plumer

Dictated [typescript] War Office
SECRET. Personal 10 December 1917

I do not know that there is much in your letters of the 2nd and 4th instant which calls for an answer. No doubt you have been put out by the repeated postponement of the despatch of the fifth and sixth divisions, but I am afraid that this is war. Haig did very well at Cambrai on the 20th and on subsequent days he consolidated his positions. But he had bitten deeply into the German lines and they were certain to make a great effort to get back what he had taken, as failing getting it back they would probably have had to come out of the salient he had created for them. They reinforced heavily and on the 30th November made a determined attack. Practically everywhere on the new line occupied by us and where the hostile attacks were by far the heaviest the enemy was thoroughly well defeated and apparently suffered very great losses. But in the south two divisions and a bit ran clean over two divisions of ours one of which was occupying part of the old line. The advance penetrated some two or three miles into our positions on a two-division front.

***

It was a piece of very bad luck for Haig, and of course has given rise here to all kinds of erroneous statements, some of them going so far as to say that Haig ought not to have attacked on the 20th whereas the sole reason is bad work on the part of two divisions. The matter is being investigated. The Germans have brought down 19 divisions to the Cambrai front since Haig attacked and as you know his troops were pretty well used up in the Ypres salient and therefore he is rather hard put to it to hold his own. As a matter of fact the incident is not altogether without value for I think it has taught the people in France that the German still has a good deal of fight in him. The diminution of German morale has been greatly overdone at General Headquarters. My opinion is that German morale will remain good until the war is over. In any case it is largely a matter of opinion and it varies from day to day and between different units. It is no sort of a basis upon which to form plans so far as the Germans are concerned.

***

LHCMA, Robertson Mss, I/34/41

200

General Sir William Robertson to Field-Marshal Sir Douglas Haig

[Holograph] War Office
Personal 11 December 1917

Your letter of the 9th instant.[18] I have not heard a word in Cabinet showing any want of confidence in *you*. You can take this for a fact. I do not think there is *any* want of it. But I have heard for *months* past complaints about Charteris. They are really very common in this country, and everybody seems to think you are ill-advised to retain him. I have seen the letter you sent to Derby on the subject. It is a matter for your consideration whether you really are doing the best for the general cause by retaining an officer in whom so many people have no confidence. The argument is that you cannot help being influenced by the advice you get.

L. G. seems determined not to give us the men we want. He is arguing from figures, which show the Allies are greatly superior in numbers on the west front. He will not listen to other points of view. Also he quotes your Memorandum every hour of the day, where you said that you could attack next spring even if 30 Divisions came over from Russia. Of course we need every man possible no matter what may be said otherwise. The Army Council will play up I think, & either get the men or have a big row (as we did before we could get the so called conscription).

NLS, Acc 3155, no 120, Haig Mss

201

David Lloyd George to General Sir William Robertson

10, Downing Street

[Typescript] 11 December 1917

I see it suggested in one of your telegrams which came in today that Howitzers should be removed from Egypt to another theatre. I trust you will not do this without bringing it before the War Cabinet. It may involve a very important policy which will be for them to decide.

The Cabinet ought at the earliest possible moment to decide whether the advance in Palestine should be exploited. It is quite clear that the information which had been given to us about the number of Turkish troops available in that theatre was utterly wrong, and that the more recent information supplied to me as to the complete breakdown of the Turkish transport is nearer the mark. Under these circumstances it is surely worth our while considering the exploitation of our victory with a view at least to securing the whole of Palestine.

H. of Lords RO, Lloyd George Mss, F/44/3/38

202

David Lloyd George to General Sir William Robertson

[10, Downing Street
Whitehall]

[Typescript] 14 December 1917

In preparing your appreciation of future military policy in the Palestine theatre, I should be glad if you would supply the War Cabinet with an estimate of the number of troops and the amount of shipping which could be released for other theatres of war as the result of the successful occupation by British troops of the Aleppa railway junction.

LHCMA, Robertson Mss, I/19/13

203

General Sir William Robertson to General Sir H. H. Wilson

[In other hand] General Headquarters
Copy 16 December 1917

I am glad to hear you have been here and had a talk with Haig. It would be useful to you both, and as you have recently said you fear mischief makers may I say that Haig told me he felt quite *sure* you intended to do *nothing* inconsistent with playing the game. You must forgive me saying this. I do so because of what you wrote to me, and to assure you of Haig and myself being quite untouched by mischief makers. I told you in Italy I had decided to do my best, and that I felt you would. Until you hear differently from me, I want you to work on this assurance.

This extension of the line is a d__d nusiance. Haig certainly ought not to go anywhere near Berry au Bac.[19] Our Divisions are played out & want a rest. I have come here to get some changes made. Charteris is going. Maxwell has also been told to go (He is not up to the job & is not helping us with man power). I have still something to say to Haig about others, regarding which I will tell you later.

IWM, Wilson Mss, 2/1A/6

204

General Sir William Robertson to Lieutenant-General Sir H. C. O. Plumer

Dictated [typescript
with holograph additions] War Office
SECRET & personal 28 December 1917

... I hope your Italian friends will keep their end up properly. There is no reason why they should not do so if they will but learn how to fight and have the necessary stomach for fighting. We shall have a rather hard time during 1918. It is bad luck just as the Russians go out[20] that the Italians should be such a burden to us. We have got to look forward to a big battle or battles on the French and Italian fronts and I confess that I have some anxiety as to the course of events, because whatever may be said to the contrary it is a fact that military operations are now conducted by the politicians. The Supreme War Council as you know is formed entirely of politicians who naturally cannot have the educated military mind and I foresee that they will become very rattled when the Bosch gets on the move and will want to rush the troops about from one end of the front to the other wherever a feint may be made. The Bosch will no doubt conduct his operations in the orthodox way and endeavour to mislead us as to where he intends to strike, and nothing but a cool head and deliberate plan will beat him, and we cannot expect to have either one or the other. I hope therefore that you will do what you can to assist me in this matter in the telegrams you send. The Bosch will I am sure make feints at different places and set about all sorts of stories through the different neutral embassies which will find their way to the capitals of France, England, and Italy with results that I fear may not be good.

***

LHCMA, Robertson Mss, I/34/43

205

General Sir William Robertson to Field-Marshal Sir Douglas Haig

Dictated [typescript with holograph additions] War Office
SECRET & PERSONAL 12 January 1918

I have returned from my interview with Pershing[21] in a by no means sanguine state of mind. He seems to have no grasp of the task in front of him and to have far too much administrative work to do. Further he is certainly in no hurry to get his divisions in front of the Germans. His one idea seems to be to amass an enormous Army before doing anything. It is necessary that he should be convinced that he must hurry up, and he must give us some idea as to what assistance he hopes to be able to afford in the near future.

There will be another Conference at Versailles in the course of a week or two, and before it meets it is necessary that we should have a clear understanding as to plans and all possibilities in the immediate future. The Versailles people are doubtless doing their best, but they cannot well help being a probable source of mischief unless we responsible people have made up our minds on all points *beforehand* and are in accord with the French.

I am therefore suggesting to Foch that you, Petain, Pershing, Foch, and myself, should have a talk before the Versailles Conference. We can then all get at Pershing and ascertain what he is doing and hopes to do, while Foch and I can also hear what you and Petain are proposing to do and so be in a position to get done what you want done without the interference of the young men at Versailles.

The latter have been very busy with war games which is their panacea for everything. I suggested to them on Thursday that there was not much doubt as to what the enemy can do and may do, but there is a good deal of difficulty in providing the means we need to defeat the enemy, and that that is the direction in which they should put their energies chiefly. I hear that these wise men have settled the extension of your front to their satisfaction by recommending that you should go about half-way between Barisis and Berry-au-bac. You were prepared to go to the first place and the French wanted you to go to the second. What the Versailles experts have done is to effect a compromise, which is no more than any political Conference would have done and has done in the past. No doubt you will have something to say about this recommendation and you may depend upon my support. I hear that the French base their argument on numbers and kilometres; Cadorna took a somewhat similar method; while the English people played their usual war game to decide the matter. It would be all very funny if it was not such a nuisance, not to say serious. I hope you feel all the better for your rest. Good luck to you.

LHCMA, Robertson Mss, I/23/78

206

General Sir William Robertson to Field-Marshal Sir Douglas Haig

Dictated [typescript] War Office
SECRET 21 January 1918

Many thanks for your letter of yesterday.

You ask me what I am going to talk about at the Conference. I am really aiming at getting a better knowledge of what you and Petain think of things and what you propose to do. It is only by having full knowledge of these matters that I can give the War Cabinet the information it asks for and generally conduct my own particular share of the business. The Chief points that occur to me are as follows:—

(a) American assistance. I want to hear from Pershing himself in the presence of you and Petain what it is he hopes to do for us in every respect.

(b) Seeing that there will almost certainly be a big battle on the West front, and perhaps in Italy also, it is necessary that we should consider the possibility of forming a Central Reserve of French and British troops. I do not mean remove them from their Commanders, of course, in any way, but to consider what we can do in the way of ear-marking troops to be used either on the French or British fronts or even in Italy. No doubt you and Petain have talked this over but I know nothing about it. If you were in command of the whole of the West front you would I am sure have a general reserve of your own. The question is therefore what can we do in this respect, seeing that there are two Commanders on the West front, and I think there will continue to be two. At the same time it is an elementary military principle that there should be a central reserve. The question is how near can we get to this.

(c) In connection with the Central Reserve it is necessary to consider the relative value of the different parts of the front. As we are fighting on the defensive we must expect to be made to give ground at some points perhaps and it is necessary that we and the French together should make up our minds what ground we could give if compelled to give ground somewhere and on what part of the front we could not give ground.

(d) Railway communications, with special reference to movements of troops to and from Italy. Whether any improvement can be made and if so what.

***

I am glad to hear that your relations with Petain are so good. I only hope that he will represent them as being equally good when we come to the discussion of the extension of the front. I daresay this will be difficult for him because his politicians wish for you to take over more front.

LHCMA, Robertson Mss, I/23/82

207

General Sir William Robertson to Lord Stamfordham

[Typescript] War Office
COPY 22 January 1918

His Majesty may like to know that I am going over to France tomorrow to meet in Conference Haig, Petain, Foch and Pershing, to ascertain their views and plans and to ensure as far as possible a clear understanding and mutual support, including, I hope, the formation of a General Reserve of British and French troops available for use when and where most needed in the forthcoming Battle, which we may expect to open at any time after the middle of February. Afterwards I go to Paris (we are having our Conference at Compiegne, well away from the politicians!) to confer with Bliss and Pershing about the 150 American Battalions I am trying to get, and for which the American Government have to-day cabled their approval to Bliss, subject to certain shipping conditions, which may be difficult for us to meet or circumvent: I hope for the best. Afterwards apparently there is likely to be another Versailles Conference! As to it I say nothing!

RA, Geo V. F. 1259/3

208

General Sir William Robertson to H. H. Gwynne

War Office
[Holograph] 22 January 1918

I am 'going across' tomorrow for a few days—probably for a week or so. Will see you on return. Meanwhile let me thank you for your help. What a d__d disgraceful position for a Government to be in, to have to resort to such vile and unmanly tactics to get rid of those they don't like![22] But this time, & for the moment, they have over done it.

IWM,Gwynne Mss, Pt. III, fol. 359

209

General Sir William Robertson to Field-Marshal Sir Douglas Haig

Hôtel de Crillon
Place de la Concorde
Paris

[Holograph] 24 January 1918

I find that Versailles have just sent in a paper advocating an offensive in Palestine to 'annihilate' & knock out the Turk. The paper is d__d rot in general. It simply advocates doing all sorts of wonderful things in Palestine, and a great offensive in the west, quite regardless of means. I have told the War Cabinet they cannot take on Palestine & I shall stick to my guns and clear out if I am overruled. It is of no earthly use filling a post & having one's advice overruled. From a rational point of view it is *wrong* I think.

NLS, Acc 3155, no. 123, Haig Mss

210

General Sir William Robertson to David Lloyd George

[Typescript] PARIS
SECRET 1 February 1918

1. I have now had an opportunity of more closely considering the Scheme put forward by the French Staff today for the control

of the General Reserves on the Allied front, and am of opinion that it goes unnecessarily far. In its place I enclose a Note giving what I consider to be the simplest, most practical and constitutional system to ensure adequate control of these reserves, which does not interfere with the Supreme War Council system, but merely provides executive means which that Council does not possess.

2. As regards the alternative proposals which you wished to have considered, namely, that the control of the General Reserves should be vested (a) in the Supreme War Council; or (b) in representative General Officers of the Allies attached to the Supreme War Council under the Presidency of General Foch, they appear to me to be identical in principle in that they place executive power in the hands of a new body—and one not under ministerial control. I may note that General Weygand already acts under the orders of General Foch and reports to him daily. The only difference therefore in this respect in the two schemes would be that General Foch would in (b) be recognised as a Member, while in (a) he would not.

3. If it were decided to adopt (b) I feel inclined to think that General Foch's powers might gradually become very like those of a Generalissimo. Either (a) or (b) would, in short, probably work to the entire satisfaction of the French for in addition to General Foch's position he has at his disposal the whole of the Administrative machinery of the French War Office and is in direct touch with the French Minister of War.

4. With us the case is different. No British officer in France who is not a Member of the Army Council and in direct touch with that body can have the necessary information as to the state of the troops, the supply, munition and medical situation and other questions essential to the effective control of military operations. On these questions I feel that both the Secretary of State for War and the Army Council should be consulted, as they affect vitally the principles of command and administration of our troops in the field.

5.[23] There are also constitutional questions to be considered. As to these I speak with diffidence and lack of knowledge, and suggest it is necessary you should consult the Secretary of State for War before deciding to adopt either of these two alternatives. I do not quite see how a British Commander-in-Chief can be made, constitutionally, to obey the orders of an Allied body, or indeed of anyone except the Army Council and the Secretary of State for War—a Minister of the Crown. If the C.I.G.S. were made a member of the Versailles body, as is proposed in the case of General Foch, this difficulty could be more easily surmounted perhaps.

LHCMA, Robertson Mss, I/24/5/1

211

General Sir William Robertson, 'Note on Control of the General Reserves'

[Typescript enclosed in above]

PARIS

SECRET

1 February 1918

1. It is decided to establish a Higher Control in order to ensure that the General Reserves available on the whole front from the North Sea to the Adriatic may be employed in the most effective manner.

2. This Higher Control will consist of the British and French Chiefs of the General Staff. When the British Chief of the General Staff cannot be present he will be represented by a British General Officer. Representatives of the American and Belgian Armies will be attached for the purposes of keeping their Commanders-in-Chief and Governments informed as to the situation in regard to reserves. When America has a larger force available this arrangement will require review.

3. The functions of the Higher Control will be:–

(a) To form general reserves. Instructions will be issued by each of the two Chiefs of the General Staff to their respective

Commanders-in-Chief in accordance with the general situation and with the plans approved by the Supreme War Council. The troops composing the General Reserve will remain under the orders of their respective Commanders-in-Chief but are at the sole disposal of the Higher Control and are not to be engaged by the Commanders-in-Chief without its sanction.

(b) To supervise the arrangements for movement of the General Reserve. In order to assure the timely movement of the General Reserve the Commanders-in-Chief will make all necessary arrangements for their transportation and concentration. These arrangements will be submitted to the Higher Control for its approval.

(c) The employment of the General Reserve. The General Reserve will be employed by the Commanders-in-Chief in accordance with instructions issued by the Higher Control.

4. If the Italian Government is prepared to appoint a General officer to the proposed Higher Control, the same procedure as above will apply to Italy. If their Constitution does not admit of this, then the only course is to attach an Italian Representative to the Higher Control, without executive functions, to keep the Italian Commander-in-Chief informed of the views of the Higher Control as to the possibilities of reinforcing the Italian front or of Italian troops reinforcing the Franco-British front.

LHCMA, Robertson Mss, I/24/5/2

212

'The following note was given by the Field-Marshal Commanding-in-Chief to the Prime Minister during the Conference, and so far as I know no reply was given to him.' (signed) W. R. R.

[Typescript] [Versailles]
SECRET 2 February 1918

I presume that definite orders or instructions will be sent to the Commander-in-Chief B.E.F. notifying the change in the channel of communication, and also as to the onus of responsibility for the effect of such orders as are given by the Foch Committee.

LHCMA, Robertson Mss, I/24/7

213

General Sir William Robertson to Lord Derby

Dictated [typescript with holograph additions] Versailles
SECRET 2 February 1918[24]

We had our final meeting this morning. The most important questions discussed at the Conference were Palestine, taking over the line, and the formation of Inter-Allied General Reserves. The extension of the line has been left more or less to be settled between Haig and Petain. It was discussed only very briefly in full Conference (You will understand that the Ministers had several Conferences by themselves and I think that probably some give and take on the more contentious questions was there arranged).

The question of Palestine was bound up with the question of

our ability to hold the Western Front. In this discussion the question of Man-Power was much to the fore and Foch made a very long statement showing the great things the French had done and the small effort that had been made by England, and pointed out the great reserves of men still in the country, in Ireland, and in the colonies, and alluded to the fact that we had as yet called up none of the older classes. The Prime Minister replied at some length explaining the other demands that are made upon us. Foch returned to the charge rather vehemently and in the end the Prime Minister appealed to the President to stop the discussion as he declined to be further criticised on matters of government and policy by a foreign General. The Proceedings at this point were decidedly of a warm nature. A fresh lot of figures were got out by the Staffs as a result of Foch's speech and were produced the next day. The different Staffs were more or less in accord with the figures they produced, and they all went to show that men would be very short this year. Petain told us that without any serious fighting he would have to reduce during the year some 25 divisions, while Haig also made a long statement about his deficiencies.

We passed on from the figures to the question of Palestine, the Prime Minister suggesting that the recommendation of the Versailles people to take the offensive there with a view to annihilating the Turk should be adopted in principle. This was supported by Orlando. Clemenceau proposed however that it should be rejected because it was quite obvious from the figures regarding man-power that we should with difficulty hold our own on the West front. Upon this the Prime Minister made a long speech much on the lines of his Paris speech, alleging great want of courage, imagination and so forth, and pointing out the admirable position we should now have been in if we had but knocked out Turkey, as we could have done a year or more ago. Clemenceau made an equally vehement reply which was to the effect that he could not for a moment think of supporting any such enterprise in Palestine when the enemy were practically knocking at the doors of Paris. In fact he might have been Maxse by the way he spoke with respect to side-shows, and he added that there had been too much 'imagination' and that if there had not been so much we might have saved many hundreds of thousands of men in Palestine, Mesopotamia, and Salonika, and by now have won the war. He also refused to accept the Prime Minister's statement that Germany had beaten Russia. He said that Russia had beaten herself and that if she had not betrayed us in the way she has we would have won the war this year. The result of these two long speeches was that we broke up on Thursday night in a state of considerable tension. The Prime Minister was very badly mauled and I never saw him look more knocked out. The situation in general was very tense, and anything might have happened. The following morning the enclosed Resolution[25] was proposed by the Prime Minister and was agreed to. There had been some previous consultation between Ministers and I understand that the Resolution was supposed to be a compromise. When it was put to the Meeting I felt it my duty to ask to make some observations, and I then expressed the opinion I have many times expressed, namely, that we have not the means for the conquest of Palestine and that to attempt such an operation would be dangerous and detrimental to our prospects of winning the war. Nothing further happened than that the Resolution was passed. Afterwards I expressed regret to the Prime Minister that I had had to intervene, but that I could not let the resolution go & remain silent. He did not agree, was much annoyed, & I daresay contemplates 'taking action' against me before long. I can't help it. I must give my opinion.

As to the question of Inter-Allied Reserves you will find the whole case in the Papers enclosed. Of course it never was a question of reserves. The real question was one of command, and for all practical purposes we now have a French Generalissimo. I do not know how or by whom powers are to be delegated to an officer, not on the Army Council and not directly under you, to issue orders to a Commander-in-Chief of about two million men. However, all this is alluded to in the Papers and I cannot help thinking that there is much trouble in store. It is folly, moreover, to imagine that anyone can issue orders about what is called General Reserves and stop there. The officer to issue orders about reserves must issue orders about many other things as well. It is folly to suppose it could be otherwise. The point is every officer must be under a *Minister*. Are you prepared to be Wilson's Minister and yet have no control over him. Who is to answer for the British Army & the future 'Cambrais'. The system is impossible, in my opinion. The Prime Minister got me out of it by saying I could not be excused from London, but surely I could find time to do on a part of one front what Ludendorf does on 2 fronts.

P.S. (In the train). Forgive me for saying so, but the matter is a very serious one for *you*. The Army, the Army Council, the C.I.G.S., and Commanders-in-Chief will look to you, their Minister, to see that they are not placed in an impossible, unfair, and unpractical position.

Liverpool Record Office, 920DER (17) 27/7, Derby Mss

214

General Sir William Robertson to General Sir E. H. H. Allenby

Dictated [typescript
with holograph
additions] War Office
SECRET & PERSONAL 2 Febuary 1918

I am sending you officially by Colonel Kirke[26] certain documents regarding the question of offensive operations in your theatre, about which Smuts is coming to see you.[27] In your dealings with Smuts you will of course be concerned mainly with your own theatre, but it seems to me to be folly for you to try to give advice as to what can be attempted in it without having some information with respect to the main theatre the security of which is now authoritatively admitted to be vital to the Allied interests. What I mean chiefly is that you should in giving your information as to your own theatre remember what is likely to happen in others and what the effect of that may be upon you. For instance, I see no prospect whatever of sending you more divisions than you now have, except perhaps one from Mesopotamia and even this is doubtful. Similarly as regards drafts. We may expect very heavy fighting indeed on the West front this year, and to meet it we shall have to supply the necessary drafts. I see no insuperable difficulty in your going further forward for a considerable distance, but I fail to see any useful gain thereby. You need to go so far and do so much. More especially I am doubtful as to the extent to which we can continue holding on to a more advanced position for a time which is quite indefinite. Lastly, I am doubtful of the Turk being knocked out by an effort you can make with your present forces plus such small additions as we may be able to give. I have not mentioned this in the official letter I am sending you because I do not wish you to think that I am trying to tie your hands, but I do wish to prevent you finding yourself in the cart later on.

LHCMA, Robertson Mss, I/32/80

215

General Sir William Robertson to General Sir H. C. O. Plumer

Dictated [typescript with holograph additions]
SECRET

War Office
4 February 1918

With regard to the newspaper attacks they do not bother me in the least. Any man occupying a position such as mine must expect to be attacked especially when we have such a disgraceful Press and one that exercises such great influence in highest political circles. At the same time I am very much obliged to you for your kind and thoughtful letter on this subject.

I shall be writing officially to you in the course of a day or two with respect to our future military policy on the Western and Italian Front. The subject has been considered at the recent Versailles Conference and I will send you the result. I am sorry to say that further complications have arisen as a result of the Versailles Soviet. As everybody knows it is desirable to have reserves to put into any desired direction and this matter has been somewhat ridden to death at the recent Conference because as a matter of fact we have not got many reserves over and above what each Commander requires. In order to make these reserves more effective it was considered that there ought to be some kind of central control and deciding authority who would step in and say where they ought or ought not to be used. This seemed to me to be a matter for the Chiefs of the General Staffs of the different Armies, but it has been decided to give the Versailles Soviet executive power so far as the reserves are concerned and a nice mess we have got into accordingly. This is so because it is impossible to have Chiefs of the General Staffs dealing with operations in all respects except reserves and to have people with no other responsibilities dealing with reserves and nothing else. In fact the decision is unsound, and [neither] do I see how it is to be worked either legally or constitutionally. However this we shall see about. Foch has been placed on the Versailles Soviet as a sort of Chairman and the English, American, and Italian Representatives form the remainder of the Committee. These sportsmen are to be the authority as to the size, composition, strength, and location of the reserves and they decide as to their employment. They are also empowered to visit the front. Therefore you may shortly expect a perambulating committee, with the powers of a generalissimo, but without his responsibility, to come round your front fussing into things which they do not understand and cannot control. It is all very trying.

***

LHCMA, Robertson Mss, I/34/45

216

General Sir William Robertson to Lord Stamfordham

War Office

[Holograph] 4 February 1918

I enclose some papers that may be of interest to His Majesty. I am afraid that the resolution will lead to more trouble. It is not practicable. A meeting of the Army Council is being held today to consider it.

We had rather a mixed discussion at the recent conference. Relations were rather strained on more than one occasion. The French were very bitter about our effort in regard to men. They made no allowance for what we do, outside the Army. Clemenceau was very severe on the 'side shows', especially the Palestine [?project]. But he was appeased a good deal by the success attending his efforts to set up a 'Generalissimo', & now that he has got *Executive* powers for the Versailles Soviet, with Foch as chairman, I have no doubt he hopes to keep control in Foch's hands.

RA, Geo V, F. 1259/13

217

General Sir William Robertson to Field-Marshal Sir Douglas Haig

Dictated [typescript] War Office

SECRET & PERSONAL 6 February 1918

On Monday last the Prime Minister gave to the War Cabinet *his* account of what had passed at Versailles. All the Papers approved at Versailles received the approval of the War Cabinet. We are sending to you to-day the necessary documents with regard to the decision with respect to the extension of your front. I am not yet able to send you instructions with respect to the Papers on the General Reserves and the control of them because the matter has not yet been fully settled. The Prime Minister told the Secretary of State to take the necessary action to give effect to the decision of the Supreme Council and the Secretary of State replied that he wished to have time to consider the system which it is proposed to establish. We then had an Army Council Meeting in the afternoon and we have had another one to-day. I enclose for your personal and private information the decisions reached by the Army Council. What the result may be I do not know, but of course until you receive instructions no action will be required.

NLS, Acc 3155, no. 123, Haig Mss

218

General Sir William Robertson to David Lloyd George

War Office

[In other hand] 7 February 1918

I rang up your Secretary last night to ascertain if you were expecting me to breakfast today and found that you were not. I want to say that I am compelled to go to the seaside for 2 or 3 days, by the Doctor's orders, to shake off the effects of the bronchitis attack of last week. Believe me, I have every wish to fix up a satisfactory and workable arrangement with respect to the Reserve. In fact I have been in communication with Haig, Petain & Foch on the subject for some weeks past, because the principle is in my opinion unquestionable. The only point in question is the method, and I trust that may be soon decided.

LHCMA, Robertson Mss, I/24/9

219

General Sir William Robertson to Field-Marshal Sir Douglas Haig

War Office
[Holograph] 7 February 1918

It would help me if you could *incidentally* drop a line to Derby and say what you think about the Reserve question, so far as concerns the proposal that the Executive Committee should issue orders to you on this subject—thus constituting 2 authorities from which orders will issue—Versailles & London. I ask this because L. G. states that you are quite agreeable to the proposal and in fact accepted it. This is what I hear. The solution is, put me on the Versailles Committee, then all is well, I think.

NLS, Acc 3155, no. 123, Haig Mss

220

General Sir William Robertson to H. A. Gwynne

York House,
St. James' Palace, S. W.
[Holograph] 7 February 1918

I am just off for 2 or 3 days. The little man is all out for my blood, & is trying to isolate me from the other members of the Army Council. Keep your eye on things while I am away. My intention is, to see him out. If he wants me to go, he should *tell* me so. But he daren't. He is trying therefore to make my position impossible. And all the trouble is that I am trying to see that the fine British army is not placed at the mercy of irresponsible people—& some of them foreigners at that. I see that the Chronicle today practically blames me because the Versailles people have had no pay. L. G. told Derby I was, this morning. Derby is supposed to have explained. But ½ hour afterwards L. G. said the same thing to another man, who told me. Of course it has *nothing* to do with me. The general situation is—I have tried to insist upon right things being done. L. G. is *sick* of me because I would not give in and trim to his ideas. The country always claims that the soldier should 'stand up' to the politician. I have stood up. What will the country do?

I go to Grand Hotel, Eastbourne.

IWM, Gwynne Mss, Pt. III, fol. 360

221

Lord Derby to General Sir William Robertson

War Office

[Holograph] 11 February 1918

This is the agreement arrived at between myself and the Prime Minister and to which Sir Douglas Haig assents. I propose to put it before the Army Council this afternoon with the exception of the last paragraph and ask their assent to it. I hope you will give me your support.

LHCMA, Robertson Mss, I/24/10/1

222

Memorandum signed by David Lloyd George

[Typescript enclosed in above]
SECRET

10 Downing Street
Whitehall, S.W. 1
[Undated but 9 February 1918]

1. The C.I.G.S. to hold office under the same conditions and with the same powers as every Chief of the Staff up to the appointment of Sir William Robertson.

2. The C.I.G.S. to continue to be the supreme military adviser of the Government.

3. The Military Representative at Versailles to be a member of the Army Council.

4. The Military Representative at Versailles to be in constant communication and consultation with the C.I.G.S., but to be absolutely free and unfettered in the advice which he gives as a member of the Board of Military Representatives sitting at Versailles.

5. When that advice is formulated it is to be submitted to the C.I.G.S. for the purpose of advising the Cabinet thereon.

6. When it is necessary to summon a Supreme Council, either to decide upon a plan of operations or to settle differences that may have arisen between the various Commanders-in-Chief, or between any one or more of the Commanders-in-Chief and Versailles, or for any other purpose, the C.I.G.S. to accompany the Ministers delegated to attend the Council for the purpose of advising them as to the decisions to be taken, after hearing what the Military Representatives and the Commanders-in-Chief have to say from their respective points of view.

7. As prompt decisions may have to be taken as to the sending of reserves to one part or other of the battle front, and time lost in referring to London may be fatal, full powers must be given to the Military Representatives in accordance with principles already settled to give the necessary orders in respect of divisions included in the General Reserve.

8. The C.I.G.S., even when not accompanied by a Minister, to have the right to go to France to consult in person with any one or all of the Military Representatives of the Supreme Council.

9. The Military Representative at Versailles to be Sir William Robertson and the C.I.G.S. to be Sir Henry Wilson.

LHCMA, Robertson Mss, I/24/10/3

223

General Sir William Robertson to Lord Stamfordham

War Office

[Holograph] 11 February 1918

The King has always shown such great kindness and consideration towards me, that it is on that account alone right I should send you a copy of a letter I have just sent to Lord Derby. I have reached my decision after very careful thought and with great reluctance. For one thing it probably means an end to my military career of more than 40 years, but the matter is much too serious to allow these questions to intrude. The ridiculous system of setting up, practically, two CIGSs must result in failure and destruction of confidence amongst the troops as to who really is their Commander. Men will not die for *Committees*.

RA, Geo V, F. 1259/15

224

General Sir William Robertson to Lord Derby

[Typescript enclosed in above]

War Office
SECRET
11 February 1918

You have informed me this morning that the War Cabinet have decided to appoint General Sir H. Wilson as C.I.G.S., and to appoint me, with my present position as Army Councillor, British Military Representative to the Supreme War Council, vice General Wilson.

With respect to the first decision you informed me that the reason for removing me from my appointment is because the Prime Minister cannot 'get on' with me. For this I can only express my deep regret, because I have always tried to serve him loyally and to tell the truth fearlessly. Will you please say when I am to hand over my duties to General Wilson.

With respect to the second decision you will remember that at a meeting on the 6th instant the four Military Members present advised you that, in order to give effect to the intention of the Supreme War Council with respect to the formation and control of the Allied General Reserves, the Army Councillor holding the appointment of C.I.G.S., who is fully acquainted with the resources and needs of the British military forces, is the proper officer to be delegated as British Military Representative on the Executive Committee at Versailles. After careful consideration I am convinced that there would be no difficulty in making such arrangements as would permit of the British C.I.G.S. carrying out the duty without interference with essential duties at home.

I am still unable to see any other practical and workable system, for the reasons given in the various Papers submitted to yourself and to the Prime Minister during the last fortnight, as well as for those put forward by Army Councillors at the meetings recently held. I need not further refer to them except to say that it is impossible in practice to separate action in connexion with

General Reserves from action concerning innumerable other matters which go to make up 'military operations'; and that the decision of the War Cabinet leaves, as before, the issue of orders affecting military operations in the hands of two different authorities—one the C.I.G.S. and the other the British Military Representative at Versailles. The fact of my remaining an Army Councillor does not in my judgment remove this defect.

It seems to me absolutely necessary that the General Staff officer who is to give orders regarding the reserves in question must be in constant and direct touch with the various departments of the War Office—the Great Headquarters of the Imperial Military Forces—and be directly served by, and in close touch with, the Intelligence Branch of the General Staff. Only the C.I.G.S., residing normally at the War Office, can be in this position, and for an officer who is not in that position to attempt to interfere with the employment and location of Reserve troops under the British Commanders-in-Chief in France, Italy, and the Balkans, upon the right use of which final victory depends, would inevitably lead to confusion and perhaps to disaster. So strongly am I convinced of this that I am compelled to say that I cannot undertake the very great responsibility involved. I say this with the deepest regret because I am keenly desirous of doing my utmost to assist His Majesty's Government in their difficult task of winning the war, but on reconsideration I feel sure that you will see that it is asking too much of me to carry out and perpetuate a system which the Adjutant-General, Master-General of the Ordnance Deputy C.I.G.S. and myself consider to be fundamentally defective.

I desire to thank you for so kindly telling me that I would not suffer financially by vacating my present post and going to Versailles.

RA, Geo V, F. 1259/16

225

Lord Derby to General Sir William Robertson

Derby House,
[Typescript] Stratford Place, W
Very Secret 11 February 1918

It is with the greatest regret that I received your letter and I still will not take 'No' for an answer and hope that tomorrow morning may find you ready to reconsider your refusal to accept the post now offered to you.

You must allow me however to demur to that sentence in which you say that I informed you that the reason for removing you from your appointment was because the Prime Minister could not get on with you. I never gave that as a reason.

If that had been the reason for what you call your removal from your appointment I certainly should not have acted as an agent in conveying that decision to you as under those circumstances I should certainly have felt it my duty to resign. The reason for making the change is an entirely different one. As you know at the last Versailles Conference certain resolutions were unanimously accepted by the Ministers representing the various Nations and these have now got to be put into effect. They differed from the previous resolutions in that they gave executive power to the Military representatives, thus largely increasing their duties and their responsibilities. To show how this was appreciated by the French it is only necessary to bring to your notice the fact that General Foch was at once substituted for General Weygand as the French Military Representative. It became obvious that our Government must also reconsider our position.

I have always pointed out to you (and publicly) that the Government are perfectly justified in making any changes that they may think proper with regard to their Military Advisors and the Secretary of State's duty is either to carry them out if he thinks them proper decisions or to resign if he considers that they are contrary to the safety and welfare of the troops for whom under the Constitution he is responsible. The Government suggested to me that just as the French had put on their Chief of the Staff and the Americans had put on their Senior Officer, so should we put you on as our representative, in view of the fact that decisions might have to be taken at a moment's notice, and it was very desirable that if they were, they should be taken by a man in whom the Army had such complete confidence as yourself.

If I had thought this was derogatory to you I should not have assented but I do not so consider it. On the contrary I think it is placing you in a position where your knowledge can be put to even greater use than in your present position. You have never failed to impress upon me in conversation, and on myself and others at Army Council meetings, that much power had been taken away from the Army Council and put in the hands of the Military Representative at Versailles and now when I ask you to take that place you tell me you are not prepared to accept it. You contend that it would be possible for the C.I.G.S. to combine the two posts of C.I.G.S. at home and Military Representative in Paris. The Cabinet have considered this and they have come to the conclusion that it would not be possible and I agree with them. When the Committee at Versailles was purely advisory it might have been done, though even then I do not think it would have been advisable. Now that it is executive I think it is absolutely impossible. C.I.G.S. living in London cannot possibly give a decision, delay in the giving of which might be fatal in France.

I admit that your Deputy the Deputy C.I.G.S. and Master-General of the Ordnance are in agreement with you as to the proposal being fundamentally defective. You expressly omit the Quartermaster General and I do not think that you should include Adjutant-General in your statement. From what he said this afternoon and from what I have gathered from him in conversation, although he thinks that your proposal is the ideal one, I do not think you would find he went to the extent of saying the proposed arrangement is fundamentally defective.

Again may I beg you to reconsider your decision. You are being offered no inferior post. On the contrary you are being asked to take one which I think entails even more responsibility than your present one and where your influence and the weight that you can bring to bear on this Committee will be invaluable in upholding the views and contentions with regard to the Reserve which Sir Douglas Haig may put forward.

You and I have been on such friendly terms that I should feel miserable if I thought I was doing anything that would mean that your services would be lost to the Nation. I look upon it as indispensable that they should be retained and I ask therefore that whatever your personal feelings may be you will as a soldier accept the position and by so doing I feel convinced you will be doing a great national service.

LHCMA, Robertson Mss, I/24/12

226

Brigadier-General G. S. Clive to General Sir William Robertson

General Headquarters

[Holograph] 12 February 1918

Yesterday morning I took over to Sir Douglas a copy of General Pétain's letter, answering the official demands of the Supreme War Council as to reserve divisions to be placed at their disposal.

This appears to have the only official communication sent; it was signed by the members of the Executive Committee, and General Pétain was asked to get the compliance of Sir Douglas.

General Pétain's reply said that our operations are for the present defensive, that the defensive plan is based on a large number of circumstances, and that any displacement or alienation of his reserves will dislocate, or any how delay, the execution of the plan.

Sir Douglas told me what was passing in London during last weekend, for communication to General Pétain. The latter said that nothing would give him greater satisfaction than your appointment, as a member of the Army Council, to the Supreme War Council. Since the last Conference, his view has been that so long as he and Sir Douglas work closely together, with you to back them up, the Versailles body cannot effectively interfere. If unsuitable instructions were received from Versailles, and the Commanders in Chief had to ask for the questions to be re-submitted, General Pétain intended to ask you to be their joint representative.—He criticises General Foch very much for his action in the matter, which he considers crooked; but at the same time he thinks that General Foch has ruined any chances that Versailles had, by forcing the pace since the Conference, and making the presumptous demand for 30 divisions without any attempt to get the Commanders in Chief into a mood to agree.

If, therefore, circumstances should bring you to Versailles, you would be regarded here as having changed your role from that of protecting the British Army from undue interferences by the British Government, to that of protecting the Allied Commanders in Chief from their collective Governments, and incidentally, of preventing, crooked dealings.

LHCMA, Robertson Mss, I/36/95

227

General Sir William Robertson to Lord Stamfordham

War Office

[Holograph] 12 February 1918

Needless to say I am both touched and honoured by your letter of today, conveying His Majesty's confidence in me. My one desire is to serve the King and my country, fearlessly and to the best of my power, and I regret that His Majesty should be caused anxiety regarding a matter in which I am concerned. But it is absolute folly to set up two authorities to deal with Sir D. Haig. No one would be responsible for anything. And there is no occasion for the trouble. All that is necessary is to follow the French example, and put our C.I.G.S., whoever he may be, on this Executive Committee—& the thing is then settled. The C.I.G.S. has *no* need to be constantly at Versailles. On the contrary he must normally be at the War Office, in order to do the work entailed. I hear there was a long Cabinet meeting this morning, and that no decision was reached. I hope it soon may be—*I* shall give no trouble. All I request is that I may not be asked to participate in what I feel, as do the military members of the Army Council, to be an unsound and unworkable system of command.

RA, Geo V, F. 1259/18

228

General Sir William Robertson to Lord Derby

[Typescript with holograph addition]

War Office

SECRET

13 February 1918

You have asked me whether I would regard the Prime Minister's undated Note (prepared I understand on the 9th instant) as a workable arrangement—so far as concerns the control of the Inter-Allied Reserves—if I remain as C.I.G.S. and do not go to Versailles as Permanent British Military Representative.

In the first place I desire to repeat my earnest desire to serve His Majesty's Government to the best of my power and to carry out such instructions as they may issue so far as that can possibly be done.

With regard to para 1 of the Note I have no remarks to make. The matter is one for His Majesty's Government.

With regard to the control of the Inter-Allied Reserves, there is no doubt that such Reserves are necessary, and I pointed the necessity out to the Prime Minister in my Note of 30th January,[28] before the meeting of the Supreme Council. The only question still at issue is how this control can be exercised. This is in my judgment primarily a military question and I have never varied in the advice which I have given, namely, that the control should be exercised by the C.I.G.S., and in this I am supported by the Military Members of the Army Council. I stated in my Note to you of the 11th instant that for any officer other than the C.I.G.S. 'to attempt to interfere with the employment and location of Reserve troops under the British Commanders-in-Chief in France, Italy, and the Balkans, upon the right use of which final victory depends, would inevitably lead to confusion and perhaps to disaster'. After further consideration I am more strongly convinced than ever of the truth of this.

There need be no difficulty in the C.I.G.S. being represented on the Executive body, in his absence, by a Deputy who would keep him fully informed of the work of the Executive, warn him when his presence was required, and act for him in case of necessity. Nothing in this arrangement need in any way affect the position or duties of the British Military Representative to the Supreme War Council. The Deputy, if desired, could be made an Army Councillor, as in the case of the present Deputy C.I.G.S. at the War Office, and he could further, if desired, be British Military Representative on the Supreme War Council.

LHCMA, Robertson Mss, I/24/15

229

General Sir William Robertson to Lord Stamfordham

War Office

[Holograph] 14 February 1918

I hope you were able to get Lord Derby on the telephone and deny the statement he seems to have made about any change in my views. He had no ground for making such a statement. On the contrary when, to my surprise, after lunch he broached the subject I vehemently stated that I could carry out neither in London nor at Versailles the scheme unless it were amended by placing on the Executive Committee the CIGS whoever he might be. He replied I ought not to reply in that way, & I remarked that I was really tired of repeating my views.

The scheme can easily be amended in the way I suggest, & without any political trouble of consequence, and I would be lost to all sense of self respect & businesslike conduct if I endeavoured to work on a scheme which I have repeatedly condemned as unworkable & dangerous. I would be false to the King & to the country to do so, and no amount of persuasion will change my mind, nor would any excuse or dialectical ingenuity serve to cover up my disgrace.

RA, Geo V, F. 1259/23

230

Lord Stamfordham to General Sir William Robertson

[Typescript]

2nd and correct Buckingham Palace

<u>COPY</u> 14 February 1918

Lord Derby has just been here. Evidently I was mistaken in thinking that during the conversation of this afternoon with him, Mr Balfour and myself he stated that you had modified the views expressed by you last evening as to the objections and indeed dangers of the Government arrangement for the control of the Inter-Allied Reserves: for he tells me he did *not* say so.

He desires me to let you know that both Lord Curzon and Mr Balfour after hearing your statement at to-day's Cabinet[29] no longer support you as they failed to see in your arguments evidence that the scheme was unworkable. Lord Derby thinks you should know this before you definitely decide[30] to decline the Government's proposal.

While writing this I received your note which is answered in the above.

I understand that Lord Derby is asking you to continue to carry on the work of the office for the present.

I have reported to the King the gist of what you told me. Needless for me to say with what deep regret His Majesty learnt of the conclusion at which you have arrived.

RA, Geo V, F. 1259/25

231
Lord Derby to General Sir William Robertson

[Typescript] War Office
CONFIDENTIAL and PERSONAL 14 Febuary 1918

I am afraid that I must at last take your 'No' as being a final decision, but I need not tell you with what deep regret I do so. You have been a faithful friend and adviser to me ever since I have been in office, and it is a great blow to think that in this matter we cannot bring our views sufficiently into harmony to enable you to stay on.

I admire extremely the courage which prompts you to adhere to your decision, even though the grounds on which you arrive at it are not those which I can endorse, and I only hope that you part from me with the same regret that I part from you.

After hearing your statement this morning, the Cabinet were quite unanimous in holding to the conditions laid down, though one and all still hoped that you would re-consider your decision. The Cabinet have decided to offer your post to Sir Henry Plumer, on the same conditions as those offered to you, and, in the event of his accepting, I am authorised to offer you the Command in Italy, which I hope you will accept, so as to keep unbroken your service to the country.

Pending an answer from Sir Henry Plumer, I would ask you to carry on your duties as C.I.G.S., and I feel sure that, with your habitual wish to do your duty, you will not refuse me in this request.

I hope I may see you again here, so that we may part with a handshake of mutual regret.

LHCMA, Robertson Mss, I/24/16

232

General Sir William Robertson to Lord Derby

Dictated [typescript] War Office,
Personal & confidential 15 February 1918

I have received your letter of the 14 instant informing me that the Cabinet have decided to offer the post of C.I.G.S. to Sir Herbert Plumer, and asking me to carry on the duties pending an answer from him. I willingly accede to your wishes. I desire to express my gratitude for the recognition you have seen fit to make of the services I have rendered you.

To me it is a matter of great concern that in the interest of the efficient prosecution of the war, the Cabinet have not been able to adopt the method I advised for carrying out their policy with respect to the Inter-Allied Reserves. This is the only question that has ever been at issue, during the last week or so, as far as I am concerned. I had greatly hoped that my advice would have been accepted when you yourself recommended in your memorandum to the Cabinet of the 13th instant, to which you will remember I at once agreed, the adoption of practically the same method.

LHCMA, Robertson Mss, I/24/18

233

Note by General Sir William Robertson on Events of February 11–15

[Typescript with holograph additions] [Undated]

On Monday [11 February] I was informed that Wilson was to be C.I.G.S., and that the Government wished me to go to Versailles.[31] Wilson arrived in London having been sent for on the previous Friday or Saturday.

On Monday afternoon I sent a written reply to the Secretary of State in which I noted that Wilson was to become C.I.G.S. and that I was to go to Versailles. With respect to the latter point I discussed the system which had been set up at Versailles and showed that it would inevitably lead to confusion and perhaps to disaster. I added 'So strongly am I convinced of this that I am compelled to say that I cannot undertake the very great responsibility involved'. There was no resignation about this. I had no appointment to resign from. I had been dismissed as C.I.G.S. and was merely being offered the Versailles appointment, my reply being as just stated.

On Wednesday [13 February] I was asked to consider whether I would remain as C.I.G.S.; the Versailles system to stand as originally stated. My reply to this (in writing) briefly alluded to what I had already said when asked to go to Versailles, and I expressed my desire to serve the Government to the best of my power and to carry out such instructions as they might issue so far as that could possibly be done but I repeated all the old objections and I put up a concrete proposal for placing the C.I.G.S. on the Executive Committee. Again there was no resignation. I was merely asked whether I would remain as C.I.G.S. (having two days before been told that I was to go away) and I could only point out that whether I was C.I.G.S. or whether I went to Versailles the bad system remained.

On Thursday [14 February] I saw the Cabinet and stated the whole case and finished up by asking (this also is now in writing):—

(1) Whether I really was the right man to remain as the Supreme Military Adviser, seeing that my advice was not being accepted on the matter in question.

(2) If nevertheless the Cabinet preferred to retain me would it be wise from their point of view to entrust me with carrying out a system, or would it be fair to ask me to assume the responsibility for working a system, which I regarded as dangerous and unworkable.

On Friday [15 February] morning I was informed that Plumer had been asked to accept the appointment of C.I.G.S. and in the event of his accepting it I was to be offered the command of Italy.

LHCMA, Robertson Mss, I/24/21

234

General Sir William Robertson to Field-Marshal Sir Douglas Haig

[Holograph] War Office
Personal and confidential 15 February 1918

I have just been informed, as underlined above, that Plumer has been wired for to come as CIGS, & if he comes, I shall be offered Italy. Notwithstanding what you said,[32] it seemed to me to be fundamentally bad & dangerous, for you to receive orders from two authorities—Versailles & London—& impossible for anyone but CIGS to give orders about Reserves any more than about anything else. When offered Versailles, therefore, I said I could not undertake the great responsibility involved by this danger. I was then offered CIGS—the Versailles arrangement standing & therefore the danger remained. I could not possibly accept a system as C.I.G.S. which I had already condemned as dangerous and said so. It would have been disgraceful. I may have acted wrongly but I do not think so. My proposal was either that I should be on the Executive Committee with a deputy acting in my absence, or have a deputy on the Committee permanently. This was not accepted. The whole thing is, in fact, a plot to get me out of here. I would have been a useless fool at Versailles, with Wilson here as CIGS, who could always have scotched me. Also there is the real danger involved by dual council & dual responsibility. It was best to be firm & not [. . .] to [. . .]. This I have done. I hope all may soon go well if & when I go, as I suppose I shall. My dealings with you have ever been of the most pleasant nature, & I wish you God speed & good luck.

Please remember this is a personal & confidential communication, & for you *alone*.

NLS, Acc 3155, no. 123, Haig Mss

235

General Sir William Robertson to David Lloyd George

Dictated — War Office
[typescript] — 16 February 1918

I desire to express my thanks for the appreciative words you saw fit to say to me this morning. I have considered the appeal you made to me to endeavour to acquiesce in the system of controlling the Reserves, by which the C.I.G.S. is not on the Executive Committee. Indeed I have considered the same question over and over again during the last fortnight. I deeply regret to say that my conscience will not allow me to depart from the views I expressed to the Cabinet on Thursday last, and in the various papers you had previously seen.

It is a matter of real concern to me that you cannot see your way to adopt the method I have ventured to advise for carrying out your policy in this matter, for I still feel that the method you have decided to adopt must prove unworkable and dangerous. Believe me, it is with the deepest regret that I cannot send you any other reply to your kind personal appeal.

LHCMA, Robertson Mss, I/24/19

236

General Sir William Robertson to Field-Marshal Sir Douglas Haig

[Holograph] — War Office
Personal — 16 February 1918

In continuation of my letter of yesterday I think you should see the two enclosed minutes I sent to Derby. The more I think of it, & the more I am advised, the more I am convinced that the system is fraught with such danger that I could not try to work it without getting into much deeper trouble later. I understand that when the case is stated by the Government in the House of Commons main reliance will be placed on the fact that you said the system was satisfactory. I think you should know this.

NLS, Acc 3155, no. 123, Haig Mss

237

General Sir William Robertson to H. H. Asquith

[Holograph] War Office
Private 16 February 1918

Your advice helped me greatly yesterday, and comprised all I felt.

I feel sure that my actions will be misrepresented next week in the House of Commons, and therefore, at the risk of boring you, I attached a statement,[33] for your personal information, repeating what I said yesterday as to what had passed with respect to the vacating of my appointment. I don't think any one can fairly say I *resigned*, or that I could have said either more or less than I did in order to make my meaning clear.

I thought the 'Evening Standard' was the organ of L. G., but it seems I was wrong, judging from the attached cutting, which puts my views so lucidly that I send it you. I might have written it myself.

Please don't reply or return anything.

P.S. You will understand that, if a separate and independent authority is set up at Versailles, whatever unity of control we may have amongst the Allies, we shall have the exact opposite within the British Army.

Bodleian, Ms Asquith 32, fol. 189

238

General Sir William Robertson to Lord Derby

Dictated [typescript with holograph additions]

War Office
17 February 1918

You will remember that on Thursday evening you informed me that the appointment of C.I.G.S. had been offered to General Plumer, and that pending a reply you wished me to continue to carry on the duties. Last evening you informed me that he had not accepted the offer, and I then reminded you that I awaited your further instructions. These you promised to give me in due course, and in the meantime you requested me to continue to carry on the duties of C.I.G.S. About 8 p.m. last evening a Press representative brought to my house a Press Bureau notice to the effect that the Government had accepted my resignation. I informed him that I had not resigned, and this is so.

Now however that it has been publicly announced that General Sir H. Wilson is to become C.I.G.S. will you please say when you wish me to hand over the duties to him.

LHCMA, Robertson Mss, I/24/20

239

General Sir William Robertson to Lord Stamfordham

War Office
[Holograph] 20 February 1918

It was with something more than usual regret that I took leave of the King last evening as His Majesty's C.I.G.S. Indeed I felt so moved that I fear His Majesty may have thought me indifferent and callous. Quite the reverse was the case, and in fact I scarcely knew how to get through the interview. I have for many years now experienced nothing but the kindest consideration from His Majesty, and at this particular time to be prevented from carrying on the important and difficult work to be done, for the welfare and safety of the country and the throne, is to me a real sorrow. Nothing less than absolute necessity would have caused me to act as I did, and looking back, I still think that in the end my actions will prove to be in the best interests. I believe, and I certainly hope, that His Majesty does not disagree with this view. The King's last act of kindness in allowing me to stay on in York House makes me think that if I did wrong I have been forgiven. No answer is expected to this.

RA, Geo V, F. 1259/37

240

Note by Sir William Robertson

War Office

[Typescript minuted by Robertson[34]] [Undated]

For some months before I ceased to be C.I.G.S. the advice I gave to the War Cabinet on certain vital questions of strategy and general military policy was either unheeded or rejected, and it daily became more evident that, for practical purposes, I did not possess their confidence. On the 11th February last, when the Secretary of State for War informed me that two days earlier he and the Prime Minister had decided to replace me as C.I.G.S. he told me, that the P.M. could not 'get on' with me, and the Prime Minister himself, in my final interview with him on the 16th of February, told me that, notwithstanding our friendly personal relations, we had for some time past differed on important military questions.[35] This was so, as for instance, when at the last Versailles conference which I attended I felt it to be my duty, greatly to my regret, to oppose the Prime Minister's proposal to adopt the dangerous and impracticable plan put forward by the M.A.[36] of the Versailles Council for an offensive campaign against Turkey.

The military situation is, in my opinion, now so grave and difficult as to demand that the War Cabinet shall, subject to the general policy of the Allies, leave the responsible Generals they employ absolutely free and unfettered in the conduct of military operations, and for this it is obvious that they must have complete confidence in those Generals. It would be idle, in view of what has been said above, to pretend that they have any confidence in me, or that I have faith in the methods which they have hitherto pursued in the military conduct of the war.

This absence of mutual confidence between the War Cabinet and myself was the real cause of my ceasing to be C.I.G.S., and, as I have frequently reminded the War Cabinet in the past, without such confidence—and especially at the present time—it is futile to hope for the best results. These facts, which I submit with full respect to the War Cabinet, are so important and far reaching in their consequences that they cannot be ignored.

While I am anxious to do everything I can to help to retrieve the serious position in which the Empire is now placed, I am nevertheless of the opinion that to undertake the appointment on the pretence of giving help when I feel that it is not possible for me to give it, must eventually cause disappointment to His Majesty's Ministers and bring disgrace upon myself.

LHCMA, Robertson Mss, I/24/22

Notes

1. The standard biographical sources for Robertson are Frederick B. Maurice's essay in the *Dictionary of National Biography*; Robertson's two books, *From Private to Field-Marshal* (Houghton Mifflin Company, Boston and New York, 1921), and *Soldiers and Statesmen 1914–1918* (Charles Scribner's Sons, New York, 1926, 2 vols); and Victor Bonham-Carter, *Soldier True: The Life and Times of Field-Marshal Sir William Robertson* (Frederick Muller Limited, London, 1963).
2. Bonham-Carter, *Soldier True*, p. 5.
3. Quartermasters and ridingmasters, of course, were a separate category and not counted in these figures. Ian F. W. Beckett and Keith Simpson, eds. *A Nation in Arms: A Social Study of the British Army in the First World War* (Manchester University Press, 1985), p. 64.
4. Robertson, *Private to Field-Marshal*, p. 77.
5. Ibid., p. 17.
6. Ibid., p. 79.
7. Brian Bond, *The Victorian Army and the Staff College 1854–1914* (Eyre Methuen, London, 1972), p. 162.
8 Robertson, *Private to Field-Marshal*, p. 103.
9. Ibid., p. 170; General Sir George de S. Barrow, *The Fire of Life* (Hutchinson & Co., London, c. 1942), p. 120.
10. Robertson, *Private to Field-Marshal*, pp. 169–85; Bond, *Victorian Army and Staff College*, pp. 275–88; and Keith Jeffery, ed., *The Military Correspondence of Field Marshal Sir Henry Wilson 1918–1922* (Published for the Army Records Society by The Bodley Head, London, 1985), p. 6.
11. Robertson, *Private to Field-Marshal*, p. 184.
12. See Ian F. W. Beckett, ed., *The Army and the Curragh Incident* (Published for the Army Records Society by The Bodley Head, London, 1986), pp. 22–3, 69–70, 277–8.
13. E. L. Spears, *Prelude to Victory* (Jonathan Cape, London, 1939), p. 33.
14. Ibid., p. 35.
15. Robertson once told a fellow officer, George Barrow, never to argue with politicians. 'If you do he will gently push and shoulder you until he gets you into a road with a dead end, then you are done. But, mind you, don't say anything, or he will settle the matter under discussion over your head.' How, Barrow wanted to know, could the give and take of debate be avoided. Robertson picked up a piece of geranium and said: 'Every time he argues, you say "This is a geranium." When he says, "It looks to me like a camelia" or "I think it's a carnation," or "It smells like a rose," or "It might be a hibiscus," you don't try to prove that it is not a camelia, or a carnation, or a rose, or hibiscus; you simply repeat "It's a geranium."' Barrow, *Fire of Life*, p. 164.

16 Spears, *Prelude to Victory*, p. 34.
17 Lord Hankey, *The Supreme Command 1914–1918* (George Allen and Unwin Limited, London, 1962, 2 vols.), II, p. 446.
18 Tim Travers, *The Killing Ground: The British Army, the Western Front and the Emergence of Modern Warfare 1900–1918* (Allen & Unwin, London, 1987), p. 19.
19. RA, Geo V, Q. 2522/3/172, Robertson to Wigram, 24 March 1915.
20. See Richard Holmes, *The Little Field-Marshal* (Jonathan Cape, London, 1981).
21. Diary entry of 1 June 1915, Hankey, *Supreme Command*, I, p. 339.
22. See the perceptive comments on the formulation of British strategy, 1914–1915, in John Gooch, *The Plans of War: The General Staff and British Military Strategy c. 1900–1916* (John Wiley & Sons, New York, 1974), pp. 299–300.
23. Hankey had indeed been furnishing the civilians with strategic appreciations. Major-General Sir Charles E. Callwell had returned to service as Director of Military Operations in the War Office, 1914–1915. LHCMA, Robertson Mss, I/12/3, Robertson to Lord Stamfordham, undated.
24. NLS, Acc 3155, no. 103, Haig Mss, Robertson to Haig, 17 November 1915.
25. Robertson, *Soldiers and Statesmen*, I, p. 162.
26. Ibid., p. 205.
27. Bodleian, Mss Selborne 95, fols. 22–23, Robertson to Selborne, 24 March 1927.
28. RA, Geo V, Q. 838/61, Robertson to Wigram, 11 December 1915.

NOTES TO CHAPTER I

1 Robertson, *Private to Field-Marshal*, p. 246.
2. British Library, Northcliffe Mss, 62335, Robertson to Northcliffe, 14 February 1917.
3. It has been suggested by David French in his excellent study that the use of 'easterners' and 'westerners' to describe the schism over British grand strategy is 'a caricature of the debate about war policy conducted within the British government'. It is undoubtedly correct that the shorthand use of 'easterner' and 'westerner' has led to oversimplification. But in Robertson's and Haig's case, it can be argued, this characterisation is both valid and useful. Both men believed, as Haig expressed it, that the war had 'to be won in London'. In other words, the high command must keep the

strategic control of the war out of the hands of the civilians so that British war resources would be mobilised and concentrated on the western front and the 'side shows' either limited or eliminated. The readers of these documents can decide for themselves whether the paradigmatic use of 'easterner' (or indirect) and 'westerner' (or direct) contributes to an understanding of the conflict over the deployment of British military resources during the Great War. See David French, *British Strategy & War Aims 1914–1916* (Allen & Unwin, London, 1987), p. x; for Haig's remark quoted above, see chapter II, document 78.

4. Robertson, *Soldiers and Statesmen*, II, p. 83.
5. H. of Lords RO, Lloyd George Mss, D/18/2/19, Memorandum by Lloyd George, 17 June 1916.
6. For the Kitchener-Robertson compact, a copy of which Robertson forwarded to Lloyd George on 24 June 1916, see Robertson, *Soldiers and Statesmen*, I, pp. 168–71; Bonham-Carter has reproduced most of the Robertson-Lloyd George correspondence, 26 June, over the terms of Lloyd George's position as Secretary of State for War in his *Soldier True*, pp. 179–81.
7. For a perceptive discussion of the conscription crisis during this period, see R. J. Q. Adams and Philip P. Poirier, *The Conscription Controversy in Great Britain, 1900–18* (Ohio State University Press, 1987), pp. 144–70.
8. Bodleian, Mss Dawson 66, fols. 49–52, 'Notes of interview with Robertson', 14 April 1916.
9. See Travers, *Killing Ground*, pp. 127–46.
10. The toe of Gallipoli Peninsula which Britian still retained control of after the evacuation of the Anzac and Suvla Bay beachheads. The last British troops were evacuated from Helles during the second week of January 1916.
11. Sir Henry B. Jackson had been appointed First Sea Lord after Fisher's resignation in May 1915.
12. Egypt was the base for all British troops operating in the Mediterranean theatre. Evacuated troops from Gallipoli were being refitted, some of whom were being sent to the new Salonika front in the Balkans. General Sir Archibald J. Murray, whom Robertson had replaced as CIGS, had just been appointed to command a British force (later to be known as the Egyptian Expeditionary Force) behind and on the Suez Canal. Lieutenant-General Sir John Grenfell Maxwell, however, remained the General Commanding Force in Egypt. The muddled command and administration of the ever-growing forces in Egypt were unacceptable to Robertson.
13. Reginald McKenna became Chancellor of the Exchequer in 1915 when Lloyd George became the head of the new Ministry of Munitions.

14. Balfour joined Lloyd George, who had vigorously lobbied for a great campaign in the Balkans in 1915, in opposing a large-scale British offensive on the western front in 1916. Balfour, when asked how Germany could be beaten if not in the West, had argued that 'the weakest part of the German line was the Russian front'. Balfour also prepared a memorandum critical of Robertson's strategy, which Robertson refused to answer with one of his own. See PRO, Cab 42/6/14, War Committee, 28 December 1915; Robertson to Haig, 5 January 1916, Robert Blake, ed., *The Private Papers of Douglas Haig, 1914–1919* (Eyre & Spottiswoode, London, 1952), pp. 122–23; and PRO, Cab 42/7/5, memorandum by Balfour, 27 December 1915.
15. Lloyd George, who favoured operations in Mesopotamia, Palestine or Salonika over the Western front, had gained the War Committee's support for an Anglo-French conference to discuss munitions requirements for a successful offensive against the German trenches. PRO, Cab 42/7/5, War Committee, 13 January 1916. Robertson had written Haig on 13 January that Lloyd George's interest in Allied discussions on munitions was 'the thin end of the wedge for deferring matters'. Blake, *Private Papers of Haig*, pp. 124–25.
16. The War Committee refused to give unequivocal support to Haig's and Robertson's western strategy (which had earlier been accepted by the Allied generals meeting at the Chantilly military conference). Robertson's memoranda of 23 December 1915 and 1 January 1916 in favour of concentrating British military power in France and Flanders can be found in PRO, Cab 42/6/14 and 42/7/1 respectively. On 28 December 1915, the ministers had only agreed to preparations for—not the launching of—an offensive: 'Every effort is to be made to prepare to carry out the offensive'. On 13 January 1916, they continued to hedge on a commitment to a large-scale British offensive: 'Every effort is to be made to prepare for carrying out offensive operations next spring in the main theatre of the war in close co-operation with the Allies, and the greatest possible strength, although it must not be assumed that such offensive operations are finally decided on.' PRO, Cab 42/6/14 and 42/7/5, War Committee, 28 December 1915 and 13 January 1916.
17. Second-Lieutenant Brian Robertson, the CIGS's eldest son, became an aide-de-camp to Haig. He later served on the general staff of the XI. Corps before becoming an infantry brigade-major. He was awarded both the Military Cross and the Distinguished Service Order for his wartime service. He subsequently had a long and most distinguished military career, rising to the rank of general.
18. Written above 'most' is 'the rest'. It is written in a different ink from the rest of the letter and is followed by a question mark.

19. Lieutenant-General Sir H. C. Sclater.
20. Lieutenant-General Sir J. S. Cowans.
21. Note prepared by the CIGS for the War Committee on the assistance that diplomacy might render to naval and military operations. PRO, Cab 22/8, 12 February 1916.
22. John Arbuthnot Fisher, the former First Sea Lord, 1904–10 and 1914–15, was involved in an unsuccessful effort to be re-instated as First Sea Lord. Churchill, who commanded a battalion in France, 1915–16, agreed with many of Fisher's criticisms of the Admiralty and demanded in a speech in Parliament on 7 March 1916 that Fisher be returned to the Admiralty. Churchill suffered a severe humiliation when he gathered almost no support in Parliament or the press for this suggestion.
23. On 8 March 1916, Robertson sent an identical letter to Haig. LHCMA, Robertson Mss, I/22/30.
24. The British force in Mesopotamia advancing on Baghdad had been driven back and encircled in Kut-el-Amara, on the Tigris.
25. The papers mentioned are apparently: Memorandum by the CIGS regarding the supply of personnel, PRO, Cab 22/80, 21 March 1916, and Note by the CIGS on the situation at Salonika, PRO, Cab 22/14, 22 March 1916.
26. The Military Service Act of January imposed conscription on bachelors and childless widowers (ages 18–41). Ministers, the population of Ireland, the medically unfit, conscientious objectors and men in essential employment, however, were excluded.
27. Underlining is apparently Haig's. Kut-el-Amara surrendered on 29 April 1916.
28. Robertson has written in margin opposite: 'Castelnau is at the bottom of all the trouble I believe'.
29. Underlining is apparently Haig's.
30. An abortive Irish Republic had been proclaimed in Dublin by rebels on Easter Sunday.
31. Haig has written in margin opposite: 'Our Navy is mentally licked'.
32. Asquith introduced on 2 May a bill in Parliament making compulsory service universal. Lloyd George had strongly backed the Army Council, threatening to join this body in resignation if Asquith refused to conscript married men. See diary entry of 17 April 1916, A. J. P. Taylor, ed., *Lloyd George: A Diary by Frances Stevenson* (Hutchinson, London, 1971), pp. 105–6; and Adams, *Conscription Controversy*, pp. 157–64.
33. Lieutenant-General Sir Francis J. Davies. Murray had sent Davies home on a month's leave. Davies stayed on in the capacity of Military Secretary in the War Office.
34. External evidence would seem to suggest that this letter was written on or

about 24 May 1916 and probably reflects Robertson's and the Army Council's concern that some members of Asquith's coalition government favoured a compromise peace. In February 1916 Colonel E. M. House, President Woodrow Wilson's special emissary, and Sir Edward Grey, the British Foreign Secretary, had agreed on conditions for U.S. mediation of the conflict, but the War Committee had not then thought that a peace effort by Wilson was either militarily necessary or politically advantageous from the British point of view. In two communications (19 and 23 May), House pressed the British government to make use of the so-called House-Grey agreement. The Army Council, whose members included Robertson and Kitchener, threatened resignation if the civilians took up the U.S. offer of mediation. When the War Committee discussed the question on 24 May, the military advisers and the secretary Hankey were excused. No record was kept of the discussion. See diary entry of 24 May 1916, Steven Roskill, *Hankey, Man of Secrets*, vol. 1: *1877–1918* (Collins, London, 1970), p. 274; John Milton Cooper Jr., 'The British Response to the House Grey Memorandum: New Evidence and New Questions', *Journal of American History* 59 (March 1973), pp. 958–71; and David R. Woodward, 'Great Britain and President Wilson's Efforts to End World War I in 1916', *Maryland Historian* 1 (Spring 1970), pp. 45–58.

35. Lloyd George, and even more so, Hankey, were critical of the military information being provided by Robertson to the War Committee. Hankey wrote Asquith on 23 May 1916: '... I would submit that the information they [members of War Committee] at present receive, both from the Admiralty and the War Office, is utterly inadequate for the proper discharge of their responsibility'. PRO, Cab 42/14/12.
36. Underlining is apparently Haig's.
37. Haig gave Robertson mixed signals on his intentions. This letter would appear to indicate that he was not contemplating a breakthrough, but this was misleading. His 1806 reference in this letter refers to Napoleon's cavalry exploitation of the defeated Prussians at Jena. According to Travers, the result of Haig's bold objectives and General Sir H. Rawlinson's cautious or 'bite and hold' tactics was that the 'final Somme plan was a mixture of limited objectives and unlimited offensive'. Travers, *Killing Ground*, p. 136.
38. The knowledgeable newspaper correspondent, Philip Gibbs, described Haig's attitude towards the press at this meeting as follows: 'The Commander-in-Chief was sympathetic, but his sympathy was expressed in words which revealed a complete misunderstanding of our purpose and of our work, and was indeed no less than an insult, unconscious but very hurtful'. It must be stressed, however, that Haig relaxed censorship. *Now It* Can *Be Told* (Harper & Brothers Publishers, London, 1920), p. 29.

NOTES TO CHAPTER II

1. John Keegan, *The Face of Battle: A Study of Agincourt, Waterloo & the Somme* (Vintage Books, New York, 1977), p. 255.
2. Travers, *Killing Ground*, p. 153.
3. A good recent account on the Imperial General Staff's strategic appreciation of the situation in Russia and the Balkans can be found in Keith Neilson, *Strategy and Supply: The Anglo-Russian Alliance, 1914–17* (George Allen & Unwin, London, 1984), pp. 141–70.
4. RA, Geo V, Q. 1200/6, memorandum by Stamfordham, 12 October 1916.
5. PRO, Cab 42/22/14, memorandum by Hankey, 31 October 1916.
6. David R. Woodward, *Lloyd George and the Generals* (Published for the University of Delaware Press by the Associated University Press, Newark, N. J., 1983), pp. 118–19.
7. Hunter-Weston must share some of the blame for the ineffective artillery. He refused to allow his heavy artillery to continue firing after zero hour; in fact, he halted the barrage ten minutes before zero hour. See Travers, *Killing Ground*, p. 158.
8. Joffre and Haig had had a strong disagreement about the direction in which Haig should continue his attack. Haig looked to his right, but Joffre ordered him to attack Thiepval and Pozières on his left. Standing his ground, Haig reminded Joffre that he—not Joffre—commanded the BEF.
9. This unsuccessful attempt to break the German trenches in September 1915 was the greatest Entente offensive since trench warfare had replaced the war of movement of the first months of the war. The British were assigned a supporting role at Loos.
10. Neutral Roumania was at this time negotiating the terms of an alliance with the Entente. One condition of her alliance was that she receive help from the Allied force at Salonika and from the Russians in the Dobrudja.
11. On this day the British campaign on the Somme began its second stage with a resounding success by Rawlinson's Fourth Army. Rawlinson's tactics (which had been initially opposed by Haig) were much closer to Robertson's tactics of limited objectives than Haig's grand tactical scheme of 1 July which had aimed at a breakthrough.
12. On 4 August 1916, Baron Friedrich Kress von Kressenstein, who commanded a Turkish force that included German artillery and trench mortar units, launched an attack on Murray's force which was advancing into the Sinai towards the Palestinian frontier.
13. Robertson's forecast proved to be too optimistic. Paul von Lettow-Vorbeck, a master of guerrilla warfare, kept a force in the field against the British until two weeks after the 11 November 1918 Armistice.
14. Grand Duke Nicholas Nikolaevich, the uncle of Tsar Nicholas II.

Formerly the Russian Commander-in-Chief, the Grand Duke was now viceroy of Transcaucasia and commander of the Caucasian front.

15. On 5 June 1916, Sherif Husein, the ruler of Hejaz, or northwest Saudi Arabia, on the Gulf of Aqaba and Red Sea, had launched a successful revolt against his Turkish overlords.
16. Major-General Herbert Lawrence, who had been in charge of the successful evacuation of Helles; replaced Kiggell as Chief of General Staff, BEF, in 1918.
17. Robertson had written Haig on 29 July 1916, warning him that: 'The Powers that be are beginning to get a little uneasy in regard to the situation. The casualties are mounting up and they are wondering whether we are likely to get a proper return for them'. Haig had been much provoked, writing on this letter: 'Not exactly the letter of a CIGS. He ought to take responsibility also'. Bonham-Carter, *Soldier True*, p.182.
18. Sir Frederick E. Smith, Attorney-General, 1915–1919, and Churchill were the most vocal critics of the results of the Somme Offensive. A critical analysis, written by Churchill with an introduction by Smith, was circulated to the War Committee on 1 August 1916. PRO, Cab 37/153/3.
19. Haig was assured of the War Committee's 'full support' despite his blunt warning that his offensive must 'go well into the autumn' and that another large-scale offensive would be required in 1917. PRO, Cab 42/17/3, War Committee, 5 August 1917.
20. Lieutenant-Colonel Brinsley Fitzgerald was close to Lord French. As one of his ADCs in May 1915, he had represented his commander-in-chief's views to Lloyd George, Bonar Law and Balfour during the political crisis over the shortage of shells.
21. Haig, and even more so, Robertson, had sought a promotion for Lieutenant-General Sir R. C. Maxwell, the BEF's Quartermaster General. Lloyd George did not then or later approve this promotion.
22. Underlining is apparently Haig's.
23. See note 19 above.
24. In early August there had been some concern in the government that Germany might seek American mediation to avoid defeat on the battlefield.
25. The Battle of Jutland, 31 May 1916.
26. Lieutenant-General A. S. Cobbe, Lieutenant-General F. S. Maude, Lieutenant- General Sir P. H. N. Lake, Major-General W. T. Furse, Major-General E. M. Perceval, Major-General J. E. Capper, Lieutenant-General G. F. Gorringe, Major-General G. T. Forestier-Walker, Major General R. Fanshawe, and Lieutenant-General R. G. Broadwood.
27. Roumania joined the Entente on 27 August 1916. Lloyd George urged the General Staff to prevent Britain's newest ally from meeting Serbia's fate.

H. of Lords RO, Lloyd George Mss, E/1/5/6, Lloyd George to Director of Military Operations (Maurice), 4 September 1916.

28. The tank was first used in warfare on 15 September 1916 on the Somme.

29. There was at this time already strong disagreement between the intelligence authorities at the War Office and GHQ about the reporting of the war to the British public. Major-General George M. W. Macdonogh, the intelligence chief in the War Office, enjoyed the confidence of Robertson while Haig had complete faith in the often exaggerated estimates of German losses and morale given him by his friend and chief intelligence officer Brigadier-General John Charteris. See LHCMA, II/3, Clive Diary, 6 and 26 September 1916.

30. On a recent trip to the front, Lloyd George had angered Haig and his staff when he had undiplomatically asked French officers about differences in French and British artillery and infantry tactics. See Woodward, *Lloyd George and the Generals*, pp. 105–6.

31. See PRO, Cab 42/19/6, memorandum by Robertson, 9 September 1916; and PRO, Cab 42/19/6, War Committee, 12 September 1916.

32. Lloyd George's outburst against what he alleged to be the Imperial General Staff's indifference to the Balkans in general and the enemy threat to Roumania in particular can be found in PRO, Cab 42/21/3, War Committee, 9 October 1916.

33. Rabegh, a port on the Red Sea between Medina and Mecca, became significant when Sherif Husein, after taking Mecca, failed to capture Medina, which remained under Turkish control. When Turkish reinforcements arrived on the scene, some British civilians led by Lloyd George wanted to send a small British force to Rabegh to keep Mecca out of the hands of the Turks. The political considerations, primarily British prestige in the East, were emphasised by the civilians. See PRO, Cab 42/19/1 and 42/20/3, War Committee, 1 and 18 September 1916; V. H. Rothwell, *British War Aims and Peace Diplomacy 1914–1918* (Clarendon Press, Oxford, 1971), pp. 87–95.

34. Paul Manatoux; French history professor who served as interpreter when Lloyd George met with Albert Thomas, the French Minister of Munitions.

35. Lord Northcliffe had earlier in the day invaded the War Office and threatened to launch an all-out press assault if Lloyd George did not stop interfering with strategy. See Woodward, *Lloyd George and the Generals*, p. 110.

36. Lloyd George did get the Army Council to go on record opposing 'unauthorised communication from official sources to the Press'. PRO, WO 163/21, Army Council (190), 13 October 1916.

37. This was the second British division that the War Committee (over Robertson's objections) had decided to divert to the Balkans. Robertson, however, did get the War Committee's support for not extending the

British military role in Salonika. PRO, Cab 42/21/6 and 42/22/5, War Committee, 12 and 24 October 1916; PRO, Cab 28/1/I.C.–11, Allied Conference (Boulogne), 20 October 1916.

38. Lieutenant-Colonel A. G. Stern, Director, Ministry of Munitions.
39. See Robertson to Lloyd George, 27 September 1916. David Lloyd George, *War Memoirs* (Odhams Press Ltd., London, 1938, 2 vols.), I, pp. 463–64.
40. Lloyd George had used Robertson's realistic appreciation of the military situation to question the efficacy of concentrating British resources in France and Flanders. For Robertson's views on the course of the war, see 'A general review of the situation in all theatres of war, together with a comparison of the military resources of the Entente and of the Central Powers', PRO, Cab 24/2/G.85, October 1916; and PRO, Cab 42/23/4, Robertson's minute read to War Cabinet by Lloyd George, 3 November 1916.
41. Misspelled. General Porro was Cadorna's Chief of Staff.
42. Leonido Bissolati, Italian socialist politician and Commissioner for War Services in 1916; Lloyd George had suggested to Hankey on 1 November that his opposition to the present conduct of the war was so great that he might jointly resign with Bissolati and Albert Thomas. See Churchill College, 1/1, Hankey Diary, 1 November 1916.
43. Lieutenant-General Sir Henry H. Wilson was disliked by both Haig and Robertson, who thought him in the camp of Lord French and in league with certain politicians.
44. Since Robertson left London in the company of Asquith on 14 November, this letter must be misdated.
45. Lord Lansdowne had circulated a paper in mid-November to the War Committee suggesting a compromise peace. Robertson, egged on by Lloyd George, had responded in intemperate language to any suggestion of a negotiated peace. He wrote: 'There are amongst us, as in all communities, a certain number of cranks, cowards, and philosophers, some of whom are afraid of their own skins being hurt, whilst others are capable of proving to those sufficiently weakminded to listen to them that we stand to gain more by losing the war than by winning it ... We need pay no attention to those miserable members of society'. PRO, Cab 37/160/15, 24 November 1916.
46. Gwynne was plotting to remove Asquith. His group was called 'All the Talents'. IWM, Gwynne Mss, Pt. III, fols. 281–82, Lord Milner to Gwynne, 27 November 1916.
47. See PRO, Cab 37/160/20, 27 November 1916.
48. Robertson minuted (3 December 1916) this note as follows: 'Secretary of State. I attach a note. A very great deal depends, of course, upon the Chief Command of the Entente Forces'.

49. See PRO, Cab 24/2/G.85, October 1916.
50. At this time a rumour was circulating in London that Robertson (working with Northcliffe) was behind the political crisis. There is, however, no evidence to support this conspiracy thesis. See LHCMA, II/3, Clive Diary, 4 December 1916.
51. The debate over the introduction of national service played a role in Asquith's downfall, but Robertson seems to have exaggerated its importance and misunderstood the chain of events that led to a new government. See Adams, *Conscription Controversy*, pp. 171–89; and Woodward, *Lloyd George and the Generals*, pp. 116–32.

NOTES TO CHAPTER III

1. PRO, Cab 42/19/2, memorandum by Hankey, 8 December 1916. This memorandum was never officially numbered and was filed incorrectly with the Cabinet Papers for September 1916.
2. Woodward, *Lloyd George and the Generals*, pp. 133–59.
3. PRO, Cab 23/2, War Cabinet (92), 9 March 1917.
4. PRO, Cab 23/13, War Cabinet (135A), 9 May 1917.
5. See document 136.
6. General Robert G. Nivelle had become Commander-in-Chief of the French Armies in the West. Joffre, given a marshal's baton, was pushed into the background.
7. The French were now requesting an additional two British divisions for the Balkan front. The Allies had agreed at the recent Chantilly Conference to launch simultaneous attacks from the Danube and Salonika, but Robertson argued that the collapse of Roumania made such an offensive policy impossible. PRO, Cab 23/1, War Cabinet (1), 9 December 1916.
8. On 12 December 1916, Germany and her allies had made an insincere proposal for peace negotiations. President Wilson on 18 December had then asked all belligerents to state their peace terms.
9. Sir Rennell Rodd, British Ambassador to Italy, 1908–1919.
10. An identical letter, written on the same day, was sent to Lloyd George. H. of Lords RO, Lloyd George Mss, F/44/3/5.
11. Major-General Sir Robert Dundas Whigham.
12. Lieutenant-General Sir J. S. Cowans, Quartermaster-General, 1912–1919.
13. Turkish outpost south of frontier of Palestine; captured by Murray on 23 December 1916.
14. Austen Chamberlain, Secretary for India, 1915–1917; member of War Cabinet, 1918.

15. Second Turkish frontier post to fall to Murray; captured on 9 January 1917 by five brigades of light horse, yeomanry and camelry.
16. PRO, Cab 24/3, Cabinet Paper G 106 of January 1917. Hankey had played the key role in preparing this strategic appreciation.
17. General Henri J. E. Gouraud, the French commander at Gallipoli.
18. General Sir Ian Hamilton, the British commander at Gallipoli.
19. For these instructions, see PRO, Cab 23/1, War Cabinet (36), 17 January 1917.
20. The memorandum (then in an early draft) of which Robertson speaks must be the one in which he argued that 'the question of success or failure may hang in the balance for some considerable time'. Robertson also drove home the point that Nivelle's plan might endanger Haig's planned offensive to clear the Flanders coast of German U-boat bases in 1917. LHCMA, Roberton Mss, I/21/50/2, Memorandum by Robertson, 24 January 1917.
21. Instructions along this line by order of the War Cabinet were sent to Haig. See PRO, Cab 23/1, War Cabinet (50), 31 January 1917.
22. General N. N. Baratov, Russian cavalry commander who had lost ground against the Turks in northern Persia after some initial success.
23. In February the Army Council warned that the prior failure of the government to provide additional recruits now made it impossible to keep the armies in France up to strength in the coming months. See Adams, *Conscription Controversy in Great Britain*, pp. 199–200.
24. The War Office classified British recruits from categories 'A' to 'E' according to their fitness and availability.
25. See PRO, Cab 23/1, War Cabinet (64), 13 February 1917. Appendix I.
26. See Adams, *Conscription Controversy in Great Britain*, pp. 200–203.
27. Lloyd George had given the ministers the impression that Haig's position vis-a-vis the French high command was little changed because Haig, on Lord Kitchener's instructions, had always subordinated British to French strategy on the western front. PRO, CAB 23/1, War Cabinet (82), 28 February 1917.
28. Major-General Sir W. E. Peyton was head of the Military Secretary's Branch.
29. Presumably this refers to the memorandum in which Robertson argued that he had signed the Calais agreement subordinating Haig to Nivelle because the War Cabinet's decision left him constitutionally no other alternative. PRO, Cab 24/6, Cabinet Paper G. T. 93, 2 March 1917.
30. Lord Milner had just returned from leading the British delegation to the Petrograd Conference, an Allied meeting which had its origins in Lloyd George's proposal to send Robertson to Russia in September and later in November 1916.

31. Nivelle wanted and got Sir Henry Wilson (who was wrongly suspected by Haig and others of being too favourable to the French point of view) as head of the British mission at French General Headquarters.
32. On 7 March the French government had demanded that Haig be forced to comply with the Calais agreement. Nivelle also secretly got in touch with Lloyd George and suggested that General Sir Robert Gough, the Commander of the Fifth Army, replace Haig. See Woodward, *Lloyd George and the Generals*, p. 151.
33. On 9 April the day Haig launched a successful attack at Arras to assist Nivelle's forthcoming offensive, the French Minister of War Paul Painlevé, who had just replaced Lyautey, came to London and appeared to suggest to Lloyd George that four British and four French divisions be sent to the Italian theatre. See PRO, Cab 23/2, War Cabinet (116), 10 April 1917.
34. In March (new style calendar) the Romanov dynasty had been overthrown and replaced by the Provisional Government.
35. The number and quality of the BEF's artillery had improved dramatically since the opening of the Somme offensive. Haig had almost doubled his heavy guns and howitzers since mid-1916. It should be noted, however, that the British still remained behind the French in howitzers and heavy guns. French divisions had twice the number of a British division. See Trevor Wilson, *The Myriad Faces of War: Britain and the Great War, 1914–1918* (Polity Press, Cambridge, 1986), p. 449.
36. Smuts had come to London in March to attend a conference of dominion prime ministers. Delighted to have on hand a man who considered the political as well as the military aspects of strategy, Lloyd George had asked the South African to assess present Allied strategy.
37. At the beginning of 1916, Lieutenant-General Lord Cavan had taken command of the XIV Corps; thought by many to be the best corps commander in the BEF; Lloyd George considered him as Haig's replacement in July 1918.
38. General Sir H. S. Horne, Commander of First Army; his troops had captured Vimy Ridge (9–10 April 1917).
39. Major-General Tom Bridges.
40. Boris V. Sturmer, incompetent who was Rasputin's choice as Russian Prime Minister; thought to be pro-German; even accused in Duma (without evidence) of being a German agent.
41. Lloyd George was eager for Smuts to replace Murray as Commander-in-Chief of the Egyptian Expeditionary Force.
42. Foch had replaced Pétain as Chief of the General Staff when the former had succeeded Nivelle as Commander-in-Chief.
43. Lloyd George had agreed to support the removal of British troops from the

Balkans, but only if these troops were transferred to Egypt instead of France. See Robertson, *Soldiers and Statesmen*, II, p. 143.

NOTES TO CHAPTER IV

1. Lloyd George, *War Memoirs*, II, p. 1252.
2. IWM, Sir Henry Wilson Diary, 8 June 1917.
3. C. à Court Repington, *The First World War 1914–1918* (Constable and Company Ltd., London, 1920, 2 vols.), I, p. 571. In June Haig had shown his displeasure towards the Imperial General Staff's appreciation of the military situation by underlining the statements: 'the morale of the German troops has not been affected by their reverses or by the adoption of a purely defensive role to such an extent as to make a decisive success for the Entente probable in the near future' and 'there is no reason to doubt the ability of the Central Powers to continue the war into next year'. NLS, Acc 3155, no. 114, 'Summary of the Military Situation in the Various Theatres of War for the Seven Days ending 14th June, with comments by the General Staff'.
4. PRO, W.O. 106/1513, 'Conference held at Abbeville on the 7th June, 1917, between General Foch and Sir William Robertson'.
5. Diary entry of 9 June 1917, Blake, *Private Papers of Haig*, p. 236.
6. PRO, Cab 23/3, War Cabinet (159), 8 June 1917.
7. Bonar Law was not an official member, but he was usually in attendance.
8. Robertson to Haig, 13 June 1917, Blake, *Private Papers of Haig*, p. 239.
9. NLS, Acc 3155, no. 161, Haig Mss, Haig to Lady Haig, 30 May 1917.
10. Woodward, *Lloyd George and the Generals*, pp. 181–82.
11. Robertson gives no date for this meeting. See Robertson, *Soldiers and Statesmen*, II, p. 262.
12. PRO, Cab 23/13, War Cabinet (225 A), 28 August 1917.
13. PRO, Cab 27/8, W.P. 52, Allenby to Robertson, 9 October 1917; for Robertson's suggestion that five additional divisions were necessary to hold the Jaffa-Jerusalem line, see PRO, Cab 27/8, G.T. 2242, 'Occupation of Jaffa-Jerusalem Line', 9 October 1917.
14. PRO, Cab 27/6, War Policy Committee (21), 9 October 1917 (misdated 11 October 1917).
15. Haig's planned operations included a surprise attack from the sea as his forces approached the enemy-held ports of Ostend and Zeebrugge.
16. See PRO, Cab 27/7, W.P. 43 and 45, 'War Policy on West Front', 19 July 1917, and 'Palestine', 19 July 1917.
17. At the beginning of July (new style calendar), the Russians launched their last offensive of the war. After making initial progress in Galicia against the

equally war-weary Austrians, the Russians were driven back in disarray by an Austro-German counteroffensive. On July 16–17, demonstrations (the so-called 'July Days') erupted in Petrograd.

18. See document 104, chapter III.
19. This important letter is in Blake, *Private Papers of Haig*, pp. 251–52.
20. Ellipsis points are Haig's.
21. Russian socialists had invited socialists from all countries to meet in Stockholm to consider a compromise peace. On 10 August a special Labour Party conference voted to send a British delegation, a decision opposed by a majority of the British people, including many in the labour movement. Henderson, the Labour representative in the War Cabinet, was forced to resign on 11 August over this controversy. Refused passports, no British delegates attended this international socialist conference.
22. Robertson had just returned from a visit to GHQ where Haig had upbraided the government for considering side shows and not providing him with more men and guns. John Terraine, *The Road to Passchendaele: The Flanders Offensive of 1917, A Study in Inevitability* (Leo Cooper, London, 1977), pp. 229–30.
23. An enduring myth is that the British government kept a secret army in Britain, denying Haig reinforcements. See David R. Woodward, 'Did Lloyd George Starve the British Army of Men Prior to the German Offensive of 21 March 1918', *Historical Journal*, 27, 1 (1984), pp. 241–52.
24. At the Battle of Langemark on 16 August, the Allied attack, hampered by pill-boxes and enemy counterattacks, had actually achieved little. Quite incorrectly Haig characterised the day's fighting as 'a decided success for the Allies'. J. H. Boraston, ed., *Sir Douglas Haig's Despatches (December 1915 – April 1919)* (J. M. Dent & Sons Ltd., London, 1919), p. 119.
25. Misspelled. Major-General C. Delmé-Radcliffe, the British military liaison officer attached to the Italian Army.
26. News had arrived from the British ambassador in Rome that the Eleventh Battle of the Isonzo might result in the 'complete smashing of the Austrian Army'. See H. of Lords RO, Lloyd George Mss, F/56/1/47 decypher telegram from Sir R. Rodd (Rome), 26 August 1917.
27. Lloyd George was taking a much needed break at Sir George Riddell's house near Hurstpierpoint in Sussex. On 28 August, with Lloyd George still in Sussex, Robertson told the War Cabinet that the despatch of guns to Cadorna would force Haig to stop his offensive. Moreover, the guns would almost certainly arrive too late to help the Italians. PRO, Cab 23/13, War Cabinet (225A), 28 August 1917.
28. A telegram had been sent to Rome offering British support, although it would involve 'breaking off the offensive in Flanders', if Cadorna would

guarantee a decisive victory over the Austrians. H. of Lords RO, Lloyd George Mss, F/56/1/48, cypher telegram to Rennell Rodd, 29 August 1917.

29. Robertson was referring to the so-called 'Korniloff Affair'. It was believed at this time that General Lavr Korniloff, the new Commander-in-Chief of the Russian Army, was involved in an attempt to overthrow the Provisional Government headed by Alexander F. Kerensky.

30. Brigadier-General Sir A. W. F. Knox, the British military attaché in Russia, was an enthusiastic supporter of Korniloff, urging the War Cabinet on 7 September to put diplomatic pressure on Kerensky to accept Korniloff's demands. PRO, Cab 23/4, War Cabinet (229), 7 September 1917.

31. Following his failure to shut down Haig's offensive by diverting men and guns to Italy, Lloyd George, suffering from nervous exhaustion, had retired to Criccieth, his Welsh home, to consider ways of undermining Robertson's and Haig's domination of British strategy.

32. General Erich von Falkenhayn, after being replaced as Chief of the German General Staff by Hindenburg, directed the successful campaign against Roumania. In early 1917 he briefly commanded the so-called Asiatic Corps before being sent to Palestine in July as chief of Army Group F.

33. Sir Joseph McClay.

34. What Robertson did not then know was that the War Cabinet had been discussing what appeared to be a German offer of a compromise peace at the expense of Russia. Haig was consequently going to be asked if the demise of Russia made it necessary to consider German peace feelers. Later at the conference with Haig, Robertson summarised Lloyd George's position as follows: 'Russia is practically finished for the purposes of the war—a view he held himself. The Italians are not fighting, and the French are not fighting. How, then, does the war look? We cannot singlehanded defeat the German army'. See David R. Woodward, 'David Lloyd George, A Negotiated Peace with Germany, and the Kuhlmann Peace Kite of September 1917', *Canadian Journal of History*, 6, 1 (1971), pp. 75–93; PRO, Cab 1/25/16, Hankey's notes, 26 September 1917.

35. The military stalemate, conscription, inflation, food shortages, the growing perception that Britain had imperialistic war aims and war-related changes in the work place were causing increased labour discontent in 1917. The small Independent Labour Party, supported in its anti-war stance by the Union of Democratic Control, was demanding a compromise peace. Moreover, for the week ending on September 26, an especially large number of strikes—75—had been reported.

36. On 5 October Robertson and Lloyd George had quarrelled over the Prime

Ministers's desire to send one and perhaps even two divisions to Allenby to act as a reserve for the East. Following this meeting of the War Policy Committee (5 October, no record being kept), Robertson had been instructed to wire Allenby for his requirements to defeat the Turkish forces in front of him.

37. Haig made extravagant (and untrue) claims about German casualties, claiming that since April his forces had defeated seventy-seven German divisions, some of them more than once. No matter what happened to Russia, he remained confident of success if—and this was a big if indeed—his forces were kept up to strength. Robertson supported Haig, arguing that 'the right military course to pursue is to act on the defensive in Palestine and the east generally, and continue to seek a decision in the west'. PRO, Cab 27/8, G.T. 2242, 9 October 1917, and G.T. 2243, 8 October 1917.

38. In truth the Battle of Poelcappelle, fought in an appalling quagmire on 9 October, was by any measure a British setback.

39. Robertson noted in this memorandum that Haig had not received all of the airplanes that he had requested or needed. Lloyd George chose to consider this comment an attack on the civilians by the military professionals. PRO, Cab 24/28, 'Air Raids and the Bombing of Germany', 6 October 1917.

40. Unknown to Robertson, Lloyd George had invited Painlevé and Foch to London to implement his plan of placing Foch in command of the entire western front. The establishment of an inter-allied war council with a permanent general staff was to be the first step towards this goal. See Woodward, *Lloyd George and the Generals*, pp. 207–8.

41. Lloyd George had decided for the moment to get a second opinion on future Allied strategy from Sir Henry Wilson and Lord French rather than push for an inter-allied war council.

42. Robertson was apparently on the verge of resignation over Lloyd George's use of Wilson and French. Haig, however, told Whigham, who had been sent to GHQ by Robertson, that the CIGS must not resign. He also wrote Robertson expressing the same sentiments. Diary entry of 11 October 1917, Blake, *Private Papers of Haig*, p. 259.

43. On 24 October, an Austro-German attack had shattered the defences of the Italian Second Army on the Isonzo front near the town of Caporetto. The Italian withdrawal became a rout and it was feared that Italy might be knocked out of the war.

44. Initially, two crack British divisions, the 23rd and 41st, were sent to Italy.

NOTES TO CHAPTER V

1. PRO, Cab 23/4, War Cabinet (263), 2 November 1917.
2. Lloyd George, *War Memoirs*, II, p. 1441.
3. *The Globe*, 15 November 1917.
4. *H. C. Deb*, 5th series, vol. 99, 19 November 1917.
5. LHCMA, Robertson Mss, I/17/5, 'Future Military Policy', 19 November 1917. The Cambrai disaster, however, which indicated that Germany was far from cracking, led Robertson to announce to the War Cabinet on 19 December that 'it was fully realised by Sir Douglas Haig that we must act on the defence for some time to come, and he had no offensive plans in mind at present'. PRO, Cab 23/4, War Cabinet (302), 19 December 1917.
6. IWM, Wilson Diary, 30 December 1917.
7. PRO, Cab 28/3/ I.C.–41, Supreme War Council, 1 February 1918.
8. See document 213, Chapter V.
9. Maurice, Robertson's alter ego, proposed this to the Prime Minister. It is almost unthinkable that Maurice would have done so without Robertson's knowledge and approval. LHCMA, 4/3, Maurice Diary, 10 January 1918.
10. Bodleian, Milner Ms, dep. 374, Memorandum by Milner, misdated 14 February 1918.
11. PRO, Cab 23/13, War Cabinet (345 A), 14 February 1918.
12. On 12 November the Army Council informed the War Cabinet that 'it presumed that the technical advice given by the British Military Representative will be given on behalf of the Army Council, and that he will be subject to the authority of, and receive his instructions from, the Army Council'. PRO, W. O. 163/22, Army Council (236), 12 November 1917.
13. Major-General W. T. Furse.
14. On 20 November 1917, elements of the British Third Army, making superior tactical use of tanks and artillery, had achieved a brilliant success at Cambrai. British infantry and tanks, supported by airplanes, penetrated the German defences to a depth of four miles, an advance as great as had been achieved in months of hard fighting at Passchendaele.
15. Allenby had opened the door to an advance on Jerusalem with his capture of Gaza on 7 November 1917.
16. On 15 November, President Poincaré had asked Georges Clemenceau to replace Painlevé who had resigned.
17. Allenby is referring to Robertson's R 184 telegram of 4 December 1917, which is not to be found in the Robertson papers at LHCMA.
18. Haig had offered his resignation if he no longer had the government's confidence. This letter is printed in full in Blake, *Private Papers of Haig*, pp. 271–72.

19. Pétain and Clemenceau were putting intense pressure on the British to extend their line. Pétain said that he could no longer defend his front and Clemenceau hinted that he would resign if the British did not agree to defend the front to Berry-au-Bac, which was thirty-seven miles beyond Barisis, the furthest point that Haig had agreed to consider.
20. The Bolsheviks, after overthrowing the Provisional Government in early November (new style calendar), had signed an armistice with the Central Powers on 15 December and begun peace negotiations at Brest-Litovsk on 22 December.
21. To alleviate their manpower crisis, the British had been unsuccessfully trying to persuade Pershing to amalgamate temporarily American units into British ranks.
22. Lloyd George had sent Smuts and Hankey to tour the British sector to search for a possible successor to Haig. On the day they crossed the Channel, 21 January, Northcliffe's *Daily Mail* attacked western strategy, calling it 'the strategy of the Stone Age'. On 24 January the Unionist War Committee in Parliament passed a resolution supporting Robertson and Haig and demanding that the government speak out against the press campaign being conducted against the British high command. See Woodward, *Lloyd George and the Generals*, pp. 245–46.
23. Original misnumbered '4'.
24. Misdated '1916'.
25. In the margin Robertson writes, 'please destroy. You will see the real thing later'.
26. Walter M. st. G. Kirke, Deputy Director of Military Operations, 1918–1920.
27. Lloyd George used Smuts to make certain that the Egyptian Expeditionary Force followed the wishes of the War Cabinet. See David R. Woodward, 'The Imperial Strategist: Jan Christiaan Smuts and British Military Policy, 1917–1918', *Military History Journal* 5 (December 1981), pp. 141–42.
28. LHCMA, Robertson Mss, I/24/3, Robertson to Lloyd George, 30 January 1918.
29. 'Statement by General Sir William R. Robertson', PRO, Cab 23/13, War Cabinet (345 A), 14 February 1918.
30. This statement minuted as follows: 'In the original letter sent to Sir William Robertson this sentence ran as follows: "before you definitely decide to accept the Government's proposal"—When this mistake was found out Sir William Robertson agreed to alter his copy in accordance with the wording set forth in *this* copy'.
31. Minuted: '11 February '18. A Note from the Prime Minister including this information was read out at the 243rd meeting of the Army Council'.
32. While in London Haig bluntly informed Robertson that 'it was his *duty* to go to Versailles or anywhere else if the Government wished it'. Haig also

dismissed Robertson's arguments against his becoming Permanent Military Representative at Versailles. See diary entry of 11 February 1918, Blake, *Private Papers of Haig*, p. 284.

33. Presumably this is document 233, Chapter V.
34. Minuted, 'not sent in', and initialled by Robertson.
35. Derby had written Haig concerning Robertson's standing with the Prime Minister on 7 February, noting: 'between you and me, whatever happens I think he [Lloyd George] is quite determined to get rid of him'. NLS, Acc. 3155, no. 123, Derby to Haig, 7 February 1918.
36. Presumably 'M.A.' stands for Military Advisors.

BIOGRAPHICAL NOTES

Alekseev. General Mikhail Vasilevich. Son of an officer who had risen from the ranks; Chief of Staff of the Southwestern Army Group during the Galician campaign; appointed Commander of northwestern front in March 1915. When Nicholas II assumed personal command of the Russian Army, September 1915, Alekseev became his Chief of Staff; suffered heart attack in late 1916, but resumed his position on the eve of the March Revolution; Commander-in-Chief of army after fall of Romanovs, but dismissed in May 1917.

Allenby, Field-Marshal Sir Edmund Henry Hynman, first Viscount Allenby of Megiddo. Nickname 'the Bull' was prewar; son of country gentleman; one of Robertson's student contemporaries at Staff College; appointed to command Third Army in October 1915; not congenial with Haig and tended to be tongue-tied in his presence; succeeded Murray as Commander of Egyptian Expeditionary Force at end of June 1917; conquered Jerusalem in December 1917 and delivered knock-out blow to Turks in 1918; field-marshal, 1919. Known for his strong temper and roughness of manner.

Asquith, Herbert Henry, first Earl of Oxford and Asquith. Son of a nonconformist wool spinner and weaver; matriculated at Balliol College, Oxford; Liberal M.P. who became Prime Minister in 1908; held office for nearly nine years, the longest continuous period for which it had been held since Liverpool; called the 'last of the Romans'; brilliant politician who was not a natural war leader; generally sided with 'westerners' in strategic debate and had harmonious relationship with Robertson with the exception of the issue of compulsion; lost his eldest son Raymond in action on the Somme.

Bacon, Admiral Sir Reginald Hugh Spencer. Son of a rector. Appointed Commander of Dover Patrol, 1915, which protected vital British shipping and played an active role on the sea flank of Haig's forces. Removed from his command when Jellicoe was dismissed in late 1917.

Balfour, Arthur James, first Earl of Balfour. Unionist Prime Minister, 1902–1905; established Committee of Imperial Defence; resigned as Unionist leader, November 1911; Earl, 1915; First Lord of the Admiralty, 1915–1916; Foreign Secretary, 1916–1919; of a philosophical bent.

Barnes, George N. Son of a journeyman machine-maker. Labour leader who gave strong support to war; appointed first Minister of Pensions, December 1916, by Lloyd George. Replaced Henderson as Labour spokesman in War Cabinet in 1917.

Barter, Lieutenant-General Sir Charles St. Leger. Division commander, September 1914—September 1916; replaced Lieutenant-General Sir John Hanbury Williams as head of the British Military Mission at Russian military headquarters in May 1917; strong supporter of General Kornilov's efforts to restore discipline in the Russian army following the disorders that accompanied the overthrow of the Romanovs.

Birdwood, Field-Marshal Sir William. Commanded Australian and New Zealand Army Corps, 1914–1918, and Australian Imperial Force, 1915–1920; Commander-in-Chief of Mediterranean Expeditionary Force, 1915–1916; and Commander of Fourth Army in France, 1918–1919. Hankey attributed his unpopularity with Haig and Robertson to the fact that he did not belong to the 'Aldershot ring'. More likely his standing with the British high command was explained by his strong defence of Australian national interests and his occasional opposition to Haig's strategy.

Bliss, General Tasker Howard. The son of a classics professor; America had no more erudite general. He knew geology, French, Spanish, Italian, Latin, and Greek. After a brief term as Chief of Staff, U.S. Army, Bliss served as the U.S. representative on Supreme War Council after it was created in November 1917. During early phase of amalgamation controversy, Bliss accepted Pershing's views over his own more conciliatory position to present a solid front to the Allies.

Bonar Law, Andrew. Canadian-born son of a Presbyterian minister; iron merchant in Glasgow; headed Unionists, 1911–1921; Secretary of Colonies in Asquith's War Committee, 1915–1916; favoured evacuation of Gallipoli; key role in creation of coalition that made Lloyd George prime minister; Chancellor of Exchequer, member of Lloyd George's War Cabinet and leader of House of Commons; lost two elder sons in 1917, one in France and the other in Palestine; usually supported Lloyd George on big issues.

Briand, Aristide. Aptly described as the 'hardy perennial' of French politics; member of Union Sacrée government in 1914; believed in deployment of men and equipment away from western front, especially in Balkans; leading supporter of General Sarrail; replaced Viviani as Premier in October 1915 (also held position of Foreign Minister); favoured major operations in Balkans at Rome Conference in January 1917; fell from power in October 1917 after eighteen months in office; played no further role in war leadership.

Burnham, Viscount (Lawson, Sir Harry Lawson Webster Levy). Newspaper proprietor (*Daily Telegraph*). Held commission in Royal Bucks, Hussars; commanded regiment, 1902–1913; rejoined to train second reserve regiment when war started.

Butler, Lieutenant-General R. H. K. Educated at Harrow and Sandhurst. Haig's Chief of Staff, First Army, 1915; became Deputy Chief of General Staff when Haig was appointed Commander-in-Chief of the BEF. Neither he nor his superior Kiggell were innovative or assertive on tactics or strategy. Rejected by the government as Kiggell's replacement, he was given command of III Corps in 1918.

Byng, Field-Marshal Sir Julian Hedworth George, Viscount Byng of Vimy. Cavalryman. Commander-in-Chief of Canadian Corps, 1916–1917. Captured Vimy Ridge, April 1916, and planned Cambrai offensive in November 1917; Commander-in-Chief of Third Army, 1917–1919; field-marshal, 1932. His personable ways won him many friends.

Cadorna, General Count Luigi. Appointed Chief of Staff in July 1914. Offensive-minded Italian Army commander who frequently feuded with his political superiors. Replaced in November 1917 by General Diaz after the collapse of Italian front following Austro-German offensive at Caporetto. Retired to private life after brief service on the Supreme War Council at Versailles.

Callwell, Major-General Sir Charles E. Recalled from retirement to serve as Director of Military Operations in War Office. 1914–1915; briefly served under Robertson as Director of Military Intelligence; sent to Russian GHQ twice in 1916. Author of many works on military history, including the edited diary of Field Marshal Sir Henry Wilson.

Carson, Edward Henry. Zealous opponent of Irish Home Rule; called 'King of Ulster'; Attorney General, 1915; First Lord of the Admiralty 1916–1917; member of War Cabinet, 1917–1918. A lawyer by profession and of an emotional nature, he has been characterised by Lord Beaverbrook as 'a clever lawyer and a rebellious politician'. British high command could usually count on his defence of the Army against civilian interference.

Castelnau, General Edouard de. Descended from a long line of important aristocratic French military leaders; commanded Second Army at start of war; appointed Joffre's Chief of Staff by Galliéni to restrain the French Commander-in-Chief's propensity for prolonged and costly offensives. His pronounced Catholicism and long association with Joffre kept him from being selected over Nivelle as Commander-in-Chief in 1917. Commanded Eastern Group of Armies under Pétain, 1917–1918.

Cecil, Edgar Algernon Robert Gascoyne-, Viscount Cecil of Chelwood. Deputy Foreign Secretary and Minister of Blockade, 1916–1918. He was suspicious of Lloyd George and supported British High Command in its conflict with politicians. Of high character and religious, he was greatly respected and admired.

Chalmers, Robert, Baron Chalmers of Northiam. Classical scholar and public servant. Chairman of Board of Inland Revenue, 1907; appointed Permanent Secretary, Treasury, 1911, and then Governor of Ceylon, 1913; returned to Treasury in 1916 as Joint Permanent Secretary, 1916–1919, with brief interlude, May–September 1916, as Chief Secretary of Ireland. His younger son died of wounds in May 1915.

Chamberlain, (Arthur) Neville. Only son of Joseph Chamberlain; half brother was (Sir Joseph) Austen Chamberlain. Businessman-turned statesman. Elected to House of Commons in 1918 at age of fifty. No British Prime Minister has ever made such a late start in Parliament. As Director-General of National Service, 1917, he was responsible for the voluntary recruitment of labour for war industries. Unhappy relationship with Lloyd George led to his resignation after only seven months.

Charteris, Brigadier-General John. Haig's unkempt Head of Military Intelligence (Haig thought him 'dirty and fat') who drank brandies before breakfast; fed Haig a steady diet of inflated estimates of German casualties. Robertson questioned his competence and judgment and succeeded in getting him replaced at GHQ at the beginning of 1918. In Lloyd George's purple prose, 'His computations were not mathematical, but temperamental. From the mass of information that came into his office he chose his facts and figures by attraction and not reflection'. Yet Charteris's last intelligence forecast (a German offensive in March 1918) was right on the mark. Later wrote extensively on Haig's command.

Churchill, Winston Spencer. Grandson of Duke of Marlborough; First Lord of the Admiralty, 1912–1915; Chancellor of the Duchy of Lancaster, 1915; commander of Sixth Royal Fusiliers in France, 1915–1916; Minister of Munitions, 1917–1918; distrusted by Haig, Robertson, and many Unionists; Lloyd George viewed him as a much greater threat outside rather than within the government.

Clemenceau, Georges. The 'Tiger'. First elected to Chamber of Deputies in 1876; leader of Radical Republicans. Issued fighting words, 'I wage war', when he became French Premier in November 1917. Frequently in conflict with British civil and military leaders, he was convinced that Britain was holding back secret reserves from the western front. At the same time, his strong leadership was admired in London.

Clive, Lieutenant-General Sir (George) Sidney. Educated at Harrow and Sandhurst. Reported to both Haig and Robertson as Chief of British Mission at French General Headquarters from December 1916 to September 1918; excellent relations with Pétain.

Curzon, George Nathaniel, Marquess Curzon of Kedleston. Conservative statesman and zealous imperialist; given office of Lord Privy Seal in coalition government of May 1915, but excluded from War Council; strong supporter of compulsory service; became member of War Committee in July 1916; also in charge of Shipping Control Committee before becoming President of Air Board in May 1916; joined Lloyd George's new government; member of War Cabinet and leader of House of Lords. Called Lloyd George's 'gilded door mat', but his support of Robertson, backed at times with the threat of resignation, restrained the Prime Minister; interested in military operations against Turkey that furthered British imperial interests.

Davidson, Major-General Sir John Humphrey. 'Tavish'. Served under Robertson when the latter was Commandant of Staff College. Head of Operations Section, GHQ, 1915–1918; major-general, 1918.

Delmé-Radcliffe, Brigadier-General Sir Charles. Head of British military mission at Italian General Headquarters, 1915–1919. Robertson apparently did not believe that he always 'played the game' correctly.

Derby, Seventeenth Earl of, Stanley, Edward George Villiers. 'K.G.'; lieutenant, Grenadier Guards, 1885–1895; Conservative M.P., 1892–1906; raised five battalions of the King's Regiment on his Knowsley estate at start of war; Director-General of Recruiting, October 1915—July 1916; Under-Secretary of State for War and President of Army Council, July—December 1916; Robertson's choice as Secretary of State for War, December 1916–April 1918; godfather to Haig's son and strong supporter of military leadership; Haig, however, unkindly likened him to 'the feather pillow, bears the marks of the last person who has sat on him'; broke with Robertson over command of the Allied general reserve; said to have two primary ambitions, to win the Derby and become Prime Minister; denied the latter he won the Derby twice.

Diaz, General Armando. After Caporetto disaster, he replaced Cadorna as Chief of Staff; Served as the real Commander-in-Chief of the Italian Army although King Victor Emmanuel III was Generalissimo. Cyril Falls has written that Diaz was 'eleven years Cadorna's junior and livelier in every way'.

Donald, Sir Robert. Editor of *The Daily Chronicle* (later *News Chronicle*). Member of National Liberal Club and on close terms with many Liberal leaders. Urged Lloyd George's government to create a Department (subsequently Ministry) of Information; became its director.

Esher, Viscount, Brett, Reginald Baliol. Chairman of Committee on Reconstruction of War Office, 1903–1904; permanent member of Committee of Imperial Defence, 1905–1918; extremely well connected in social, political and military circles; sent on a secret mission to France in September 1914 by Lord Kitchener; remained there on instructions from Asquith and then from Lloyd George; important source of information on political and military trends in France; prolific correspondent with almost everyone who mattered; lover of intrigue.

Fayolle, General Marie-Emile. Son of a lace manufacturer; taught at War College with Pétain and Foch. He briefly commanded the French Tenth Army sent to rescue Italy after Caporetto. Returning to the western front in March 1918, he commanded the multinational reserve army under Foch's direction.

Foch, General Ferdinand. Son of civil servant; fought as a private in

Franco-Prussian War; taught strategy and military history at War College before becoming its head in 1911; General Joffre's chief assistant and Commander of Northern Army Group which fought alongside BEF in 1916; position suffered when Nivelle supplanted Joffre; Nivelle's demise and Clemenceau's selection as premier dramatically improved his fortunes; held many important posts, including Chief of the General Staff, French Permanent Military Representative on the Supreme War Council and Generalissimo; frequently at sixes and sevens with Robertson; Sir Henry Wilson's friend.

French, Field-Marshal Sir John, First Earl of Ypres. Best cavalry officer in Boer War; Commander-in-Chief, Aldershot Command, 1902–1907; Inspector-General of Forces, 1907; CIGS, 1912–1914; field-marshal, 1913; Commander-in-Chief, BEF. August 1914—December 1915; Commander-in-Chief, Home Forces, 1916–1918; Lord Lieutenant of Ireland, 1918–1921. Robertson and Haig sought his removal as head of BEF. He never forgot or forgave their role in his dismissal. When negotiating his recall to London in 1915, he facetiously proposed that he be given the title of Lord St. Omer, or 'sent home-r'. First World War I British general to write his war memoirs.

Galliéni, General Joseph Simon. Recalled from retirement at the beginning of the war; he was appointed Military Governor of Paris in August 1914 and played an important part in First Battle of the Marne; Briand appointed him Minister of War, 1915; his bitter quarrel with Joffre over the respective prerogatives of the Commander-in-Chief and Minister of War led to Galliéni's resignation in 1916; he died in May 1916 after undergoing two operations.

Geddes, Major-General Sir Eric Campbell. Born in India. As a young man, he held many odd jobs, ranging from a brakesman on a freight train to a lumberman. In 1914 he was forty years old and the General Manager designate of the North Eastern Railway. His energy and enterprise greatly impressed Lloyd George; appointed Haig's Director-General of Transportation, 1916. In May 1917 Geddes became Controller of the Navy and an additional member of the Board of Admiralty with the temporary and honorary rank of vice-admiral. Since he retained his honorary military rank, he became one of the select few to hold senior naval and military rank at the same time; later became First Lord of the Admiralty, 1917–1918. Very regular in his habits, he sat down to dinner at precisely 7:30 p.m. and rose from the table at 8:15.

George V, H. M. Second son of Edward VII. Blue-eyed and of medium height, the King had impeccable bearing. Oddly his trousers were creased at the sides instead of front and back. His disciplined personal habits were a reflection of his cherished naval career. After attending the Royal Naval College, he attained the rank of commander. Ascending the throne in 1910, he took seriously his monarchial responsibilities in the military realm. During the war he visited the Western Front seven times and the Grand Fleet five times. In 1915, a visit to the front almost had tragic consequences when he was trapped beneath his fallen horse, fracturing his pelvis and suffering severe shock. Close to Haig and Robertson, he trusted them as much as he distrusted Lloyd George, whom he suspected of wanting a republican government.

Grey, Sir Edward, third Baronet, Viscount of Fallodon. Son of army officer and country gentleman; Foreign Secretary from December 1905 to December 1916; his dominant position in foreign affairs declined with the outbreak of war; inclined to leave military questions to the professionals, but did at times intervene in military sphere to keep the anti-German alliance intact; influence hurt by perceived failures in Balkan diplomacy; denied membership in War Committee; thought by Lloyd George, Robertson and others to be inclined towards a compromise peace in 1916.

Gwynne, Howell Arthur. 'Taffy'. War correspondent for Reuters in Balkan, African and China wars; editor of *Morning Post*, 1911–1937; Robertson's friend and ally who made his paper the organ of the War Office; determined to expose civilians who interfered with professional soldiers' conduct of the war; his right-wing paper had influence in ruling circles far beyond its modest circulation.

Haig, Field-Marshal Sir Douglas Haig, first Earl Haig. 'Lucky' Haig; son of a Scottish distiller; family motto was 'Tyde What May'; Robertson's contemporary at Staff College; headed I Army Corps at start of war; given command of First Army (I Corps, Indian Corps and IV Corps) in early 1915; replaced Lord French as Commander-in-Chief of BEF on 19 December 1915; field-marshal, 1917; although his generalship during the Somme and Passchendaele battles has been criticised, both then and now, a better commander-in-chief could not be found; skillfully conducted offensives of 1918 represented the high point of his career.

Hankey, Lieutenant-Colonel Sir Maurice Pascal Alers. Entered Royal Marine Artillery, 1895; retired 1912; secretary to Committee of Imperial Defence, 1912–1938; Lieutenant-Colonel Royal Marines, 1914; held secretaryship of War Council, Dardanelles Committee, and the War Committee; chief of Cabinet Secretariat when it was established in December 1916; most important behind-the-scenes individual in wartime government; tactful individual of temperate habits who, despite Lloyd George's efforts to use his strategic appreciations as a substitute for the advice of the Imperial General Staff, got on well with Robertson.

Henderson, Arthur. Son of a Scottish cotton-spinner. Labour leader and statesman who supported the war; when Ramsay MacDonald resigned in August 1914. Henderson replaced him as Chairman of Parliamentary Labour Party, 1914–1917; became minister without portfolio in Lloyd George's ministry, December 1916. Resigned in August 1917 over controversy surrounding conference of international socialists at Stockholm.

Hindenburg, Field-Marshal Paul von Beneckendorf und von. Son of an East Prussian aristocratic army officer. Became a national hero after the Battle of Tannenberg, September 1914; replaced General Falkenhayn as Chief of the German General Staff, August 1916. Hindenburg and his First Quartermaster General Erich Ludendorff then dominated both military and civil policy during most of the rest of the war.

Hunter-Weston, Lieutenant-General Sir Aylmer Gould. Commanded 29th Division and then VIII Corps in Gallipoli; continued to command VIII Corps when it was sent to western front until the end of war.

Jellicoe, Admiral Sir John Rushworth, first Earl Jellicoe. Commander-in-Chief of newly created Grand Fleet at start of war; criticised for drawn battle of Jutland in May 1916; appointed First Sea Lord, November 1916, with major responsibility of containing U-boat threat; supported Haig and Robertson over launching Passchendaele offensive; dismissed on Christmas Eve 1917; raised to peerage as Viscount Jellicoe of Scapa, in January 1918; promoted Admiral of the Fleet 1919.

Joffre, Field-Marshal Joseph Jacques Césaire. Son of a barrel-maker. Commander-in-Chief of French armies of north and north-east, 1914, and all French forces in west, December 1915–December 1916. Worked closely with his deputy General Castelnau. After being replaced by Nivelle, he took the largely ceremonial position of Marshal of France. Robertson shared his dim view of politicians and respected him for his steadiness in a crisis.

Kiggell, Lieutenant-General Sir Launcelot Edward. 'Kigg'; son of an army officer and justice of peace; succeeded Robertson as Commandant, Staff College, 1913–1914; Director of Home Defence, War Office, 1914–1915; Chief of the General Staff, BEF, December 1915–January 1918; owed his position more to friendship with and subservience to Haig than to his ability; more servant than advisor. Robertson critical of his understanding of trench warfare and successfully pushed Haig to remove him after Cambrai setback.

Kitchener, Field-Marshal Horatio Herbert, first Earl Kitchener, of Khartoum and of Broome. 'K'; son of army officer; Britain's most famous soldier on eve of World War I because of his role in colonial wars in Sudan and South Africa; Asquith appointed him Secretary of State at beginning of war; dominated strategy, 1914–1915; expanded army from twenty to seventy divisions, 1914–1916; influence and reputation steadily declined with government leaders but not with public; drowned in June 1916 when his ship bound for Russia struck a mine off the Orkneys.

Lansdowne, Fifth Marquess of. Former Secretary of State for War and Foreign Secretary, he served as leader of the Conservatives in the House of Lords, 1906–1916. Became a minister without portfolio in Asquith's coalition government in May 1915. In November 1916 he circulated a paper within the Cabinet that advocated a compromise peace. A year later, in semi-retirement, he expressed similar views in a controversial letter to the *Daily Telegraph*.

Lloyd George, David. Welshman son of a schoolmaster; Liberal M.P., 1890–1945; Chancellor of the Exchequer, 1908–1915; Minister of Munitions, 1915–1916; Secretary of State for War, 1916; Prime Minister, 1916–1922; many consider equal of Churchill as war leader; conflict with generals continued after war with publication of his polemical memoirs; limited military experience in the pre-Haldane militia did not deter him from developing grand strategic schemes; considered use of his correct surname 'George' as almost an insult. Only minister to serve from beginning to end of war.

Lucas, Major C. C. 'The Monument'; Robertson's faithful A.D.C. who accompanied him to London from France when he was appointed CIGS; Robertson described him thus in *From Private to Field-Marshal*; 'Lucas had been, as always, a devoted comrade, displaying ability and initiative much above the ordinary, and having but one object in life—to serve me to the utmost of his power'.

Ludendorff, General Erich. As Hindenburg's chief assistant, Ludendorff was Germany's primary strategist for the last two years of the war. He and Hindenburg also dominated the German government from August 1916 until the last weeks of the war.

Lyautey, General Hubert. Colonial administrator; Resident General of Morocco during first two years of war; Briand appointed him Minister of War in December 1916; skeptical of Nivelle's grand offensive plan, once calling it 'a plan for the Grand Duchess of Gerolstein'; unable to work effectively with political leaders, he resigned in March 1917. Hard of hearing, he was inclined to dominate a conversation much to the annoyance of Robertson.

Macdonogh, Lieutenant-General Sir George M. W. Served as Robertson's very capable head of intelligence when the latter was Chief of the General Staff, BEF, and CIGS. His views on Germany's staying power were in sharp contrast with the optimistic appreciations of Haig's chief of intelligence

Charteris. A furious Haig once even alleged that Macdonogh's Roman Catholicism perhaps unwittingly led him to rely too much on unreliable Catholic sources that exaggerated German strength.

McKenna, Reginald. Graduate of Trinity Hall, Cambridge. Prominent Liberal politician and banker. While First Lord of Admiralty, 1908–1911, he pushed for expanded dreadnought construction. Replaced Lloyd George at the Treasury when the latter became Minister of Munitions in 1915. The chemistry was never right between the two men. As the *DNB* has noted, 'A mind that saw everything in pictures clashed with one that saw everything in figures'. Another source of conflict was McKenna's staunch support of Robertson in his conflicts with Lloyd George. Quite athletic, McKenna was also an excellent chess and bridge player.

Macready, General Sir C. F. Nevil. Director of Personal Services, 1910–1914; Adjutant-General, BEF, 1914–1916; replaced Sclater as Adjutant-General in War Office, 1916–1918. With the exception of Robertson's first days as CIGS the two men served together from August 1914 until February 1918. In the summer of 1918, Macready left the War Office to become Commissioner of the Metropolitan Police.

MacMahon, Sir (Arthur) Henry. Military political officer; Indian Political Department, 1890–1914. Served as Kitchener's replacement as High Commissioner for Egypt until he was recalled in late 1916.

Mahon, Lieutenant-General Sir Bryan Thomas. Commanded 10th Division at Gallipoli; transfered to Salonika and commanded British forces there until Robertson replaced him with Milne; commanded the Western Frontier force in Egypt for a month before returning to England; sent to Ireland as Commander-in-Chief, 1916.

Maude, Lieutenant-General Sir Frederick Stanley. 'Joe'; fellow student of Robertson's at Staff College; appointed to command 31st Division, July 1915; sent to assume command of 13th Division at Dardanelles; appointed to command Tigris Corps, July 1916; assumed command of army in Mesopotamia, August 1916; occupied Baghdad on 11 March 1917; died of virulent cholera on 18 November 1917.

Maurice, Major-General Sir Frederick B. 'Freddy'; served under Robertson at Staff College before war; Robertson's alter ego as Director of Military Operations, 1915–1918; E. L. Spears, in his *Prelude to Victory*, has written: 'He and his chief evoked the idea of Don Quixote and Sancho Panza reversed, if it is possible to imagine a short and portly Knight of La Mancha, followed by an elongated attendant'; ended his army career with a controversial letter to press in May 1918 concerning the BEF's strength; became a distinguished professor of military history.

Maxse, Leopold James. 'Leo'. His father, an admiral, bought him the *National Review* in 1895. Influential wartime editor who launched especially severe attacks on civilian leaders who dared interfere with the generals' conduct of the war.

Maxwell, Lieutenant-General Sir Ronald C. Robertson's successor as Quartermaster-General, BEF; replaced by Lieutenant-General Sir Travers Clarke over Haig's objections at the insistence of Robertson and the Army Council in late 1917.

Milne, Lieutenant-General George Francis, first Baron Milne. One of Robertson's student contemporaries at Staff College; later worked under Robertson in the Foreign Intelligence Section of the War Office; general staff position in III Corps and Second Army in France before commanding 27th Division and XVI Corps in Balkans; assumed command of British forces in Salonika from Mahon, 1916.

Milner, Alfred, first Viscount Milner. German-born bachelor. Freemason and member of Brooks. Conservative peer and advocate of New Imperialism; opposed Home Rule and Parliament Bill of 1911; supported national service prior to war; before his appointment as Minister without Portfolio in War Cabinet, 1916–1918, he presided over committees on food and coal production; replaced Derby as Secretary of State for War on 19 April 1918; Lloyd George's most important ally in late 1917 and early 1918 in conflict with Robertson.

Montgomery, Field-Marshal Sir Archibald Armar (took name of Montgomery-Massingberd, 1926). 'Archie'. Chief of Staff IV Corps, 1915, and Rawlinson's Fourth Army, 1916–1918; field-marshal, 1935. Described by E. L. Spears as 'one of the handsomest men I have ever met, with the profile of a Greek statue, big, fair, and blue-eyed; a tiny lisp added to his charm'.

Monro, General Sir Charles Carmichael. Commanded 2nd Division before succeeding Haig as Commander of I Corps, 1914; given new Third Army in July 1915; replaced Sir Ian Hamilton as commander of the Mediterranean Expeditionary Force at Gallipoli; supported complete withdrawal from Gallipoli; Commander of First Army in France, January 1916; Commander-in-Chief in India, 1916–1920.

Murray, General Sir Archibald James. Son of country gentleman; student with Robertson at Staff College; Lord French's Chief of Staff in 1914; fainted at an inn in St. Quentin on 26 August 1914 and his fitness for command a topic of discussion by senior officers; replaced by Robertson, January 1915; became Deputy CIGS in February and CIGS in September 1915; replaced by Robertson in December 1915; arrived in Egypt in January 1916 to take command there; nine of his fourteen divisions were sent to France in preparation for Somme offensive; initial success in local battles against Turks but his reputation damaged in London by his failure to take Gaza in March and April 1917; replaced by Allenby on 29 June 1917.

Nivelle, General Robert Georges. Son of a French army officer and an English mother; his fluency in English a considerable asset in dealing with British politicians; a colonel in the artillery when war started; became a national hero during Battle of Verdun because of his employment of sophisticated artillery tactics in local battles; promoted from Commander of Second Army to Commander-in-Chief, replacing Joffre; persuaded Lloyd George in early 1917 to support a big offensive in west employing 'new' artillery tactics and to subordinate Haig to his command; replaced by Pétain in May 1917 after failure of his offensive; cleared of serious misconduct by a military court of inquiry; sent to North Africa for remainder of war; one of few leading generals not to write his memoirs.

Northcliffe, Viscount, Harmsworth, Alfred Charles William. 'King Alfred'. Proprietor of influential *The Times*; holdings included the *Evening News* and *Daily Mail*; his papers perhaps accounted for half the London circulation during the Great War; attacked Kitchener but generally supported Robertson and Haig against the politicians until the Passchendaele and Cambrai offensives. Made violent attacks on public figures but kept critical comments about himself from being published in his papers.

Orlando, Vittorio Emanuele. Became Italian Premier on 30 October 1917 after Caporetto disaster; brought new fighting spirit to government, proclaiming a policy of 'resist, nothing but resist'. He kept both radicals in the streets and the Italian military leadership under control.

Painlevé, Paul. Brilliant Professor of Mechanics and Mathematics at Ecole polytechnique; socialist politician; gave strong support to Balkan projects of General Sarrail, the favourite of the left; appointed Minister of War, March 1917; opposed Nivelle's 1917 Spring offensive and threw his support to Pétain; served as both Minister of War and Premier. September–November 1917.

Pershing, General John J. Nickname 'Black Jack' a reference to his having once led Black troops; ramrod straight and with extraordinary self-discipline, he was every inch a soldier. Stood only five feet and nine inches tall, but he had such a formidable presence that many thought he was above six feet. Commander-in-Chief of the American Expeditionary Force. Called the '100-per cent American' by Captain B. H. Liddell Hart because he usually put American interests above the general interests of the anti-German coalition.

Pétain, Marshal Henri-Philippe. Son of a peasant family; one of first generals to recognise that new military technology greatly strengthened defence and required a new style of warfare. Gave particular attention to artillery preparation prior to an attack and advocated 'elastic defence'; given command of Second Army, 1915; in charge of centre Army Group, which included

Verdun sector, 1916; promoted to Chief of the General Staff and then Commander-in-Chief, 1917.

Plumer, Lieutenant-General Sir Herbert Charles Onslow, first Viscount Plumer of Messines. 'Plum'; succeeded Smith-Dorrien in the command of the Second Army, May 1915; popular with men and achieved great success at Messines; sent to Italy to take over Allied force of six French and five British divisions in November 1917; refused to replace Robertson as CIGS in February; returned to France, 13 March, to lead Second Army in great battles of 1918; model, unjustly so, for David Low's cartoon character, Colonel Blimp, because of his walrus moustache, beefy complexion and rotund figure; considered one of great British generals of the war.

Poincaré, Raymond. Native of German-occupied Lorraine; influential wartime President of France. In military matters he supported Allied commitment to Balkan theatre and Nivelle's 1917 Spring offensive. Respected as a man of strong principles.

Rawlinson, General Sir Henry Seymour, second Baronet and Baron Rawlinson, of Trent, 'Rawly'; at Staff College with Sir Henry Wilson; temporary Commander of First Army in 1915 before becoming Commander of new Fourth Army in 1916; advocated limited attacks to open battle of Somme, but was overruled by Haig who wanted to break through first and second German lines of defence in one great blow; selected to command secret forces for a naval-military attack on Belgian coast, July 1917; replaced Wilson as Permanent Military Representative at Supreme War Council, February 1918; worked with Haig to undermine general reserve; at end of March 1918 he took command of broken Fifth Army which was reconstituted as part of Fourth Army. 'Rawly had a way of floating over and away from his troubles', E. L. Spears has written.

Repington, Charles à Court. Soldier and military writer; brilliant though traditional military mind; army career came to an early demise because of an affair with wife of British official; failed to keep his word as an officer to break off affair; well-connected with ruling circles; leading military correspondent of his day; worked for *The Times*, 1904–1918, until he fell out with Lord Northcliffe; moved his pen to *Morning Post*; charged, along with his editor Gwynne, with contravention of the Defence of the Realm regulations because of an article on Allied General Reserve; found guilty and fined.

Ribot, Alexandre. Son of a banker. He began his forty-five year parliamentary career when he was elected to Chamber of Deputies in 1878. An Anglophile he served as both Premier and Foreign Minister before World War I. Served as Finance Minister during first two years of war. Became Premier in March 1917, succeeding Briand. As Premier he strongly supported Allied commitment to Balkan front and played a decisive role in removal of Greece's pro-German monarch. Fell from power on 7 September 1917.

Robinson, (George) Geoffrey. Changed his name to Dawson in 1917. Graduate of Magdalen College, Oxford. Twice editor of *The Times*, 1912–1919 and 1923–1941. Close to Milner, he was an important member of the Tory intelligentsia.

Rodd, James Rennell, first Baron Rennell. Graduate of Balliol College, Oxford. Intellectual and diplomatist who served as British Ambassador to Rome, 1908–1919. Later wrote his memoirs.

Sarrail, General Maurice Paul Emmanuel. Radical, freemason and Dreyfusard; served under reforming General André in War Ministry, 1900–1907; started war as Commander of VI Corps; appointed Commander of Third Army; Commander of French forces at Salonika, 1915–1917; made Commander-in-Chief of the Allied Army of the Orient at Rome Conference, January 1917; recalled to France in December 1917 after military failures; career much advanced by Radical Republicans because he was recognised as the leading Republican general in an army dominated by clerical and monarchist officers.

Smith, Frederick Edwin, first Earl of Birkenhead. Brilliant jurist; in prewar years he was known for his extravagant life style which included a love of cards, horses and night life. Solicitor-General, 1915; Attorney General, 1915–1919. Briefly headed Press Bureau and was criticised for his handling of the British retreat from Mons. A close friend of Churchill, he did not get on well with the military. 'He did not understand soldiers, nor they him', the *DNB* has noted.

Smuts, Jan Christiaan. South African statesman and general of Dutch origin. His South African opponents called him 'Slim Jannie'. Appointed Commander of Imperial Forces in East Africa in 1916; given rank of lieutenant-general in British Army; came to London in January 1917 as member of Imperial War Cabinet; Lloyd George appointed to War Cabinet, 1917–1918; geopolitical thinker who supported at different times both Lloyd George and Robertson; in 1918 he made extraordinary proposal to Lloyd George that he replace Pershing as Commander of the American Expeditionary Force.

Stamfordham, Lord, Bigge, Arthur John. Educated at Rossall School and at the Royal Military Academy; retired lieutenant-colonel Royal Artillery, 1898; private secretary to Queen Victoria, 1895–1901; to Prince of Wales, 1901–1910; to George V, 1910–1931.

Thomas, Albert. Son of a baker. Socialist politician. Thomas found a soul mate in Lloyd George. Both men worked to mobilise their countries for total war and served as ministers of munitions. Like Lloyd George, Thomas thought his country's military leadership hidebound and unimaginative. Special ambassador to Russia following March Revolution.

Trenchard, Major-General Hugh Montague, first Viscount. Nicknamed 'Boom' because of his loud and dominating voice. Has been called the 'Father of the Royal Air Force'. As a student he was good in sports and games and weak academically. A faltering military career was reversed when he took up flying in 1912. Commander of Royal Flying Corps in France, 1915–1918; first Chief of new Air Staff, January–May 1918. Resigned when he could not get along with his superior Air Minister Lord Rothermere; returned to France to command an independent bombing force. Loved a controversy and evoked strong feelings from friend and foe alike.

Waters, Brigadier-General Wallscourt H.-H. Hanbury Williams' temporary replacement at Russian military headquarters in 1916 as head of the British Military Mission; had been Robertson's superior during the latter's brief posting to the Asia and Russia Section of the Intelligence Branch of the War Office in the late 1890s.

Weygand, General Maxime. Born in Belgium, his parentage remains a mystery today. Entered St. Cyr as a foreigner. Served as General Foch's alter ego and assistant for most of the war. 'He is my doormat', Foch once unfairly commented, 'I use him to wipe my boots on'. In truth they formed an effective military combination. Replaced Foch on Supreme War Council. When Foch became Allied commander, Weygand became his Chief of Staff.

Whigham, Major-General Sir Robert Dundas. Served under Robertson at Staff College at Camberley and on western front during the war; became Deputy CIGS when Robertson went to War Office; commanded 62nd Division in France after Robertson's removal from power in 1918.

Wigram, Clive, first Baron Wigram. Commissioned in Royal Artillery, 1893; service on North-West Frontier, 1897–1898; Military Secretary to Commander-in-Chief at Aldershot, 1908–1910, when Robertson was on General Staff of Aldershot Command; Assistant Private Secretary to the King, 1910–1931; Private Secretary of George V, 1931–1936; brevet lieutenant-colonel, 1915.

Wilson, (Thomas) Woodrow. President of the U. S., 1913–1921. Former president of Princeton University. Told a friend on the eve of his inauguration, 'It would be the irony of fate if my administration had to deal chiefly with foreign affairs'. His world view was based on strongly-held religious and ethical values. Believed that the U.S. had a special role to play in international affairs. Many British leaders viewed his idealistic diplomacy and defence of U. S. neutrality with suspicion and guarded hostility.

Wilson, Field-Marshal Sir Henry Hughes, Baronet. Lanky Irishman who was as glib as he was humorous; suspected by some of his fellow officers of being more the politician than the soldier; Commandant of Staff College, 1907–1910; succeeded by Robertson when he moved on to War Office as Director of Military Operations; unpleasant disagreement with Robertson over money for items which Wilson alleged he had left in Commandant's house; neither apparently forgot nor forgave; played key prewar role in giving Britain military role on continent; a friend of Ferdinand Foch, he advocated closer Anglo-French ties; supported Ulster cause during Curragh incident; Robertson chosen over him as Lord French's Chief of Staff in early 1915; chief liaison with French headquarters, January 1915; commanded IV Army Corps, December 1915; headed mission to Russia, December 1916; returned as chief liaison officer with French headquarters until he returned to London in May 1917; Eastern Command, September 1917; Permanent Military Representative at Supreme War Council, November 1917–February 1918; CIGS, 1918–1922; field-marshal, 1919; assassinated by Sinn Feiners on the doorstep of his London home.

INDEX

ARMY RECORDS SOCIETY
(FOUNDED 1984)

Members of the Society are entitled to purchase back volumes at reduced prices.
Orders should be sent to the Hon. Treasurer, Army Records Society,
c/o National Army Museum,
Royal Hospital Road,
London SW3 4HT.

The Society has already issued:

Vol. I:
The Military Correspondence of Field Marshal Sir Henry Wilson 1918–1922
Edited by Dr Keith Jeffery

Vol. II:
The Army and the Curragh Incident, 1914
Edited by Dr Ian F. W. Beckett

Vol. III:
The Napoleonic War Journal of Captain Thomas Henry Browne, 1807–1816
Edited by Roger Norman Buckley

Vol. IV:
An Eighteenth-Century Secretary at War The Papers of William, Viscount Barrington
Edited by Tony Hayter